Colonialism and Genocide

This is the first book to link colonialism and genocide in a systematic way in the context of world history. It fills a significant gap in the current understanding on genocide and the Holocaust, which sees them overwhelmingly as twentieth century phenomena.

Raphael Lemkin, the man who invented the term 'genocide' in 1944, regarded genocide as an intrinsically colonial phenomena. In his own unpublished writings on a global history of genocide since antiquity, he wrote chapters on the European settlement of the Americas, Africa, and Australia.

This book recognises the need to examine the colonial prehistory of twentieth century genocides and publishes Lemkin's account of the genocide of the Aboriginal Tasmanians for the first time. Other chapters cover the exterminatory rhetoric of racist discourses before the 'scientific racism' of the mid-nineteenth century and Charles Darwin's preoccupation with the extinction of peoples in the face of European colonialism. The result is an accessible and valuable resource for social theorists and historians alike.

This book was previously published as a special issue of *Patterns of Prejudice*.

A. Dirk Moses is Senior Lecturer in History at the University of Sydney, Australia

Dan Stone is Professor of Modern History at Royal Holloway, University of London

Colonialism and Genocide

Edited by
A. Dirk Moses and Dan Stone

Routledge
Taylor & Francis Group
LONDON AND NEW YORK

First published 2007 by Routledge
2 Park Square, Milton Park, Abingdon, Oxon, OX14 4RN

Simultaneously published in the USA and Canada
by Routledge
270 Madison Ave, New York NY 10016

Routledge is an imprint of the Taylor & Francis Group, an informa business

Transferred to Digital Printing 2008

© 2007 Taylor & Francis Group Ltd

Typeset in by Datapage International Ltd., Dublin, Ireland.

British Library Cataloguing in Publication Data
A catalogue record for this book is available from the British Library

Library of Congress Cataloging in Publication Data
A catalog record for this book has been requested

ISBN10: 0-415-40066-x (hbk)
ISBN10: 0-415-46415-3 (pbk)

ISBN13: 978-0-415-40066-4 (hbk)
ISBN13: 978-0-415-46415-4 (pbk)

COLONIAL GENOCIDE
A. Dirk Moses and Dan Stone

Contents

Introduction

The title 'Colonial Genocide', is not meant to signal that the editors believe in an overdetermined link between colonialism and genocide. As Nicholas Thomas noted a decade ago, a belief in the omnipotence of the colonizers and the impotence of the colonized fails to see the fragile negotiation and mutual relationships that existed between the two groups. Often the rule of colonizers was barely discernible, and the colonized—or some of them—drew benefits from the relationships into which they entered:

> It is misleading even to attribute uniformly to colonizers an imagining of, or a will to, total dominance: colonial rule was frequently haunted by a sense of insecurity, terrified by the obscurity of 'the native mentality' and overwhelmed by indigenous societies' apparent intractability in the face of government.[1]

Claiming that colonial genocides did not occur as often as many scholars like to believe, Thomas suggests that this belief is an unconscious reworking of the longstanding fantasy of the inevitable 'extinction' of 'primitive races', a theory held throughout the nineteenth century and well into the twentieth that maintained that, in the face of a superior civilization, primitive peoples would, through no fault of their own, simply 'pass away'.[2] Both this racist discourse of the necessary disappearance of primitive races and the modern, condemnatory notion of colonial genocide rest, according to Thomas, on the same fallacy: that of the helpless native destined to die at the hands of the white man.

In contrast to the relatively beneficent position of Thomas, Nancy Scheper-Hughes has observed that modern anthropology 'was built up in the face of colonial and postcolonial genocides, ethnocides, population die-outs, and other forms of mass destruction visited on the "non-Western" peoples whose lives, suffering and deaths provide the raw material for much of our work'.[3] In other words, Thomas's revisionism might be less justified than those who entertain a notion of empire's essential beneficence would like to think.

1 Nicholas Thomas, *Colonialism's Culture: Anthropology, Travel and Government* (Cambridge: Polity Press 1994), 15.
2 Patrick Brantlinger, *Dark Vanishings: Discourse on the Extinction of Primitive Races, 1800–1930* (Ithaca, NY: Cornell University Press 2003); Russell McGregor, *Imagined Destinies: Aboriginal Australians and the Doomed Race Theory, 1880–1939* (Melbourne: Melbourne University Press 1997).
3 Nancy Scheper-Hughes, 'Ishi's brain, Ishi's ashes: anthropology and genocide', in Nancy Scheper-Hughes and Philippe Bourgois (eds), *Violence in War and Peace: An Anthology* (Oxford: Blackwell 2004), 61.

Mike Davis has shown that the British empire had a distinctly dark side, if not because of a Nazi-like ideology of destruction, then certainly because of a willing disregard for those who lost out at the hands of a rigid and ultimately murderous free-trade policy.[4] And other scholars have begun to advance the argument that genocides in colonial contexts have occurred in many parts of the world but that they have been neglected by western scholars for fear of the implications for their own nations' histories. Gavan McCormack, for example, argues that Japanese colonialist policy in China between 1931 and 1945 and Korea between 1894 and 1945 clearly aimed at destroying both as national groups by assimilating them into Japan. But, as he notes,

> the use of the term 'genocide' carrying as it does extreme legal and moral opprobrium, to describe acts committed by imperial Japan but not to describe acts committed by the Western powers must be problematic. If Japan was genocidal in China or elsewhere in Asia, what then shall we say of the French in Algeria or Indochina, the Americans in Korea and Indochina and the Gulf, the Russians in Chechnya?[5]

The relationship between genocide and colonialism is clearly a vexed question that admits of no easy answers and even stumps seasoned analysts. For instance, Leo Kuper pointed rightly to the absence of automism between colonialism and human destruction: 'the effects of colonial settlement were quite variable, dependent on a variety of factors, such as the number of settlers, the forms of the colonizing economy and competition for productive resources, policies of the colonizing power, and attitudes to intermarriage or concubinage.' But was it plausible to conclude, as he did, that unintended 'genocidal processes' were the main culprits, namely, 'massacres, appropriation of land, introduction of diseases, and arduous conditions of labor'?[6] When is a massacre the unintended result of an uncontrolled process? He concluded more plausibly by pleading for a qualified 'affinity between colonialism and genocide'.[7] Thus, although colonialism does not necessarily

---

4 Mike Davis, *Late Victorian Holocausts: El Niño Famines and the Making of the Third World* (London: Verso 2001).

5 Gavan McCormack, 'Reflections on modern Japanese history in the context of the concept of genocide', in Robert Gellately and Ben Kiernan (eds), *The Specter of Genocide: Mass Murder in Historical Perspective* (Cambridge: Cambridge University Press 2003), 270.

6 Leo Kuper, 'Other selected cases of genocide and genocidal massacres: types of genocide', in Israel W. Charny (ed.), *Genocide: A Critical Bibliographical Review* (London: Mansell 1988), 156.

7 Leo Kuper, *Genocide: Its Political Use in the Twentieth Century* (Harmondsworth: Penguin 1981), 45.

issue in genocide, the two phenomena are profoundly connected, as many examples from around the world illustrate. Tasmania, for example, is often cited as the site of a successful genocide, with the white settlers wiping out the indigenous Tasmanians. In this regard, we are proud to be able to publish here a chapter by Raphaël Lemkin on Tasmania, unearthed in the New York Public Library by Ann Curthoys, who sets it in historiographical context. Intended as part of his world history of genocide, which was to include many colonial cases, it constitutes an important statement on a controversial topic by the man who invented the term 'genocide'. Regrettably, Lemkin's study was never published. The correspondence from publishers held in the Lemkin archives in New York and Cincinnati reveal a lack of interest in such a topic in the 1950s. This was also the time when Raul Hilberg found it exceedingly difficult to find a house for his monumental manuscript on the 'destruction of the European Jews'. Remarkably, this neglect of Lemkin's broad interest in world history was continued by the new discipline of 'comparative genocide studies' in the 1980s and 1990s. With the rediscovery of Lemkin's unpublished manuscripts, we are better placed to understand that he did not conceive of genocide as a synonym for mass murder. His concern was the protection of culture-bearing groups rather than contingent ones like political associations. The former could be destroyed by a range of policies that undermined their ability to reproduce themselves culturally as well as biologically. Consequently, their genocidal destruction—or crippling, a term he also used—need not resemble the relentless state-centred model of the Holocaust.[8]

This book on genocide and colonialism continues the tradition of Lemkin's virtually unknown interest in colonial genocides. Historians today find themselves in a far easier situation than Lemkin did when he embarked on his analyses half a century ago. Able to draw on a mountain of secondary literature, and as specialists in their chosen case study, they can bring a powerful arsenal of intellectual resources to bear on the problem. Utilizing intellectual history and discourse analysis, for instance, Norbert Finzsch and Tony Barta investigate the various modes of racism that operated in colonizing societies to legitimate the dispossession of the land of indigenous people, their eventual 'extinction' or even massacre. To think of genocide as a phenomenon perpetrated only by Europeans on agentless 'natives' would, however, not do justice to the 'one generic notion' that Lemkin proposed. Drawing on French and Haitian sources, Philippe R. Girard is able to show how the struggle between the colonists and former slaves resulted in the genocide of the former by the latter. For all his concern with the genocides of past centuries, however, Lemkin did

---

8 A. Dirk Moses, 'The Holocaust and genocide', in Dan Stone (ed.), *The Historiography of the Holocaust* (Basingstoke: Palgrave Macmillan 2004), 533–55.

think that the Holocaust of European Jewry was distinctive: it was 'a flawless and almost scientific system, the perfection of which has still not been achieved by another people even today'.[9] Of course, he did not live long enough to witness the outcome of the revolution in 'Democratic Kampuchea' after 1975 or 'Hutu power' in Rwanda in 1994, but we know that he did not use the quasi-sacrificial term 'holocaust', or indulge in metaphysical language about its commonly regarded uniqueness. That the Holocaust did not strike as a thunderbolt, unrelated to secular trends, but was related to intellectual and political traditions, above all in Germany, would have struck him as an eminently sensible view. So it is entirely appropriate that Jürgen Zimmerer puts flesh on the bones of the now often-mentioned thesis about the continuities between the Holocaust and colonialism by investigating the links between German imperialism in South-west Africa before the First World War and the radicalized form of German imperialism on the European continent almost four decades later.

That colonialism and destruction can be conceived as far broader than even Lemkin's genocide concept allows is explored by the historian Vinay Lal. As concerned with the colonization of knowledge—or categories—as with its more well-known modalities, Lal asks the reader to entertain the destructive, indeed genocidal, consequences of Eurocentric concepts of social development, which issued in the catastrophes of the Soviet collectivization of agriculture and the Maoist 'great leap forward'. Moreover, is the West's focus on genocide a means by which to render its conscience clean? Whatever readers make of these arguments, can it be gainsaid that any critical history of genocide needs to interrogate its social and political function in discourses of human rights? This book does not pretend to cover the gamut of world history. That would be an impossible undertaking in so few pages. These contributions are designed to deepen research into the cases at hand and further the research agenda on genocide and colonialism. That agenda is still in its infancy. We hope these essays stimulate debate and further research.

A. Dirk Moses
Department of History, University of Sydney
Dan Stone
Department of History, Royal Holloway, University of London

9 Lemkin, quoted in Uwe Markino, 'Final solutions, crimes against mankind: on the genesis and criticism of the concept of genocide', *Journal of Genocide Research*, vol. 3, 2001, 55.

'It is scarcely possible to conceive that human beings could be so hideous and loathsome': discourses of genocide in eighteenth- and nineteenth-century America and Australia[1]

NORBERT FINZSCH

1 I wish to thank the two anonymous referees for constructive criticisms in the preparation of this article. The quotation in the title is from Charles Sturt, *Two Expeditions into the Interior of Southern Australia, during the Years 1828, 1829, 1830, and 1831: With Observations on the Soil, Climate, and General Resources of the Colony of New South Wales* (London: Smith, Elder and Co. 1834).

Et on tuera tous les affreux[2]
Exterminate all the brutes[3]

In the discussion about European colonialisms, it has become a common-place to assume that modern racism emerged with Darwinism and with the modern nation-state in the second half of the nineteenth century. Through Darwinian thinking, racism acquired both a biological and a scientific basis, and 'culture' ceased to be a decisive factor in the presumed difference between human 'races'. Stephen Jay Gould expressed the conventional wisdom when he remarked that, following the publication of Charles Darwin's *On the Origin of Species* in 1859,[4] 'subsequent arguments for slavery, colonialism, racial differences, class structures, and sex roles would go forth primarily under the banner of science'.[5] Nationalism, so this account continues, was racialized, just as racism was nationalized.[6] For this reason, the 'age of scientific racism' witnessed major genocides, such as the annihilation of the Hereros by German troops in South-west Africa in 1904–5, the slaughter of Armenians in Turkey in 1915, and the mass murder of Jews and other groups during the Holocaust in Europe.[7]

2 Boris Vian, *Et on tuera tous les affreux* (Paris: Le Terrain vague 1965).
3 Joseph Conrad, *Heart of Darkness and the Secret Sharer* (New York: New American Library 1950), 123.
4 Charles Darwin, *On the Origin of Species by Means of Natural Selection, or the Preservation of Favoured Races in the Struggle for Life* (London: John Murray 1859).
5 Stephen Jay Gould, *The Mismeasure of Man* (New York: Norton 1981), 72. Darwinian ideas reached both Australia and North America right after 1859; see Barry W. Butcher, 'Darwin down under: science, religion, and evolution in Australia', in Ronald L. Numbers and John Stenhouse (eds), *Disseminating Darwinism: The Role of Place, Race, Religion, and Gender* (Cambridge and New York: Cambridge University Press 1999), 39–59 (41–3); Jon H. Roberts, 'Darwinism, American Protestant thinkers, and the puzzle of motivation', in Numbers and Stenhouse (eds), *Disseminating Darwinism*, 145–72 (146–8). Even if Darwin treated human development fully only in 1871 in his treatise *The Descent of Man*, references to human biology abound in *On the Origin of Species*. Referring to the idea of constant struggle for survival, for instance, Darwin notes: 'There is no exception to the rule that every organic being naturally increases at so high a rate that, if not destroyed, the earth would soon be covered by the progeny of a single pair. Even slow-breeding man has doubled in twenty-five years, and at this rate, in a few thousand years, there would literally not be standing room for his progeny' (Darwin, *On the Origin of Species*, 45). The inclusion of humankind in Darwin's consideration is by no means exceptional, since Malthus treated humanity already as a biological entity. Another word of caution: the dates 1859 and 1871 only denote a discursive threshold after which it became acceptable to include humans into the biological realm; the question of when and where this idea of human development emerged is beyond the point I want to make.
6 Etienne Balibar, 'Racism and nationalism', in Etienne Balibar and Immanuel Wallerstein, *Race, Nation, Class: Ambiguous Identities* (London and New York: Verso 1991), 37–67 (42–4).
7 Samuel Totten, William S. Parsons and Israel W. Charny, *A Century of Genocide: Critical Essays and Eyewitness Accounts*, 2nd edn (New York: Routledge 2004); Jürgen Zimmerer,

There are good reasons, however, not to limit the concept of genocide to the application of racial theories in the late nineteenth and twentieth centuries. After all, the period before 1860 witnessed genocidal wars in both North America and Australia.[8] Then there is the fact that immigrants from various parts of the world settled in places like North America and Australia, where they drove the indigenous peoples from their lands by high and low intensity wars, infectious diseases, ecological shifts, government policies and in a process of more or less peaceful expansion of settlers and squatters that Carl Schmitt has called the 'taking of the land'.[9] White/indigenous interaction and subsequent white settlement are virtually simultaneous with processes of invasion and displacement of indigenous populations, notwithstanding that in both societies the relations between indigenous and settler societies went through periods of peaceful interaction, cultural accommodation and mutual adjustment.

The question is how killings and dispossession of the Native Americans and Aborigines before the 1860s was possible and legitimizable, given that the 'age of Enlightenment' is usually perceived as a relatively benign period for the interaction of western and indigenous populations. In this article, I argue that Darwinian thinking was preceded by and overlapped with an archaic racism with genocidal potential, constituted by the visual othering of indigenous populations in America and Australia. This contention does not exclude the possible co-existence of scientific racism and archaic racism after 1859 or early forms of scientific racism before 1859. My assertion rather tries to establish the existence of a racism based on the body, aesthetic categories and

Deutsche Herrschaft über Afrikaner: Staatlicher Machtanspruch und Wirklichkeit im kolonialen Namibia, 3rd edn (Münster and Hamburg: LIT 2003); Richard G. Hovannisian, *Looking Backward, Moving Forward: Confronting the Armenian Genocide* (New Brunswick, NJ: Transaction Publishers 2003); Dan Stone (ed.), *The Historiography of the Holocaust* (New York: Palgrave Macmillan 2004); Eric D. Weitz, *A Century of Genocide* (Princeton, NJ: Princeton University Press 2002).

8 Henry Reynolds, *Frontier: Aborigines, Settlers and Land* (Sydney: Allen and Unwin 1996), 23. Reynolds answers the question of whether these warlike acts constituted genocides in the negative because '[the] Aborigines survived the invasion', and thus falls prey to a frequent misunderstanding of the term 'genocide' and its meaning (53). Tony Barta, 'Discourses of genocide in Germany and Australia: a linked history', *Aboriginal History*, vol. 25, 2001, 43.

9 Carl Schmitt suggested that the history of peoples is the history of taking land (*Landnahme*) and that every real *Landnahme* produces a new *nomos*; a pre-state order of society is therefore based on land; Carl Schmitt, *Der Nomos der Erde im Völkerrecht des Jus Publicum Europaeum* (Cologne: Greven 1950). Pertaining to the 'taking of the land' in North America, see Ward Churchill, *Indians Are Us? Culture and Genocide in Native North America* (Monroe, ME: Common Courage Press 1994). A broad, if somewhat general, overview is presented in Robert A. Williams, *The American Indian in Western Legal Thought: The Discourses of Conquest* (New York: Oxford University Press 1990). For a Native American perspective, see Robert A. Williams, *Linking Arms Together: American Indian Treaty Visions of Law and Peace, 1600–1800* (New York: Routledge 1999).

culture.[10] This visual ideology constructed a racialized and gendered abject Other on the basis of aesthetics and an assessment of the Other's economic, societal and linguistic achievements.[11] By placing the indigenous Other at the very bottom rung of humanity, this discourse justified the Other's expulsion from native lands, economic exploitation, destruction of the indigenous ecosphere and even eventual genocide.[12] A racism emerged at the end of the eighteenth century, then, but a racism not defined by scientific definitions of 'race', as in the case of post-Darwinian biology. Accordingly, this analysis focuses on the years between 1788 and the 1850s, the crucial period of early colonialism before the publication of Darwin's *On the Origin of Species*.[13]

Eighteenth-century colonial projects had their own historic pattern and, although specific colonialisms differ in time, place and agents, they share certain attributes.[14] These commonalities constitute the basis for a comparison of British expansionism in North America and Australia.[15] English language, customs and British laws and institutions influenced the underlying cultural and political structures for the first decades, if not centuries, after settlement. And both settler societies were influenced deeply by the existence of peoples of non-European descent that had settled the country a long time before Europeans arrived. To be sure, primitivism was one of many colonial ideologies, and it does not necessarily entail a genocidal potential. Montaigne's 'On Cannibals' or Tacitus' 'Germania' do not constitute genocidal discourse, for instance. But, in the primitivism in both these settler societies, the Europeans perceived the indigenes as savage, barbaric, wild and uncivilized.[16] I draw on primary sources by white people

---

10 Thomas Jefferson is a prime example of how aesthetic judgements and proto-scientific data converge in early racisms. In his justification of slavery in *Notes on the State of Virginia*, written in 1781, he makes both aesthetic and scientific observations on the corporeal and mental abilities of Africans; Thomas Jefferson, *Notes on the State of Virginia* (Boston: Wells and Lilly 1829), 144–51, 169–71.

11 Elizabeth Elbourne, 'Domesticity and dispossession: the ideology of the "home" and the British construction of the "primitive" from the eighteenth to the early nineteenth centuries', in Wendy Woodward, Patricia Hayes and Gary Minkley (eds), *Deep hiStories: Gender and Colonialism in Southern Africa* (Amsterdam and New York: Rodopi 2002), 29–33.

12 On the intellectual origin of the stage theory, see David Armitage, 'The New World and British historical thought' and Peter Burke, 'America and the rewriting of world history', both in Karen Kupperman (ed.), *American in European Consciousness* (Chapel Hill: University of North Carolina Press 1995).

13 Charles Darwin, *The Descent of Man and Selection in Relation to Sex*, 2 vols (London: John Murray 1871), i.184; Butcher, 'Darwin down under'.

14 Elbourne, 'Domesticity and dispossession', 29.

15 Geoffrey Bolton, 'Reflections on a comparative frontier history', in Bain Attwood and Stephen Foster (eds), *Frontier Conflict: The Australian Experience* (Canberra: National Museum of Australia 2003), 161–7.

16 Terry Goldie, *Fear and Temptation: The Image of the Indigene in Canadian, Australian, and New Zealand Literatures* (Kingston, Ontario: McGill–Queen's University Press 1989).

who actually went to Australia, saw indigenous people with their own eyes and came to conclusions about the 'character' of 'savages'.

Why focus on such perceptions? Since a nation-state and a war machine capable of carrying out secret genocides did not exist before 1850, the early colonial genocides had to be brought about by 'people on the ground', meaning the discoverers, soldiers, settlers and squatters that filled the 'wilderness' by conquering, surveying, buying and ploughing native lands. 'Settler imperialism' was at the very core of premodern genocide.[17]

This is not just a story of parallels. Whereas colonial expansion in North America started as early as the seventeenth century, in Australia it began only in 1788 after the American colonies had gained their independence from England and at the height of 'the age of Enlightenment'.[18] Whereas in North America settlers were looking for political and religious freedom, in Australia the first colonizers were convicts accompanied by a detachment of British marines. Yet both military men and convicts had some previous knowledge about indigenous peoples without ever having actually seen Aborigines before their ships anchored in Port Jackson: British soldiers and officers had been fighting in the French and Indian Wars of North America (1755–63) as well as during the American Revolution and, in both colonial conflicts, native troops had played a major part, both as allies and as enemies of the British soldiers. The British in Australia, having the American experience in their heads, were ready to perceive the Aborigines as just another variety of North American Indian; in fact, they used the very same words to describe them.[19]

Discourses and *dispositives*

Any policy of genocide, extermination, colonialism or expansion rests on two pillars. It needs agents and perpetrators who serve as carriers of the

---

17 A. Dirk Moses (ed.), *Genocide and Settler Society: Frontier Violence and Stolen Indigenous Children in Australian History* (New York and Oxford: Berghahn Books 2004). For an elaboration of the concept of 'settler imperialism', see my chapter in A. Dirk Moses (ed.), *Genocide and Colonialism* (New York and Oxford: Berghahn Books 2006, forthcoming).

18 John Gascoigne, *The Enlightenment and the Origins of European Australia* (Cambridge, New York and Melbourne: Cambridge University Press 2002).

19 Jacob Abbott, *American History*, 8 vols (New York and Boston: Sheldon, Gould and Lincoln 1860). Volume 1, entitled *Aboriginal America*, refers to Amerindians as 'American Aboriginals' (60, 61, 144, 153, 257, 275, 277). Watkin Tench, referring to Australians, states: 'Like ourselves, the French found it necessary, more than once, to chastise a spirit of rapine and intrusion which prevailed among the Indians around the bay'; Watkin Tench, 'A narrative of the expedition to Botany Bay', in Tim F. Flannery (ed.), *Two Classic Tales of Australian Exploration: 1788 by Watkin Tench; Life and Adventures by John Nicol* (Melbourne: Text Pub 2002), 62.

policy, and it needs a discourse that endows these agents with the knowledge/power, justification and rationale for their practices. Mind-management necessarily complements military and economic domination in the repertoire of colonialism and imperialism. This article addresses the discourses of legitimization, namely, the 'discourses of genocide'.[20] I will not deal with the way British colonials, bureaucrats, officers and settlers treated Native Americans and Australian Aborigines *realiter*, but focus instead on the discourses of primitivism and exclusion that abounded in the Anglo-sphere after 1788. These discourses are part of colonialism in the form of a *dispositive*, that is, an apparatus of power relations that backs up types of knowledge and that is in turn supported by them. This apparatus consists of a network of various and heterogeneous elements, such as discourses, laws, prescriptions, buildings and institutions.[21]

Before the impact of scientific racism in the 1860s, these discourses helped to define not only the superiority of western explorers, colonialists and imperialists over the colonized, but lay the ground for the latter's exploitation, enslavement and eventual genocide. When I use the concept of genocide in a colonial context, I refer to the international legal definition of the crime of genocide as found in Articles II and III of the 1948 Convention on the Prevention and Punishment of Genocide. Article II describes the two elements of the crime of genocide: the *mental element*, meaning the 'intent to destroy, in whole or in part, a national, ethnical, racial or religious group, as such', and the *physical element*, which includes a range of five acts, namely, killing members of the group, causing serious bodily or mental harm to members of the group, deliberately inflicting on the group conditions of life calculated to bring about its physical destruction in whole or in part, imposing measures intended to prevent births within the group, or forcibly transferring children of the group to another group. According to this definition, a crime must include *both elements* to be called 'genocide'.[22] Since the intent, defined as 'anticipated outcome', precedes actual acts of killing or harming, it is safe to say that any form of genocide requires anticipation and discursive preparation.

20 Here I follow Barta, 'Discourses of genocide in Germany and Australia'.
21 Nancy Stepan, *The Idea of Race in Science: Great Britain 1800–1860* (Hamden, CT: Archon Books 1982), 47–9; Michel Foucault, 'Ein Spiel um die Psychoanalyse', in *Dispositive der Macht: Über Sexualität, Wissen und Wahrheit* (Berlin: Merve 1978), 123; Michel Foucault, 'Le Jeu de Michel Foucault', in Michel Foucault, *Dits et Écrits*, 3 vols (Paris: Gallimard 1994), iii.299; Michel Foucault, *Discipline and Punish: The Birth of the Prison*, trans. from the French by Alan Sheridan (New York: Pantheon Books 1977), 174.
22 United Nations, *Convention on the Prevention and Punishment of the Crime of Genocide: Adopted by Resolution 260 (III) A of the U.N. General Assembly on 9 December 1948*, United Nations Treaty Series, no. 1021, vol. 78 (New York: United Nations Treaty Series 1951), 277.

Such preparation was laid by early travellers, observers, ethnographers and amateur anthropologists who provided 'evidence' for a classification of human groups and their subsequent subjection to a hierarchy of qualities. Thus Darwin's mentor John Stevens Henslow could write in 1837:

> To obtain a knowledge of a science of observation, like botany, we need make very little more exertion at first than is required for adapting a chosen set of terms to certain appearances of which the eye takes cognizance, and when this has been attained, all the rest is very much like reading a book after we have learned to spell, where every page affords a fresh field of intellectual enjoyment.[23]

Observation was a way not only to reify the objects of the visible world but also to bestow on the colonial gaze the character of scientific truth.

Visual abjection

Central to the definition of genocide is the concept of intent, the paramount wish that the other group should cease to exist, be it as a consequence of adverse economic and ecological conditions or the kidnapping of children. Before acts of violence and dispossession could be committed in the period before the 1860s, perpetrators and silent witnesses had to agree on a taxonomy of primitivism that would allow perpetrators and witnesses to view Native Americans and Aborigines as less than equal, less than civilized and less than human. These discursive entities coalesce into an image of a 'creature' that is utterly rejected and excluded from humanity.[24] This position of abjection is analysed by Giorgio Agamben, who shows how political power is most effective when it does not deal with politics *per se*, but with human existence as an object of bio-power.[25] Bio-power constitutes a form of power/knowledge that is inscribed on bodies and that becomes

---

23 John Stevens Henslow, 'On the requisites necessary for the advance of botany', *Magazine of Zoology and Botany*, vol. 1, 1837, 115.

24 The 'exclusionary matrix by which subjects are formed requires the simultaneous production of a domain of abject beings', who hint at the 'unlivable [*sic*] and uninhabitable . . . zones of social life which are nevertheless densely populated by those who do not enjoy the status of subject, but whose living under the sign of the "unlivable" [*sic*] is required to circumscribe the domain of the subject'; Judith Butler, *Bodies That Matter: On the Discursive Limits of Sex* (New York: Routledge 1993), 3. Jonathan Swift uses the term *abject* when he discusses the Yahoos, the human 'slave race' in the country of the Houyhnhnms; Jonathan Swift, *Gulliver's Travels* [1726], ed. Herbert John Davis, vol. 11 of *The Prose Works of Jonathan Swift* (Oxford: Blackwell 1941), 265–7.

25 Michel Foucault, 'Body/power', in *Power/Knowledge: Selected Interviews and Other Writings 1972–1977*, ed. and trans. from the French by Colin Gordon (Brighton: Harvester Press 1980), 55–62.

visible on the body, especially through a panoptic gaze. Groups and individuals that remain outside of the desired effects of bio-power are 'unliveable', and are defined as unworthy of life.[26]

Two basic models for describing the indigenous had been developed during the seventeenth century: the Ignoble or Primitive Savage, and the Noble Savage.[27] The concept of the Noble Savage had been discarded by the end of the eighteenth century and was only resuscitated after indigenous populations, both in America and Australia, ceased to constitute a threat to colonial societies.[28] The image of the Primitive Savage, by contrast, continued to be used throughout the eighteenth and nineteenth centuries as a justification for chattel slavery, colonial domination and economic exploitation.[29] The assessment as 'savage' was based largely on observation, that is, the European gaze directed at the indigenous body. This gaze did not only constitute the obvious instrument of contemporary scientific research; it also served as a microtechnique of power in the sense that it empowered and engendered colonial conquest through the 'dominant gaze'.[30] With the rise

26 Giorgio Agamben, *Homo Sacer: Sovereign Power and Bare Life*, trans. from the Italian by Daniel Heller-Roazen (Stanford, CA: Stanford University Press 1998). See also Attwood and Forster (ed.), *Frontier Conflict*, 22–3.

27 See the special issue of the *William and Mary Quarterly*, 3rd Series, vol. 54, no. 1, 1997, on the construction of race in colonial America. On pre-Darwinian racial discourse in North America, see Alden T. Vaughan, *Roots of American Racism: Essays on the Colonial Experience* (New York: Oxford University Press 1995); Ivan Hannaford, *Race: The History of an Idea* (Washington, D.C. and Baltimore: Woodrow Wilson Center Press 1996); Joyce E. Chaplin, *Subject Matter: Technology, the Body and Science on the Anglo-American Frontier, 1500–1676* (Cambridge, MA: Harvard University Press 2001).

28 Socorro Babaran Cario, 'Eighteenth Century Voyagers to the Pacific and the South Seas, and the Rise of Cultural Primitivism and the Noble Savage Idea', Ph.D. thesis, University of Illinois, 1970; Terry Jay Ellingson, *The Myth of the Noble Savage* (Berkeley: University of California Press 2001); Jean Woolmington, *Aborigines in Colonial Society, 1788–1850: From 'Noble Savage' to 'Rural Pest'* (Armidale, NSW: University of New England Press 1988). In the field of morals/ethics, a trajectory of the Noble Savage was still visible, fitting the genealogical division of an older and a younger discourse; see James Cook's remarks about New Holland, in 'James Cook's Journal of Remarkable Occurrences aboard His Majesty's Bark Endeavour, 1768–1771', online edition of the original journal at the National Library of Australia, http://southseas.nla.gov.au/journals/cook_remarks/092.html (viewed 10 February 2005). However, most of the time, Aborigines are portrayed as fickle, treacherous and thieving; see Tench, 'A narrative of the expedition to Botany Bay', 59, 190. For the same mindset, see Sturt, *Two Expeditions into the Interior of Southern Australia*.

29 Louise K. Barnett, *The Ignoble Savage: American Literary Racism, 1790–1890* (Westport, CT: Greenwood Press 1975); John K. Lodewijks, 'Rational economic man and the Ignoble Savage', *History of Political Economy*, vol. 32, 2000, 1027–32; Ronald L. Meek, *Social Science and the Ignoble Savage* (Cambridge and New York: Cambridge University Press 1976); Beulah V. Thigpen, 'The Indians of *The Leather-Stocking Tales*: A Study of the Noble and the Ignoble Savage', Ph.D. thesis, East Texas State University, 1982.

30 Laura Mulvey, 'Visual pleasure and narrative cinema', *Screen*, vol. 16, no. 3, Autumn 1975, 6–18.

of 'the regime of the scopic', possession was experienced through the act of looking.[31]

Consider Anthony Ashley Cooper, 3rd Earl of Shaftesbury (1671–1713), who described the virtuous man as a 'spectator', devoted to the disinterested 'survey and contemplation' of beauty in manners and morals.[32] His conception of beauty resonates with his conception of virtue.[33] Beauty meant virtue, and hideousness meant sin.[34] For the European gaze directed at the indigenous body, it meant that the inner morality and ethics of the indigene could be measured by its external beauty or ugliness, by the shape of limbs, flatness of breasts, wooliness of hair and complexion.[35] Speaking about the eighteenth-century foundations of racism, George L. Mosse called it a 'visual ideology based upon stereotypes',[36] meaning that the appearance, the looks of indigenous peoples, carried a specific meaning. In the eighteenth century, complexion meant more than just skin colour. It also entailed a moral evaluation, especially after 1770 when the old distinction between Christians and pagans gave way to aestheticized judgements.[37] As in the case of antebellum slave markets, where slaves were looked at and examined through a (male) gaze, the aboriginal body 'was made racially legible' through inspection.[38]

Colonial gaze and indigenous speech

Intimately connected with this aesthetic theory was a theory of the origin of humanity and its ability to speak. Scottish Enlightenment philosophers developed a taxonomy of cultures that imagined a process of civilization

31 Gargi Bhattacharyya, *Tales of Dark-Skinned Women: Race, Gender and Global Culture* (London: University College London Press 1998), 337.
32 Anthony Ashley Cooper Shaftesbury, *Characteristics of Men, Manners, Opinions, Times*, 2 vols (Cambridge and New York: Cambridge University Press 1999), ii.45.
33 Paul Guyer, 'Beauty and utility in eighteenth-century aesthetics', *Eighteenth-century Studies*, vol. 35, 2002, 439–53 (439–40).
34 Cf. the depiction of the animal-like, abject Yahoos in Swift, *Gulliver's Travels*, 266–7 and also ch. 1.
35 Claude Rawson, *God, Gulliver and Genocide: Barbarism and the European Imagination, 1492–1945* (Oxford and New York: Oxford University Press 2001), 98–108.
36 George L. Mosse, *Toward the Final Solution: A History of European Racism* (Madison: University of Wisconsin Press 1985), xii.
37 Roxann Wheeler, *The Complexion of Race: Categories of Difference in Eighteenth-century British Culture* (Philadelphia: University of Pennsylvania Press 2000), 54–5.
38 Walter Johnson, *Soul by Soul: Life inside the Antebellum Slave Market* (Cambridge, MA and London: Harvard University Press 1990), 161. Lynette Russell shows how this scopism made its way into British museums after 1850; Lynette Russell, '"Well nigh impossible to describe": dioramas, displays and representations of Australian Aborigines', *Australian Aboriginal Studies*, vol. 2, 1999, 35–45.

consisting of four stages.[39] According to these philosophers, the lowest stage was marked by an economy based on hunting; this was followed by the next evolutionary step, an economy of herding. Then came cultivation, defined as labour on the land and fixed residence; the final and highest stage was industry and commerce, only lately achieved by the members of European nations. Early modern theories of language supplement the stage theory. Questions of language and speech capability were paramount for a definition of humanity. It is only fitting, then, that those at the lowest stages lack a proper language, since they are devoid of humanity: statements like Arthur Bowes Smyth's that 'their Language is excessively Loud & harsh & se[e]ms to consist of a very short Vocabulary' very much sum up what observers had to say about the indigenes.[40]

By regarding the indigenous body and listening to indigenous speech, it was possible for the eighteenth-century English-speaking spectator to place this body in a matrix of progress and civilization, morality and ethics, growth or extinction. The ethnographic episteme that was the result of this observation and discourse had the same effect, for the observer, as a peephole: it limited the gaze and transformed it into a tool of power. This thinking was a form of cultural racism, because what 'distinguished the different races was culture not biology'.[41] Racial variation was attributed to environmental rather than biological factors.[42] But this also meant that the 'savage environment' (geology, botany, climate, society and family) had to be described and evaluated much more rigorously than in the later theories of scientific racism that focused on inherent biological qualities of groups. Once fixed in written texts and published in books and journals, destined for consumption in England, this descriptive and classifying discourse became 'writing that conquers'.[43]

The allegory of America depicted as a naked woman exposed to the European gaze in many pictorial representations in books and pamphlets

---

39 See Alan Barnard, 'Hunting-and-gathering society: an eighteenth-century Scottish invention', in Alan Barnard (ed.), *Hunter-Gatherers in History, Archaeology and Anthropology* (Oxford and New York: Berg 2004). Istvan Hont, 'The language of sociability and commerce: Samuel Pufendorf and the theoretical foundations of the "four stages theory"', in Anthony Pagden (ed.), *The Languages of Political Theory in Early-Modern Europe* (Cambridge and New York: Cambridge University Press 1990), 253–76.

40 Paul G. Fidlon and R. J. Ryan (eds), *The Journal of Arthur Bowes Smyth: Surgeon, Lady Penrhyn, 1787–1789* (Sydney: Australian Documents Library 1979), 58; James Grant, *The Narrative of a Voyage of Discovery Performed in His Majesty's Vessel the Lady Nelson, of Sixty Tons Burthen, with Sliding Keels, in the Years 1800, 1801, and 1802 to New South Wales* (Adelaide: Libraries Board of South Australia 1973), 157.

41 Gascoigne, *The Enlightenment*, 149.

42 Ibid., 150.

43 Michel de Certeau, *The Writing of History* (New York: Columbia University Press 1988), xxv.

'draws on a long tradition of male travel as an erotics of ravishment'.[44] This European gaze is not only an index for a position of the indigenous Other on a scale of acculturation, but it is also a 'projection into the New World of European representations of gender—and of sexual conduct'.[45] This gaze interprets nudity at once as a sign of low evolutionary status and as a promise of effortless access. This 'coherent hermeneutical strategy of feminization and eroticization' that makes 'gendered difference' one of the meanings of the New World can also be observed in the travel descriptions of Australia after 1788.[46] In both America and Australia, European consciousness is encoded as masculine. In Johannes Stradanus's image, an emblematic Vespucci *dis*covers an *un*covered woman: America is a male 'voyeur's paradise'.[47] Territorial conquest coincided with the possession of the abstract and literal female body.[48]

What does the 'persistent gendering' of imperial conquest have to do with the discovery and settlement of America and Australia?[49] Gender is a way of portraying 'relationships of power'.[50] In Stradanus's picture, there is an important iconographic element in the background: a cannibal meal is taking place. This element refers to America as a continent of female cannibals, thus laying bare 'the mark of unregenerate savagery'.[51] America is 'simulta- neously naked and passive *and* riotously violent and cannibalistic', a combination that requires European intervention in order to restore male mastery.[52] America and Australia as the ultimate opposites of the European

44 Anne McClintock, *Imperial Leather: Race, Gender and Sexuality in the Colonial Contest* (New York: Routledge 1995), 22.
45 Louis Montrose, 'The work of gender in the discourse of discovery', in Stephen Greenblatt (ed.), *New World Encounters* (Berkeley: University of California Press 1993), 197–217 (178).
46 Margarita Zamora, *Reading Columbus* (Berkeley: University of California Press 1993), 157.
47 Johannes Stradanus [i.e. Jan van der Straet], *New Discoveries: The Sciences, Inventions and Discoveries of the Middle Ages and the Renaissance as Represented in 24 Engravings Issued in the Early 1580s* (Norwalk, CT: Burndy Library 1953); Peter Mason, *Deconstructing America: Representations of the Other* (London, New York: Routledge 1990), 171.
48 See Susan Morgan, *Place Matters: Gendered Geography in Victorian Women's Travel Books about Southeast Asia* (New Brunswick, NJ: Rutgers University Press 1996), 11. Morgan asserts the importance of gender as a structuring principle of colonial discourse. See also Sara Mills, *Discourses of Difference: An Analysis of Women's Travel Writing and Colonialism* (London and New York: Routledge 1991); Mary Louise Pratt, *Imperial Eyes: Travel Writing and Transculturation* (London and New York: Routledge 1992).
49 McClintock, *Imperial Leather*, 24.
50 Joan Wallach Scott, *Gender and the Politics of History* (New York: Columbia University Press 1988), 42.
51 Peter Hulme, *Colonial Encounters: Europe and the Native Caribbean, 1492–1797* (London and New York: Methuen 1986), 3.
52 McClintock, *Imperial Leather*, 27.

way of life and a source of male anxiety must be subjugated/penetrated. [53] Thus it becomes understandable that many American as well as Australian sources are obsessed with the question of whether or not indigenous populations were cannibals. Again the chronological structure seems to be that of a split between an older generation of texts that flatly deny the existence of cannibalism among the Aborigines and a younger set that imply that anthropophagy was rampant among them.[54]

Dying races and the land

A second concept is crucial for the understanding of both American and Australian colonial expansionism, namely, the idea that the conquered continent was either virtually uninhabited or uncultivated and, therefore, lacking an owner, a concept expressed in the term *res nullius*. Over time, the colonialists systematically downplayed the number of Indians and Aborigines, thereby echoing Cook's description of the land as thinly populated. They also conceived increasingly of indigenous peoples as 'dying races'.[55] The

---

53 Ibid., 26–7.
54 Tench, 'A narrative of the expedition to Botany Bay', 53–4; William Bradley, *A Voyage to New South Wales: The Journal of Lieutenant William Bradley RN of HMS Sirius, 1786–1792* (Sydney: Public Library of New South Wales 1969), 142; Peter Miller Cunningham, *Two Years in New South Wales: A Series of Letters, Comprising Sketches of the Actual State of Society in That Colony; of Its Peculiar Advantages to Emigrants; of Its Topography, Natural History, &c. &c.*, 2 vols (London: H. Colburn 1828), ii.15, 36–7.
55 'The aboriginal inhabitants of the country were of races formed with constitutions, both physical and mental, adapting them to obtain their livelihood by fishing and the chase—modes of life by means of which North America might sustain perhaps twenty or thirty millions of inhabitants. The Caucasian race, which was introduced from Europe, is endowed with constitutions adapting them to gain their livelihood by agriculture, commerce, and the manufacturing arts, a mode of life by which the same territory is capable of supporting *many hundred* millions—we know not how many. Under these circumstances it was an inevitable, and as much in fulfillment of the designs of divine Providence, that the old races should be supplanted by the new, as that the horse and the cow should displace the alligator and the elk, and brakes and bulrushes yield their native ground to corn'; Abbott, *American History*, i.275–6. The plantation owner and US statistician Joseph Camp Griffith Kennedy predicted both the extinction of Native Americans and of emancipated African Americans; Joseph Camp Griffith Kennedy, *Population of the United States in 1860: Compiled from the Original Returns of the Eighth Census* (Washington, D.C.: Government Printing Office 1864), xi–xii. See also Brian W. Dippie, *The Vanishing American: White Attitudes and U.S. Indian Policy* (Middletown, CT: Wesleyan University Press 1982); Patrick Brantlinger, *Dark Vanishings: Discourse on the Extinction of Primitive Races, 1800–1930* (Ithaca, NY: Cornell University Press 2003); Reynolds, *Frontier*, 54; Barry W. Butcher, 'Darwinism, social Darwinism, and the Australian Aborigines: a reevaluation', in Roy Macleod and Philip F. Rehbock (eds), *Darwin's Laboratory: Evolutionary Theory and Natural History in the Pacific* (Honolulu: University of Hawaii Press 1994), 371–94.

question of the indigenes' right to their lands became salient in the early years of colonization and the ensuing process of taking over the lands formerly possessed by Aborigines and Amerindians. Legal arguments centred on the issue of settlement versus conquest. The settlement of Australia was predicated on the notion that the native inhabitants held no territorial claims to the lands they occupied. In the American case, although both the British colonial as well as the American governments recognized the land rights of Native Americans, the latter were forced to give up the titles to their lands through military conquest and fraudulent sales.[56] In the Australian case, Aborigines were defined as occupants—not owners—of the land.[57]

By contrast, in North America, at least in the legal fiction that served as the basis for Indian treaties, Amerindians were the initial owners of the land that they subsequently sold or lost to the colonial and American governments. Yet both cases share the idea that white settlers were entitled to indigenous lands because the original owners/occupants did not use them and remained in a state of migration. It is arguable that, from 1788 onwards, well before the legal concept of *res nullius* was formalized in 1847,[58] colonials had virtually adopted this doctrine as it had been laid out previously in both international law and Blackstone's *Commentaries on the Laws of England*. In the introduction to the latter, Blackstone outlined the relationship of the 'more distant plantations in America' to England, arguing:

> Plantations, or colonies in distant countries, are either such where the lands are claimed by right of occupancy only, by finding them desart [deserted] and uncultivated, and peopling them from the mother country; or where, when already cultivated, they have been either gained by conquest, or ceded to us by

---

56 Charles D. Bernholz, 'American Indian treaties and the presidents: a guide to the treaties proclaimed by each administration', *Social Studies*, vol. 93, September–October 2002, 218–27. The legal basis for the denial of indigenous land rights in both America and Australia was almost identical: in the 1823 US Supreme Court case *Johnson* v. *McIntosh* (8 Wheaton, 543), Chief Justice John Marshall argued that, by reason of conquest, native lands became the property of the US government and Indians were to be considered occupants. In 1831 the same court ruled in *Cherokee Nation* v. *State of Georgia* (5 Peters, 1, 16–19) that tribes were 'sovereign nations' but not 'foreign nations', establishing a guardian relationship between Indians and the government.

57 Reynolds, *Frontier*, 133–8.

58 In *Attorney-General* v. *Brown* (1847) one finds confirmation for the suggestion that, upon the settlement of New South Wales, the unqualified legal and beneficial ownership of all land in the colony was vested in the Crown. Arguably, the judgement of the Supreme Court of New South Wales in this case seems ambiguous in that the judges confined the proposition to 'waste lands', which they defined as 'all the waste and unoccupied lands of the colony'. Careful reading of the judgement makes it clear that it implicitly assumed all the lands of the colony to be vacant at the time of its establishment in 1788. See *Attorney-General* v. *Brown* (1847) 2 SCR (NSW) APP 30 (FC).

treaties. And both these rights are founded upon the law of nature, or at least upon that of nations.[59]

Evidence

In order to come to grips with genocidal discourses, I constructed a matrix of fifteen categories of observations from a number of sources dealing with Australian indigenous populations.[60] This matrix is based both on the research of Australian and American scholars on the importance of Enlightenment discourse for the development of European racism, and on the connection of colonial discourse and gender. (Extensive work on Native American history is implicitly included.[61]) The matrix constitutes a system of references that follows the logic of eighteenth- and nineteenth-century 'observations' of indigenous peoples. These references presuppose types of 'institutions'—including family, law, religion, political system and economy—that do not fit the ways in which indigenous communities in nation-states dominated by settler populations structured their societies.

This coarse genealogy falls into two stages, the first being the period 1788–1800, with a rupture at the very end of the eighteenth century. This earlier phase shows an almost 'neutral' image of the indigene, whereas the later period (1800–60) is marked by contemptuous and continuing condemnations of Aboriginals and their cultures. Of the fifteen categories of observations, it turns out that those pertaining to the 'looks' and the body types of the indigenes are the most prevalent. Take the following quotation by William Dampier (1691):

59 William Blackstone, *Commentaries on the Laws of England*, 4 vols (Oxford: Clarendon Press 1765–9), i.104.

60 The complete collection of sources can be accessed online at www.uni-koeln.de/phil-fak/histsem/anglo/html_2001/matrix.htm (viewed 11 February 2005).

61 On cannibalism as a traditional European reference to Indians, see Rawson, *God, Gulliver and Genocide*, 17–91; Francis Barker, Peter Hulme and Margaret Iversen, *Cannibalism and the Colonial World* (Cambridge and New York: Cambridge University Press 1998); David English and Penelope Van Toorn, *Speaking Positions: Aboriginality, Gender and Ethnicity in Australian Cultural Studies* (Melbourne: Victoria University of Technology 1995); Terry Goldie, *Fear and Temptation: The Image of the Indigene in Canadian, Australian and New Zealand Literatures* (Kingston, Ontario: McGill–Queen's University Press 1989); Richard Drinnon, *Facing West: The Metaphysics of Indian-Hating and Empire Building* (Norman: University of Oklahoma Press 1997); Robert F. Berkhofer, Jr., *The White Man's Indian: Images of the American Indian from Columbus to the Present* (New York: Vintage Books 1979).

They have great Bottle Noses, pretty full Lips, and wide Mouths. The two Fore-teeth of their Upper jaw are wanting in all of them, Men and Women, Old and Young; whether they draw them out, I know not: Neither have they any Beards. They are long visaged, and of a very unpleasing Aspect, having no one graceful Feature in their Faces. Their Hair is black, short and curl'd, like that of the Negroes; and not long and lank like the common Indians. The colour of their Skins, both of their Faces and the rest of their Body, is coal black, like that of the Negroes of Guinea.[62]

The following quotation is by David Collins and was published in 1802:

Of those who last came, three were remarkable for the largeness of their heads; and one, whose face was very rough, had much more the appearance of a baboon than of a human being. He was covered with oily soot; his hair matted with filth; his visage, even among his fellows, uncommonly ferocious; and his very large mouth, beset with teeth of every hue between black, white, green, and yellow, sometimes presented a smile, which might make one shudder.[63]

Here, early descriptions that seem almost to be purely descriptive and resonate with the image of the Noble Savage are replaced by later utterances that reinforce an image of abject hideousness.

Equally rich is the discourse about the 'civilization' of Aboriginal culture. As in the case of physical appearance, observations shift from the earlier image of the Noble Savage to one of utter abjection. Compare the three following statements by James Cook (1771), Watkin Tench (1789) and James Grant (1803) that seem to indicate a rupture in the discursive regime around 1800:

From what I have said of the Natives of New-Holland they may appear to some to be the most wretched people upon Earth, but in reality they are far more happier than we Europeans; being wholy unacquainted not only with the superfluous but the necessary conveniencies so much sought after in Europe, they are happy in not knowing the use of them. They live in a Tranquillity which is not disturb'd by the Inequality of Condition: The Earth and sea of their own accord furnishes them with all things necessary for life; they covet not Magnificent Houses, Houshold-

62 William Dampier's account of his 1691 voyage in the *Cygnet* was published in Ernest Scott (ed.), *Australian Discovery*, 2 vols (London: Dent 1929), vol. 1, ch. 9, available online at www.gutenberg.net.au/ausdisc/ausdisc1-09.html (viewed 11 February 2005).

63 David Collins, *An Account of the English Colony in New South Wales, from Its First Settlement in January 1788, to August 1801: With Remarks on the Dispositions, Customs, Manners, &c., of the Native Inhabitants of That Country*, 2 vols (London: T. Cadell and W. Davies 1798–1802), ii.180.

stuff &Cᵃ. they live in a warm and fine Climate and enjoy a very wholsome Air, so that they have very little need of Clothing and this they seem to be fully sencible of, for many to whome we gave Cloth &Cᵃ. to, left it carlessly upon the Sea beach and in the woods as a thing they had no manner of use for. In short they seem'd to set no Value upon any thing we gave them, nor would they ever part with any thing of their own for any one article we could offer them; this, in my opinion argues that they think themselves provided with all the necessarys of Life and that they have no Superfluities—[64]

Less than twenty years after Cook, Tench writes:

If they be considered as a nation whose general advancement and acquisitions are to be weighed, they certainly rank very low, even in the scale of savages. They may perhaps dispute the right of precedence with the Hottentots or the shivering tribes who inhabit the shores of Magellan. But how inferior do they show when compared with the subtle African; the patient watchful American; or the elegant timid islander of the South Seas. Though suffering from the vicissitudes of their climate, strangers to clothing, though feeling the sharpness of hunger and knowing the precariousness of supply from that element on whose stores they principally depend, ignorant of cultivating the earth—a less enlightened state we shall exclaim can hardly exist.[65]

Writing shortly after Tench, here is James Grant in 1802:

As there is thought to be a chain in Creation, beginning with the Brute and ending with Man, were I inclined to pursue the notion, I should be at a loss where to place my Bush Native, whether as the next link above the monkey, or that below it.[66]

The same pattern can be seen with regard to the subject of Aboriginal gender relations: Dampier in 1691 admits flatly to ignorance about how marriage is organized among Aboriginal peoples, whereas Watkin Tench in 1789 goes into lengthy detail about the cruelty of indigenous men towards their wives, an attitude reproduced over and over again in the following forty years.[67] The following remark by Charles Sturt is typical in its combination of empathy for the oppressed women's plight and disgust of their physical features:

64 'James Cook's Journal of Remarkable Occurrences aboard His Majesty's Bark Endeavour, 1768–1771', online edition of the original journal at the National Library of Australia, http://southseas.nla.gov.au/journals/cook_remarks/092.html (viewed 10 February 2005).
65 Tench, 'A narrative of the expedition to Botany Bay', 252–3.
66 Grant, *The Narrative of a Voyage of Discovery*, 158.
67 Tench, 'A narrative of the expedition to Botany Bay', 161–2, 264.

Like all savages, they consider their women as secondary objects, oblige them to procure their own food, or throw to them over their shoulders the bones they have already picked, with a nonchalance that is extremely amusing; and, on the march, make them beasts of burden to carry their very weapons. ... An old woman, a picture of whom would disgust my readers, made several attempts to embrace me. I managed, however, to avoid her, and at length got rid of her by handing her over to Fraser, who was no wise particular as to the object of his attention.[68]

The assessment of the Aborigines as savages was to a large extent based on the perceived treatment of indigenous women. At the same time, the colonial gaze and a desire for indigenous women shaped gender relations of the male colonialists with Aboriginal women. The latter represented not only sexual gratification, but also symbolized Australian land and its conquest. Indigenous women thus were othered in a double sense, as part of a 'savage' society and in relation to their gender, since Enlightenment theory in large part construed European women as savages.[69] Australian sources that raise the problem of Aboriginal gender relations are often marked by a tone of tacit complicity and ironic complacency. On the one hand, Aboriginal bodies must not be objects of desire because of their abject status; on the other hand, a male-writer-to-male-reader understanding is conveyed, implying that the white male colonialist could 'possess' the indigenous woman if he wanted, because of her low morals and the promiscuity rampant in indigenous society.[70]

Another discursive field is that of work. According to the aforementioned theory of the four stages, the kind of work performed by a group determined its evolutionary status. Hunter/gatherers remained in a lower state of development than peoples working the land and were little more than human animals. William Robertson's influential *History of America* (1777) reinforced the notion that North American Indians constituted a case of arrested development because of their supposed lack of agriculture.[71] In the middle of the nineteenth century, this contention was fortified by the prediction that, because of their lack of work ethic, Native Americans would soon die out.[72] In the early sources on Aborigines, this argument figures prominently and is connected with the apparent lack of fixed habitations.

68 Sturt, *Two Expeditions into the Interior of Southern Australia*.
69 Jane Rendall, 'The Enlightenment and the nature of women', in Jane Rendall (ed.), *The Origins of Modern Feminism: Women in Britain, France and the United States 1780–1860* (New York: Schocken Books 1984), 7–32.
70 George Bouchier Worgan, *Journal of a First Fleet Surgeon* (Sydney: Library Council of New South Wales 1978), 47–8.
71 Charles Dunoyer, *L'Industrie et la morale considérées dans leurs rapports avec la liberté* (Paris: A. Sautelet 1825), 146–7.
72 Horace Greeley, *An Overland Journey, from New York to San Francisco, in the Summer of 1859* (New York: Saxton, Barker and Co. 1860), 151.

Charles Darwin laid the ground for the evaluation of the Aboriginals' attitude on work in 1836:

> They will not, however, cultivate the ground, or build houses and remain stationary, or even take the trouble of tending a flock of sheep when given to them. On the whole they appear to me to stand some few degrees higher in the scale of civilisation than the Fuegians. . . . The aborigines are always anxious to borrow the dogs from the farmhouses: the use of them, the offal when an animal is killed, and some milk from the cows, are the peace-offerings of the settlers, who push farther and farther towards the interior. The thoughtless aboriginal, blinded by these trifling advantages, is delighted at the approach of the white man, who seems predestined to inherit the country of his children.[73]

General evaluations of indigenous civilization and government are closely connected to statements about the stages of development in relation to the forms of labour performed. The argument goes as follows: since Aboriginal societies have not evolved beyond the stage of hunters and gatherers, they do not possess government in the form of hereditary chiefs or elders. According to the same reasoning the low state of civilization reflects the animal-like state of existence and *vice versa*. The following excerpt neatly sums up this assertion since it compares explicitly the Aborigines with Native Americans:

> We may, I think, in a great measure impute their low state of civilization, and deficiency in the mechanical arts, to the nature of the country they inhabit, the kind of life they lead, and the mode of government they live under. Civilization depends more upon the circumstances under which man is placed than upon any innate impulse of his own,—the natural inclinations of man tending toward the savage state, or that in which food is procured with the least possible effort; . . . . In primitive communities, generally speaking, the chiefs must be hereditary, and must have acquired power to control the others, before much improvement can take place; when, if these chiefs exercise their power with justice, and secure the inviolability of persons and property, industry will soon be encouraged, and various useful arts originated. . . . The North American tribes form an apt illustration of these observations,—the chiefs being mere advisers, as it were, possessing no power to enforce their counsel, and consequently no means of breaking up the old savage habits of the tribes, and impelling them onward in the path of civilization.[74]

73 Charles Darwin, *Journal of Researches into the Natural History and Geology of the Countries Visited during the Voyage round the World of H.M.S. 'Beagle' under the Command of Captain Fitz Roy, R.N.* (London: John Murray 1913), 462, 469.
74 Cunningham, *Two Years in New South Wales*, ii.46–7, 49–50.

Between discourse and genocide

Australian sources of the late Enlightenment and Romantic period, written between 1788 and 1850, portrayed indigenous Australian populations as non-religious, indolent, idle, hideous and as uncivilized cannibals. The men were depicted as less ugly than the women, who were, according to these commentators, constantly under the oppressive power of their men. The promiscuity and loose morals of women seemed to demand a firm hand of the men. Aborigines represented in these sources did not own the land because they did not till it; they disrespected property rights and lived as nomadic hunter/gatherers without fixed abode and useful implements. Their number was thought to be decreasing rapidly due to their cultural backwardness. Their lack of a proper language with a developed vocabulary made them less than human, almost on a level with primates.

Early racist discourses, therefore, formed the necessary preconditions for two centuries of discrimination, dissolution and genocide of indigenous peoples in the absence of scientific racism. But what was the relationship between these discourses and genocidal practice? To distinguish sharply between 'theory' and 'practice' would be to draw a false dichotomy between 'ideology' and 'reality'. The discourses analysed here *were* the reality of British/indigenous relations for the British and thereby constituted the limits of their imaginative capacity to address those relations. In this respect, two points can be made in relation to the question of genocidal intention in early colonial contexts. The first is obvious in that the British view of the abject Other, which was particularly prominent among frontier settlers who had to contend with ferocious indigenous resistance, licensed brutal suppression in the form of genocidal massacres. The second is that the wilful blindness to or impotent disapproval of such unauthorized settler actions on the part of colonial authorities can be construed as an implicit intention to destroy the indigenes, despite the fact that they were often in thrall to humanitarian ideals of just treatment of the 'natives'. For the fact is that their commitment to theodicies of civilization and modernity meant that such enlightened humanitarians were prepared to accept, if in an agonized or resigned manner, the 'inevitable extinction' of the aboriginal peoples. After all, how could they justify halting the march of progress in the form of colonization in order to save such abject creatures?[75]

Norbert Finzsch is Professor of Anglo-American History at the University of Cologne.

---

75 On this point, see A. Dirk Moses, 'Conceptual blockages and definitional dilemmas in the "racial century": genocides of indigenous peoples and the Holocaust', *Patterns of Prejudice*, vol. 36, no. 4, 2002, 30.

Mr Darwin's shooters: on natural selection and the naturalizing of genocide[1]

TONY BARTA

1 My title is borrowed from Roger McDonald, *Mr Darwin's Shooter* (Sydney: Random House 1998) but also based on testimony from Darwin himself: 'Looking backwards, I can now perceive how my love for science gradually preponderated over every other taste. During the first two years my old passion for shooting survived in nearly full force, and I shot myself all the birds and animals for my collection; but gradually I gave up the gun more and more, and finally altogether to my servant, as shooting interfered with my work...'; Charles Darwin, *The Autobiography of Charles Darwin and Selected Letters*, ed. Francis Darwin (New York: Dover 1958), 29–30. Reading Darwin has been a pleasure shared with Jones and, as always, I owe a lot to her insights. My understanding of natural selection has been much improved by the clear explanations of John Clendinnen. Any errors are of course my own. I am grateful to Dirk Moses, Raymond Evans and my colleagues at La Trobe for suggestions and criticism, to the staff of the Boroondara, Borchardt and Baillieu libraries for their willing assistance, and to Dirk Moses and Dan Stone for nurturing a project that will now need further instalments.

Let us consider in what a village of English colonists is superior to a tribe of Australian natives who roam about them. Indisputably in one, and that a main sense, they are superior. They can beat the Australians in war when they like; they can take from them what they like, and kill any of them they choose.[2]

It is a more curious fact, that savages did not formerly waste away, as Mr Bagehot has remarked, before the classical nations, as they now do before modern civilised nations; had they done so, the old moralists would have mused over the event; but there is no lament in any writer of that period over the perishing barbarians.[3]

Charles Darwin grew up with guns. Only twenty-two when he was offered the position of naturalist on the round-the-world voyage of the *Beagle*, he used his skill with a firearm to bring down the birds that started him thinking about the differences of species. Henceforth, thinking was his life. 'I discovered, though unconsciously and insensibly, that the pleasure of observing and reasoning was a much higher one than that of skill and sport.'[4] But he was neither unconscious of, nor insensible to, the role played by the gun in the distant places he visited. His voyage initiated Darwin into the long drama of evolution, and into another drama, quicker and more dire. While he began his search for specimens in South America, the settlers were shooting the Indians. Even as his party of Europeans discovered the remains of long-dead megafauna, he observed European colonists doing their best to make the indigenous people extinct.

Before Darwin understood species, he understood genocide. His diary and his published account of the voyage make that plain. With remarkable clarity, he commented on both the larger relations of genocide within the colonial world and the eruption of genocidal moments on the frontier.[5] When he again turned his attention to contemporary history he was reluctant to say as much as he had earlier; and he is less direct than the relatively sheltered Walter Bagehot.[6] Darwin became radically

2 Walter Bagehot, *Physics and Politics* (London: Henry S. King 1872), 207.
3 Charles Darwin, *The Descent of Man* (London: John Murray 1871), 239.
4 Darwin, *The Autobiography*, 29–30.
5 Tony Barta, 'Relations of genocide: land and lives in the colonization of Australia', in I. Wallimann and M. N. Dobkowski (eds), *Genocide and the Modern Age* (New York: Greenwood Press 1987); see also the introduction by the editors, and the afterword by Richard L. Rubenstein. The importance of 'genocidal moments', intentional actions within such a dynamic set of relations, is convincingly argued by A. Dirk Moses, 'An antipodean genocide? The origin of the genocidal moment in the colonization of Australia', *Journal of Genocide Research*, vol. 1, 2000, 89–105.
6 Walter Bagehot (1826–77), essayist, banker, politician and editor of *The Economist*, was influenced by Darwin's science to apply natural selection to history. In the *Descent of Man*, Darwin in turn refers to 'a remarkable series of articles' published by Bagehot in 1868, and subsequently issued as a book, *Physics and Politics*. Bagehot was only one of

unconventional in science and, with even more notoriety, in religion. In social and political questions, he retained the worldview of his class and time.[7] The basis of that view was historical: it held that the advance of civilization was a triumphant progress, morally justified and probably inevitable. When Darwin lent his great gifts and influence to making the disappearance of peoples 'natural' as well as historical, his theory—conceived amid a worldwide human catastrophe—could serve as an ideological cover for policies abhorrent to his humanitarian and humanist principles.[8] Darwin's fateful confusion of natural history and human history would be exploited fatally by others. To understand the connections to the colonial genocides of his time and to the European genocides that followed, we have to read this Darwin again.

Darwin's British contemporaries who sought to bring the natural sciences into the emerging social sciences; Greta Jones, *Social Darwinism and English Thought: The Interaction between Biological and Social Theory* (Brighton, Sussex: Harvester Press 1980) and J. W. Burrow, *Evolution and Society. A Study of Victorian Social Theory* (Cambridge: Cambridge University Press 1966).

7 The biographies contextualizing Darwin's science in the society, economy, politics and culture of his time were a long time in coming. Adrian Desmond and James Moore, in *Darwin* (London: Michael Joseph 1991), show what needed to be done. Janet Browne, *Charles Darwin: The Power of Place* (London: Cape 2002), though certainly alert to matters of 'territorial and commercial expansion' (187), race and social Darwinism, has fewer references than Desmond and Moore to the larger societal and historical context. Peter J. Bowler, *Charles Darwin: The Man and His Influence* (Oxford: Blackwell 1990) succinctly clarifies the development and significance of Darwin's ideas within the broader history of evolution. In their introduction to a new edition of the *Descent of Man* (London: Penguin Classics 2004), Desmond and Moore provide fresh insights into Darwin's efforts to research and explain race.

8 For genocide as 'disappearance', see Patrick Brantlinger, *Dark Vanishings: Discourse on the Extinction of Primitive Races, 1800–1930* (Ithaca, NY and London: Cornell University Press 2003). Frontier violence in Australia has been searchingly explored only during the past thirty years. A pioneering account, notable also for its attention to Darwinist discourse, is Raymond Evans, Kay Saunders and Kathryn Cronin, *Exclusion, Exploitation and Extermination: Race Relations in Colonial Queensland* (Sydney: Australia and New Zealand Book Company 1975). Henry Reynolds, *Frontier* (Sydney: Allen and Unwin 1987) looks at ideologies as well as actions; for further references, and his considered views on genocide, see H. Reynolds, *An Indelible Stain? The Question of Genocide in Australian History* (Melbourne: Viking 2001). A. Dirk Moses, 'Genocide in Australian history', in A. D. Moses (ed.), *Genocide and Settler Society* (New York and Oxford: Berghahn Books 2004) has the most up-to-date argument and references. Tony Barta, 'Discourses of genocide in Germany and Australia: a linked history', *Aboriginal History*, vol. 25, 2001, 37–56, connecting racist colonial violence to consequences in Europe, follows the course plotted in Hannah Arendt, *The Origins of Totalitarianism* (New York: Harcourt, Brace 1951) and explored by Sven Lindqvist, *'Exterminate all the brutes'*, trans. from the Swedish by Joan Tate (London: Granta 1997) and *A History of Bombing*, trans. from the Swedish by Linda Haverty Rugg (London: Granta 2001).

When he returned from five years at sea, Darwin still believed in a wondrous creation. It took him more than twenty years of ever-widening research, distracted by poor health, children and worries about the reception of his heresy, to complete an outline of a theory that decisively shifted modern consciousness to the realities of a world in which divine intervention played no part. Life and death belonged to nature; the causing of life and death could be construed as rational, natural and even moral within nature's harsh, amoral laws. His own summary could hardly be clearer:

> As many more individuals of each species are born than can possibly survive, and as consequently there is a frequently occurring struggle for existence, it follows that any being, if it vary however slightly in any manner profitable to itself . . . will have a better chance of surviving, and thus be naturally selected. . . . This preservation of favourable individual differences and variations, and the destruction of those which are injurious, I have called Natural Selection, or the Survival of the Fittest.[9]

These terms, which Darwin said he used 'in a large and metaphorical sense', came out of a large and literal context. It is not the case, as is generally assumed, that humans and human history entered his explanations as a kind of afterthought; they were there from the beginning, based on indelible early experience. The practices of colonialism that Darwin encountered as a young man were embedded in the vocabulary of his most influential work and its reception. His initial outrage could change to acceptance in part because of his overall acceptance of extermination in natural selection. But he was also fascinated by *intervention* in nature and the observable effects in plants, animals and peoples. From the outset, he recognized the spread of European civilization as a historic human intervention, a global process of *unnatural* selection that he kept trying to integrate into his civilized ethics and the non-ethical, biological basis of evolution.

The long historical and philosophical pedigree of Darwinism cannot be laid out here. Like colonialism, it belonged to the modern project of dominating nature; it celebrated the power of nature while promoting its disempowerment. My concern is the confusion of natural history with human history that Darwin promoted, and the consequences of fusing the two. When the interventionist ideology of eugenics was added into the mix, there were terrible consequences for nature and humans alike.[10]

9   Quoted in J. W. Burrow, 'Introduction', in Charles Darwin, *The Origin of Species* [1859], ed. J. W. Burrow (Harmondsworth: Penguin 1968), 68.
10 John C. Greene surveys the two centuries of intellectual development leading towards Darwinism in *The Death of Adam: Evolution and Its Impact on Western Thought* (Ames, IA: Iowa State University Press 1959), esp. 322–35, 372. J. C. Greene, *Science, Ideology, and World View* (Berkeley: University of California Press 1981), particularly the chapter 'Darwin as a Social Evolutionist', is an excellent account of Darwin's intellectual journey.

Darwin's colonial encounters

Darwin had read little history when he boarded HMS *Beagle*. In his captain, FitzRoy, he saw the noble type civilizing the world in Britain's image; in the strange peoples of the antipodes he would find the countertype to civilization. The natives of Tierra del Fuego were the first 'savages' he met and they made a lasting impression as primitives. Yet he had for months shared shipboard life with three Fuegians kidnapped on an earlier voyage and could not but be impressed by their ability to adapt. Much opinion, he knew, emphasized innate inferiority, biology over culture. 'But in contradiction to what has often been stated, three years has been sufficient to change our savages, into, as far as habits go, complete and voluntary Europeans.' He was sorry to leave them again 'amongst their barbarous countrymen'. It was a European who in this case failed to adapt. The *Beagle* crew had to take Mr Matthews, the would-be missionary of civilization, away with them.[11]

Then, during a long journey into the interior in 1833, he came face to face with the alternative policy towards indigenous peoples defending their lands against expropriation. General Manuel de Rosas, a cattle rancher who served as governor of Buenos Aires, and later dictator of Argentina (and who, later again, retired to Swaythling in Hampshire), was engaged on what Darwin recognized at the time as a mission 'to exterminate the Indians'. Some 112 women and children and men were 'nearly all taken or killed, very few escaped'. (Darwin notes in the margin: 'Only one Christian was wounded.') 'The soldiers pursue and sabre every man. Like wild animals however they fight to the last instant.' The reason was to be made plain. 'This is a dark picture; but how much more shocking is the unquestionable fact that that all the women who appear above twenty years old are massacred in cold blood. I ventured to hint, that this appeared rather inhuman. He answered me, "What can be done, they breed so."'[12]

It is the sadly familiar language of genocide. To the perpetrators, Darwin noticed, the killing was reasonable and even moral in the larger scheme of things. 'Everyone here is fully convinced that this is the justest war, because it is against Barbarians.' His protest echoed all the others: 'Who would believe that in this age in a Christian, civilized country that such atrocities

11 Charles Darwin, *Charles Darwin's Beagle Diary*, ed. Richard Darwin Keynes (Cambridge: Cambridge University Press 1988), 121–4, 141–3. Darwin's talent as an ethnographer was not diminished by his robust value judgements. They are as prominent in the diary as his gift for observation and description of nature.

12 Darwin, *Beagle Diary*, 179–80. The version published in chapter 5 of Darwin's *Journal of Researches into the Natural History and Geology of the Countries Visited during the Voyage of H.M.S. Beagle round the World*, 2nd edn (London: John Murray 1845), a revised edition of the original *Journal of Researches* (London: Henry Colburn 1839), is essentially the same, with exclamation marks added; the 1845 second edition was often republished in later years as *The Voyage of the Beagle*.

were committed?' In fact, those who could believe it included himself, and for the reasons of historical progress self-evident to the winners of the war for the land. The theodicy of civilization would set the pattern for Darwin in all his writings: it celebrated a new world of productivity and profit that decreed the sacrifice of barbarians who stood in its way. The shooters were the shock troops of the new relations being established.

> If this warfare is successful, that is if all the Indians are butchered, a grand extent of country will be available for the production of cattle, and the valleys ... will be most productive of corn. The country will be in the hands of white Gaucho savages instead of copper-coloured Indians. The former being a little superior in civilisation, as they are inferior in every moral virtue.[13]

In the second edition of the *Journal of Researches* (often republished in later years as *The Voyage of the Beagle*), the grand vision of colonial productivity does not appear. The remarks on the Gauchos were also edited out. However, the violence is not expurgated, and some significant remarks are added. First: 'Since leaving South America we have heard that this war of extermination completely failed.' Then, in the next paragraph: 'I think there will not, in another half-century, be a wild Indian northward of the Rio Negro. The warfare is too bloody to last; the Christians killing every Indian and the Indians doing the same to the Christians.' There follows a reflection on how the destruction of a whole people takes place in a colonial society, not always by massacre.

> It is melancholy to trace how the Indians have given way before the Spanish invaders. Schirdel says that in 1535, when Buenos Aires was founded, there were villages containing two and three thousand inhabitants. Even in Falconer's time (1750) the Indians made inroads as far as Luxan, Areco, and Arrecife, but now they are driven beyond the Salado. Not only have whole tribes been exterminated, but the remaining Indians have become more barbarous: instead of living in large villages, and being employed in the arts of fishing, as well as of the chase, they now wander about the open plains, without home or fixed occupation.[14]

This is notable not only for its observation of the fate of an indigenous remnant, and its concern with accuracy in the history (a footnote gives his source for the founding of Buenos Aires—Purchas's *Collection of Voyages*— and adds, 'I believe the date was really 1537') but for the clarity, later lost, in separating historical casualties from natural ones. In the admiration for Indian bravery evident in other sections there is a hint of the later mourning

---

13 Darwin, *Beagle Diary*, 180–1. Keynes notes that the passage about opening up the country for production was marked in pencil to be deleted.
14 Darwin, *Journal of Researches*, 2nd edn, 104.

for the more noble savages, and the way it would conventionally be combined with racist stereotyping of the degraded survivors.

Darwin would never be quite at ease with the moral questions packed into these early reflections, but he accepted and finally promoted the idea that a higher form of humanity could not evolve without the demise of the lower. In natural history, he would keep telling himself, there was no 'higher' and 'lower'.[15] In human affairs he was faced early and dramatically by the argument that even bad people and bad methods could be justified by a higher purpose. Where there was clear moral superiority he would be second to none in accepting casualties.[16]

When the *Beagle* reached Sydney, he found few traces of moral superiority in convict society. His first encounter with the not yet civilized indigenous people, on the other hand, was positive. 'They were all partly clothed and several could speak a little English; their countenances were good-humoured and pleasant and they appeared far from such utterly degraded beings as usually represented.' He knew of their 'most wonderful sagacity' in tracking and for a shilling got them to demonstrate their remarkable spear throwing. 'They will not however cultivate the ground, or even take the trouble of keeping flocks of sheep which have been offered them, or build houses and remain stationary.'[17] Darwin had read Locke for his final exams at Cambridge, and his land-owning class did not lack eloquence in justifying the appropriation of land.[18] Aboriginal Australians were obviously not interested in improving pursuits. He rated them a few degrees above the Fuegians.

Darwin knew the Aborigines were disappearing. 'Their numbers have rapidly decreased; during my whole ride with the exception of some

15 Timothy Shanahan, *The Evolution of Darwinism: Selection, Adaptation and Progress in Evolutionary Biology* (Cambridge: Cambridge University Press 2004) refers to the insistence of Stephen Jay Gould that Darwin the scientist made many compromises with Darwin the social conservative: he was not game to deny the idea of progress fundamental to his social milieu but could not believe it biologically. Shanahan goes on (288) to quote what followed Darwin's 'never say higher or lower': 'Say more complicated'.

16 On the voyage Darwin boldly argued with FitzRoy about the evil of slavery, and he would later follow the fortunes of the North in the American Civil War with a passion that left no doubt about his willingness to accept deaths as the price of progress: 'Some few, and I am one of them, even wish to God, though at the loss of millions of lives, that the North would proclaim a crusade against slavery. In the long run, a million horrid deaths would be amply repaid in the cause of humanity'; letter to Asa Gray, 5 June 1861, in Frances Darwin (ed.), *The Life and Letters of Charles Darwin*, vol. 2 (New York: Basic Books 1959), 166.

17 Darwin, *Beagle Diary*, 398.

18 Desmond and Moore, *Darwin*, 88. For the Lockean, as distinct from Darwinian, foundations of dispossession, see Alan Frost, 'New South Wales as *terra nullius*: the British denial of Aboriginal land rights', *Historical Studies*, vol. 19, no. 77, October 1977, 513–23.

boys brought up in the houses, I saw only one other party.' Their wandering life caused great numbers of children to die in infancy, he had been told, quite apart from the effects of European diseases, the drinking of spirits and 'the gradual extinction of the wild animals', especially by English greyhounds. The extinction of the Aborigines, he thought, would follow.

> The Natives are always anxious to borrow the dogs from the farmhouses; their use, offal when an animal is killed, and milk from the cows, are the peace offerings of the Settlers, who push further and further inland. The thoughtless Aboriginal, blinded by these trifling advantages, is delighted at the approach of the White Man, who seems predestined to inherit the country of his children.[19]

Did Darwin understand that Australian settlers had also employed the more direct methods of General Rosas to ensure their predestined inheritance? 'Although having bad sport, we enjoyed a pleasant ride' is his next line; he then describes in lively detail the landscape and wildlife, including the already famous platypus. He was on his way to the 'not very inviting' town of Bathurst where only ten years before (according to another reporter) 'one of the largest holders of sheep in the colony' had stood up in a public meeting and maintained

> the best thing that could be done would be to shoot all the Blacks and manure the ground with their carcasses, which was all the good they were fit for. It was recommended likewise that the women and children should especially be shot as the most certain method of getting rid of the race.

The forces of law and order obliged. 'A large number were driven into a swamp, and mounted police rode round and round and shot them off indiscriminately until they were all destroyed.'[20]

We have reason to think Darwin would have noted a massacre he heard about, and no reason to believe he ever approved of shooters in killing parties. They were not part of his class inheritance, with its consciousness of higher culture as well as practical enterprise.[21] He was intrigued by social and economic aspects of the colony and the extraordinary opportunities for prosperity. He was shown round 'one of the large farming or rather sheep grazing establishments of the Colony' and noted the return from the clip. 'I believe the value of the average produce of wool from 15,000 sheep would

19 Darwin, *Beagle Diary*, 398–402.
20 Report by the missionary L. E. Threlkeld, quoted in Barta, 'Relations of genocide', 245.
21 For the specifically British class influence on Darwin and his theorizing, see, most comprehensively, Desmond and Moore, *Darwin*, and, most incisively, E. P. Thompson, 'The peculiarities of the English', in *The Poverty of Theory and Other Essays* (London: Merlin Press 1978), esp. 56–64.

be more than 5000 pounds sterling.'[22] In Tasmania, too, he was as likely to remark on economy and society—'They enjoy an advantage in there being no wealthy Convicts'—as on ferns and forests. Did he know at what cost the prosperity there had been bought? There is a clear sign of it, significant also for the terms of its judgement. 'The Aboriginal blacks are all removed and kept (in reality as prisoners) in a Promontory, the neck of which is guarded. I believe it was not possible to avoid this cruel step; although without doubt the misconduct of the Whites first led to the Necessity.'[23]

This cruel step. Not possible to avoid. The Necessity. These thoughts did not dominate Darwin's reflections as he put his five-year voyage on the *Beagle* behind him. He warned against the boredom, the cramped quarters, the awful scourge of seasickness: 'it is no trifling evil cured in a week'. But the greater cruelties and necessities of life on earth kept returning to him in the forty-five years of reflection ahead. His own health never recovered, and would be made worse by the painstaking nature of the work, the scale of his enterprise, the difficulties of thinking things through. The moral grounding of the empire such voyages helped to acquire was not a problem for Darwin. 'The march of improvement, consequent on the introduction of Christianity throughout the South Sea, probably stands by itself in the records of history.'

> In the same quarter of the globe Australia is rising, or indeed may be said to have risen, into a grand centre of civilisation, which, at some not very remote period, will rule as empress over the southern hemisphere. It is impossible for an Englishman to behold these distant colonies, without a high pride and satisfaction. To hoist the British flag, seems to draw with it a certain consequence, wealth, prosperity, and civilisation.[24]

Darwin knew there were other consequences as well. The dispossession, destruction and disappearance of peoples were among them. Yet his skill with language also blunts the suggestion of responsibility. After noting

22 Darwin, *Beagle Diary*, 401. A few pages later (406–7), a remarkable economic commentary sees the colony's rise to be 'as grand & powerful a country as N. America' becoming 'very problematical'. A cool eye for economic interest is at work. 'The balance of my opinion is such, that nothing but rather severe necessity should compel me to emigrate.'

23 Darwin, *Beagle Diary*, 408. For the way Darwin amplified this and other parts of his account for the 1839 publication of his journal, see F. W. and J. M. Nicholas, *Charles Darwin in Australia* (Cambridge and Sydney: Cambridge University Press 1989), 86–7. More generally, on Darwin's way of returning to earlier influences, see Howard E. Gruber, *Darwin on Man: A Psychological Study of Scientific Creativity*, 2nd edn (Chicago: University of Chicago Press 1981), including an appendix, 'The many voyages of the *Beagle*', 259–99.

24 Darwin, *Journal of Researches*, 2nd edn, 505. The words are almost the same in the original; see Darwin, *Beagle Diary*, 445–6.

'evident causes', Darwin describes the 'agency' as 'mysterious', a factor 'generally at work'. And any 'extirpating' acts the 'varieties of man' might commit are naturalized in terms that would be reassuring to his readers but now sound more disturbing.

> Beside these several evident causes of destruction, there appears to be some mysterious agency generally at work. Wherever the European has trod, death seems to pursue the aboriginal. We may look at the wide extent of the Americas, Polynesia, the Cape of Good Hope and Australia, and we shall find the same result. Nor is it the white man alone that thus acts the destroyer; the Polynesian of Malay extraction has in parts of the East Indian archipelago, thus driven before him the dark-coloured native. The varieties of man seem to act on each other in the same way as different species of animals—the stronger always extirpating the weaker.[25]

The struggle for existence: natural or historical selection?

Done with his account of the voyage, Darwin for many years left his encounters with human history behind him as well. But in crucial respects they resurfaced when he was compelled to publish the great work of interpretation that he had kept putting aside.[26] By Darwin's own account, it was problems of human populations rather than his observations of plants and animals that gave him 'a theory by which to work'. It occurred to him in as early as 1838 while reading Thomas Malthus.[27]

25 Darwin, *Journal of Researches*, 2nd edn, 435. For the importance of Darwin's Australian encounter, see Barry W. Butcher, 'Darwinism, social Darwinism and the Australian Aborigines: a reevaluation', in R. Macleod and P. H. Rehbock (eds), *Darwin's Laboratory: Evolutionary Theory and Natural History in the Pacific* (Honolulu: University Press of Hawaii 1994), 371–94.

26 Raymond Evans notes that the *Origin of Species* appeared in the same year that Queensland became a separate colony, and gives numerous examples of just how explicit Queensland settlers were in their racist justifications for doing away with black people; Evans, Saunders and Cronin, *Exclusion, Exploitation and Extermination*, 12. See also Ann Curthoys and John Docker, 'Genocide: definitions, questions, settler colonies', introduction to a special genocide section, *Aboriginal History*, vol. 25, 2001, 1–15; Moses, 'Genocide in Australian history'; and Anna Haebich '"Clearing the wheatbelt": erasing the indigenous presence in the Southwest of Western Australia', in Moses (ed.), *Genocide and Settler Society*.

27 Darwin appears to have read the 1826 edition of Malthus's *Essay on the Principle of Population*, first published in 1798; see Darwin, *Descent of Man*, 131–5, as well as Darwin, *Origin of Species*, 116–17 and Darwin, *Autobiography*, 42–3. In an 1887 letter, Alfred Russel Wallace, whose almost identical ideas pushed Darwin into publishing his theory, says he, too, was directly influenced by Malthus and the checks to population of 'the struggle for existence'; Darwin, *Autobiography*, 200–1. Herbert Spencer's essay on Malthus containing the phrase 'survival of the fittest' appeared in 1852, seven years before Darwin adopted it. So often credited, or discredited, as the

Influenced more by conditions in Britain than by events in the colonies, Malthus made mathematical play of a rather obvious fact: there could not be enough room on the planet for all the progeny of every organism. The weakest, logically, would go under. That is natural; Malthus was pessimistic about mere mortals countering the reproductive force of nature. William Godwin (against whom his original essay was directed) had tried to argue that human institutions were to blame. No, said Malthus, suffering, disaster and even extinction could not be prevented by human institutions: they were 'mere feathers that float on the surface, in comparison with those deeper seated causes of impurity that corrupt the springs and render turbid the whole stream of human life'. This could be, from a Christian, an argument for original sin, but it isn't. It is about necessity, 'the inevitable laws of nature'.[28]

Such laws were Darwin's concern when he penned a title intended to draw attention away from humans and their evolution.

ON

THE ORIGIN OF SPECIES
BY MEANS OF NATURAL SELECTION

The words nevertheless stored trouble for mankind, as did the subtitle:

THE PRESERVATION OF FAVOURED RACES IN THE STRUGGLE FOR LIFE

'Races' here were not the visible divisions of the single human species, though Darwin later recalled that visible human difference had sparked his interest.

---

father of 'social Darwinism', Spencer thus helped father Darwinism itself. Desmond and Moore highlight the influence of Malthus on colonialism and, subsequently, Darwin, in *Darwin*, 264–8.

28 Thomas Malthus, *An Essay on the Principle of Population* [1798], ed. with introduction by Antony Flew (Harmondsworth: Penguin 1972), 144. For the degree to which Darwinism was from the outset also social Darwinism, see James Moore, 'Socializing Darwinism: historiography and the fortunes of a phrase', in Les Levidow (ed.), *Science as Politics* (London: Free Association Books 1986). Sven Lindqvist points out that Malthus clearly identified colonial genocide, and rejected it; though exterminating the native populations of other continents was possible as a temporary solution to Europe's food shortages, it would be morally indefensible to repeat what was happening in the United States: 'If the united states of America continue increasing, which they certainly will do, though not with the same rapidity as formerly, the Indians will be driven further and further back into the country, till the whole race is ultimately exterminated, and the territory is incapable of further extension.' It must not be allowed to happen elsewhere, either. 'To exterminate the inhabitants of the greatest part of Asia and Africa is a thought that could not be admitted for a moment'; Lindqvist, *History of Bombing*, excerpt 35.

In 1813, Dr W. C. Wells read before the Royal Society 'An Account of a White female, part of whose skin resembled that of a Negro' ... In this paper he distinctly recognises the principle of natural selection and this is the first recognition which has been indicated; but he applies it only to the races of man, and to certain characters alone.

Darwin then gives a long quotation from Wells about the ability of some African peoples to better adapt to climate and disease. 'This race would consequently multiply, while the others would decrease; not only from their inability to sustain the attacks of disease, but from their incapacity of contending with their more vigorous neighbours.'[29]

The colonial context keeps appearing: introduced plants and animals dramatically displace indigenous species when they come into competition—example after example shows 'why the competition should be most severe between allied forms, which fill nearly the same place in the economy of nature; but probably in no case could we say precisely why one species has been victorious over another in the great battle of life.'[30] In human competition it was possible, as Darwin observed on his voyage, to be quite precise about how the displacement occurred. More often than not, the gun was involved, though he did not often refer to it after his return. Like others, he preferred the language of inevitable demise. The reasons include his developing sense of evolution in history as well as nature, and his knowledge that history—human activities, however difficult to trace exactly—could be equally callous. The 'realistic' frontiersmen who were not by instruction or imitation his disciples had a broad understanding and moral ideology hard to separate from the conclusions he was developing, in part, from their example.[31]

29 Darwin's 'Historical sketch on the progress of opinion on the Origin of Species' predates publication of the *Origin of Species* in 1859; it is published in the 1968 Penguin edition of *Origin of Species*, following J. W. Burrow's introduction.
30 Darwin, *Origin of Species*, 127. James Moore notes the effect of repeated words throughout the book: 'Whatever else these terms may show, they denominate a world of competitive individualism, racial hierarchy, and imperial advantage. One could be forgiven, on this basis, for thinking the *Origin of Species* dealt with human evolution, so frequently—twice on average per page—does Darwin draw on the language of everyday social life to interpret the natural world. The point, however, is that the book *is* about human evolution. And once Darwin's language was recirculated, now under the banner of biology, familiar terms acquired a fresh authority. People not only spoke differently—more often, say, about "survival", "fitness", and "species"—but they thought differently about how they spoke and what they spoke about. Ideology had undergone a scientific translation; Social Darwinizing was the result'; Moore, 'Socializing Darwinism', 67–8.
31 Alfred Russel Wallace, who separately reached conclusions about natural selection, also commented on 'the inevitable extinction of those low and mentally undeveloped populations with which the Europeans come into contact'. Darwin marked this passage with a double line in his copy of Wallace's 'The origin of human races and the antiquity of man deduced from the theory of "natural selection"', *Anthropology Review*, vol. 2, 1864; see Greene, *Science, Ideology, and World View*, 103.

When he finally took up the challenge of diverse human populations in the *Descent of Man*, Darwin determined, as in the *Origin of Species*, that nature—with crucial help from conscious sexual selection—accounted for the many branches of the single human species.[32] 'Extinction', however, was another matter. Humans could survive in all kinds of climates and conditions; they often could not survive each other. 'Extinction follows chiefly from the competition of tribe with tribe, and race with race.' In tribal societies the contest for resources 'is soon settled by war, slaughter, cannibalism, slavery, and absorption'.[33]

The difference in the contemporary case was again 'civilization', the imposition of not only a strange culture but a completely alien and immeasurably more powerful set of economic, social and political relations. 'When civilised nations come into contact with barbarians the struggle is short, except where a deadly climate gives its aid to the native race.' Darwin, it appears, had found no grounds to alter the view he had formed from his observations on the *Beagle*. 'Of the causes which lead to the victory of civilised nations, some are plain and some very obscure. We can see that the cultivation of the land will be fatal in many ways to savages, for they cannot, or will not, change their habits.' Here there is no mention of slaughter in the competition for resources, though the younger Darwin, as we have seen, knew very well it happened. Rather, he chose the usual view of dramatic decline. 'New diseases and vices are highly destructive', as are 'the evil effects from spirituous liquors'.[34] Most significant in all cases—he carefully gives figures for Tasmania, New Zealand and Hawaii—is the sudden and persistent drop in births. But of what is it significant? He compares cases of animals unable to breed in captivity and the evidence that natives somehow lose motivation to cope with new conditions.

It appears that Darwin, so keen to resume historical enquiry, had himself lost motivation to investigate the new conditions his countrymen had created. He knew the phenomenon of population decline he more than once called 'obscure' was in effect genocidal, and that it was connected to policies of colonization, land seizure and economic development that were historical rather than natural. Darwin could have commented with more of the insight he had shown as a young man. Instead, he concentrated on the failure of

---

32 Charles Darwin, *The Descent of Man*, ed. John Tyler Bonner and Robert M. May, facsimile of 1871 edn (Princeton, NJ: Princeton University Press 1981), ch. 7. Darwin in this chapter is still settling accounts with polygenism (235) and, like almost all biologists, remained unaware of Gregor Mendel's principles of genetics, published in mathematical form five years earlier (xix). Sexual selection was such an important issue for Darwin that the greater part of the book is devoted to it. In their 2004 introduction to the Penguin *Descent*, Desmond and Moore explain why Darwin omitted human evolution from the *Origin of Species*, and the context in which he returned to it.

33 Darwin, *Descent of Man* (1871), 236–40.

34 Ibid.

indigenous peoples to reproduce, a concern much closer to the core of his natural selection theory. For his readers, he knew, it was more comfortable to admire the achievements of explorers, missionaries and settlers from the security of a prospering Britain while ignoring or mildly mourning the disappearance of peoples unable to cope with the coming of civilization. And anyone troubled by their passing found reassurance: something inevitable—apparently God's will—seemed now also to be borne out by science.

It was not, I think, Darwin's intention to give comfort in this way. Yet nowhere does he appeal for the survival of indigenous peoples; unlike slavery, a wrong that could be righted, the 'extinction' he knows about is cast as a matter of human agency but one without full human responsibility.[35] The two pages in the *Descent of Man* that give his considered view of a process that belongs entirely to human history inevitably place his observations in a context of biology as well as anthropology. Just as inevitably, he therefore contributes to the naturalizing of human population displacement—and human violence—within the eternal verities of natural selection. His two concluding paragraphs on the matter show the confusion taking place. 'The grade of civilisation seems a most important element' in the competition between peoples Bagehot saw happening in the colonies. 'Although the gradual decrease and final extinction of the races of man is an obscure problem, we can see that it depends on many causes, differing in different places and at different times.' He compares displacement of the South American 'fossil horse' by 'countless troops of Spanish horse', and then calls in a displaced people as witness: 'The New Zealander seems conscious of this parallelism, for he compares his future fate with that of the native rat almost exterminated by the European rat.'[36]

Clearly, Darwin is dealing here with *unnatural* selection: the result of historical intervention. Even the first chapter of the *Origin of Species*—Darwin was rather proud of this—locates the whole theory of natural selection in a contradictory context. 'Variation under Domestication' is his starting point, calculated to allow his readers a familiar entry into the greater drama of prehistoric mutations. Alfred Russel Wallace, the naturalist whose similar theory pushed Darwin into publication, was only one who

35 James Bonwick, Darwin's main source for Tasmania, makes the plight of the indigenous remnant vivid, but mourns more than he blames. He sees genuine warfare for the land, and then good intentions gone terribly wrong. 'No means existed for the arrest of the terrible *home sickness* which was carrying off so many of the Natives. An Old Hand told me "they died in the sulks, like so many bears"'; James Bonwick, *The Last of the Tasmanians* (London: Sampson Low 1870), 245.
36 Darwin, *Descent of Man* (1871), 238–40. On pre-Darwinian racism and extinction theory, see Brantlinger, *Dark Vanishings*, chs 1 and 2, and, on 'Darwin and after', ch. 8. For a rare history conceptualizing the present and future in the light of past population policies, see Richard L. Rubenstein, *The Age of Triage: Fear and Hope in an Overcrowded World* (Boston: Beacon Press 1982).

questioned the shift from artificial selection by domestic breeders to the grand principle of 'Nature' selecting. 'To the few this is as clear as day-light, and beautifully suggestive, but to many it is evidently a stumbling block.'[37]

It was not, alas, a stumbling block to the administrators, settlers and soldiers who thought they were somehow doing nature's work, or to the purveyors of the ideology of disappearance. It is hard to see that the popular perception would have been different if Darwin (as Wallace suggested) simply emphasized 'survival of the fittest': this was in any case the favourite of those most frank about the consequences of colonization. In later years Darwin compromised the moral universe he tried to act within by not declaring himself with continued force against the horrors of frontier expansion. He did take care to promote altruism as one way the more civilized were able to advance, but prejudice against peoples deemed lacking in virtues—most notably the Irish—was promoted as well.[38] While the latest biology and the new anthropology proved the unity of mankind, they also stimulated awareness of difference, and different stages of civilization.[39] The natural history that illuminated a common human history would light the way to pernicious discrimination, and allow human history to be made on biological principles. All editions of the *Descent of Man* began with the same set of questions about the origin of races, their distribution, and population pressure leading to 'occasional severe struggles for existence, and conse-quently to beneficial variations, whether in body or mind, being preserved, and injurious ones being eliminated'.

37 Robert Young, *Darwin's Metaphor: Nature's Place in Victorian Culture* (Cambridge: Cambridge University Press 1985), 100; Darwin's most forceful response (to Hooker and Lyell as well as Wallace) is on 104. The significance of Darwin's move from artificial to natural selection is persuasively argued by Young (85–8). I would pursue the question of metaphor even further, especially in regard to another favourite, 'colonization' by plants and animals.

38 In a quotation from Darwin's friend W. R. Greg, 'The careless, squalid, unaspiring Irishman multiplies like rabbits' while 'the frugal, foreseeing, self-respecting, ambitious Scot . . . marries late and leaves few behind him'; Darwin, *Descent of Man* (1871), 174. The importance of altruism is also argued in *Descent of Man* (100–2), where Darwin also cites Herbert Spencer, 'our great philosopher', in support. Spencer's eight volumes of comparative ethnology, *Descriptive Sociology* (1873–81), were still in the future, as were his forthright pages on European atrocities in the conquest of other peoples in *The Study of Sociology*, facsimile of 1873 edn (Ann Arbor: University of Michigan Press 1961), 188–93. See also Bowler, *Charles Darwin*, 190–201, and Greene, *Science, Ideology, and World View*, 60–94 ('Biology and social theory in the nineteenth century: Auguste Comte and Herbert Spencer'). This latter essay does much to rescue Spencer from the crudest social Darwinism, even as it reaffirms his belief in progress through competition.

39 Darwin's influential neighbour, Sir John Lubbock, author of *Prehistoric Times* (1865), and E. B. Tylor, whose *Early History of Mankind* was published in the same year, are both cited in support of Darwin's monogenesis, 'that all are descended from a common progenitor'; Darwin, *Descent of Man* (1871), 231–6.

Do the races of or species of men, whichever term may be applied, encroach on and replace each other, so that some finally become extinct? We shall see that all these questions, as is indeed obvious with most of them, must be answered in the affirmative, in the same manner as with the lower animals.[40]

Darwinism, colonialism and Nazi genocide

The deaths and the suffering and the extinction of whole peoples were proceeding before Darwin set sail and after he was buried in Westminster Abbey. Most importantly, just as the colonial frontier shaped his thinking in the Home Counties, it shaped the coming age of genocide in Europe. The route was complicated by developments in science and racism that combined with Darwinian theory and colonial practice to produce the radicalism that Hitler made his own.[41] Darwin himself was assiduous in fostering links between his English-language success and the enthusiastic *Darwinismus* of his German apostles.[42] Like them, he was swept up in the victory of Prussia over France in 1870 and the possibilities of Bismarck's new German empire.[43] No one could have foreseen how a later German empire would invoke Darwin's ideas to justify an active programme of colonizing, supplanting and killing.

The developments that would create a catastrophe in Europe stemmed from unresolved problems of society and politics in the conservative German state rather than from Darwin's science. In the second half of the nineteenth century, Germany underwent the social dislocation, demographic

40 Ibid., 9–10.
41 Paul Weindling, *Health, Race and German Politics between National Unification and Nazism, 1870–1945* (Cambridge: Cambridge University Press 1989) is an impressive history of the connections between German Darwinism and National Socialism, via eugenics and other politicized developments in science. Richard Weikart, *From Darwin to Hitler: Evolutionary Ethics, Eugenics, and Racism in Germany* (New York: Palgrave Macmillan 2004) is less interested in Darwinism than in ideas 'devaluing human life'. Richard J. Evans is critical of Weindling and an earlier essay by Weikart in a robust overview, 'In search of German social Darwinism: the history and historiography of a concept', in Manfred Berg and Geoffrey Cocks (eds), *Medicine and Modernity: Public Health and Medical Care in Nineteenth- and Twentieth-century Germany* (New York: Cambridge University Press 1997), 55–79.
42 The most important German convert was the zoologist Ernst Haeckel (1834–1919). His energy in furthering the cause was much appreciated by Darwin. Although Haeckel later widened his mission to include social life and the politics of the increasingly radical right, his books were removed from libraries by the Nazis. Daniel Gasman, *The Scientific Origins of National Socialism: Social Darwinism in Ernst Haeckel and the German Monist League* (London: Macdonald 1971) is too intent on tarring Haeckel with a Nazi brush. See Evans, 'In search of German social Darwinism', 63–6.
43 Desmond and Moore, *Darwin*, 538–43, 561–2, 576–9. Initial enthusiasm for German victory was tempered by the occupation of Paris and the Commune. By 1873 Spencer was commenting on the 'exaggerated Teutomania' that success in war had produced in German liberal and academic circles; Spencer, *Study of Sociology*, 195–6.

upheavals and political effects of industrialization.[44] Before the new century arrived, industrial development and expansionist nationalism were influencing every academic discipline and helping to create new ones: sociology, statistics, economics. Practical scientific engagement with the social realm integrated many impulses and apparently contradictory ideologies. Advances in biological science, most notably in bacteriology, cell theory and genetics, made Darwin decidedly dated in the professional research that distinguished German universities, but 'social Darwinism'—the term was just coming into use—found new adherents, not least in the medical profession that burgeoned in numbers and influence with the new social insurance schemes. Social involvement increased medical interest in links between living conditions and disease, mental illness and criminality. Emigration, colonies and imperial assertion became linked to national well-being. Vogue words with changing ideological loadings and policy consequences included *Untermensch*, *Volk* and *Lebensraum*. *Weltpolitik* abroad was associated with 'racial hygiene' at home.[45]

It had been Darwin's cousin Francis Galton who advanced the idea of creating a better society by attention to inherited characteristics. Since it was possible to intervene in nature and by purposeful selection bring about improvements in animals and plants, why not in humans as well? Galton believed that by encouraging breeding between the best examples of humans, the science he called 'eugenics' had the potential 'to further the ends of evolution more rapidly and with less distress than if events were left to their own course'.[46] As the name implied, it was all about a better world: 'what nature does blindly, slowly and ruthlessly, man may do providently, quickly, and kindly.'[47] Because eugenics was first of all a site for improving

44 For the pressures of population growth, internal and overseas migration, and declining health with increasing poverty, see Weindling, *Health, Race and German Politics*, 11–13.

45 Many reformist concerns, ranging from sexuality to class divisions, seemed to belong more 'naturally' to the left, so the role of professionals, as well as intellectuals, in the new right was significant. In 1876 there were 13,728 doctors in the Reich; by 1900 there were 27,374. They were prominently represented in all the nationalist pressure groups: between 1894 and 1914, up to 10 per cent of Pan-German League chairmen were medical doctors. Weindling, *Health, Race and German Politics*, 17, 111.

46 Quoted in Gertrude Himmelfarb, *Darwin and the Darwinian Revolution* (New York: Norton 1968), 425. Himmelfarb comments that 'it did not seem to have occurred' to Darwin that eugenics 'vitiated his essential principle, making survival independent of the natural struggle for existence'. Brantlinger, 93–5, notes Galton's extension of Darwin in his hopes of getting rid of England's 'refuse' in the colonies, and Darwin's mention in the *Descent of Man* (28) of 'the admirable work of Mr Galton'. Darwin's generosity disguised his differences. 'Some of the more obscure passages of the *Descent* can be disentangled if we read them as Darwin's reply to the degenerationist tone of Galton's work'; Jones, *Social Darwinism and English Thought*, 23.

47 Galton, quoted in Daniel J. Kevles, *In the Name of Eugenics. Genetics and the Uses of Human Heredity* (Harmondsworth: Penguin 1986), 12.

the home population without social revolution, it quickly attracted ideological allies who also saw the potential of imperialism, racism and antisemitism as populist alternatives to socialism. One of the alarm bells for Europe
was sounded by Galton himself. In 1892 he warned about ideas escaping
from the academy into the new world of democratic—or demagogic—po-
politics.

> The great problem of the future betterment of the human race is confessedly, at
> the present time, hardly advanced beyond the stage of academic interest, but
> thought and action move swiftly nowadays, and it is by no means impossible that
> a generation which has witnessed the exclusion of the Chinese race from the
> customary privileges of settlers of two continents, and the deportation of a
> Hebrew population from a large portion of a third, may live to see analogous acts
> performed under sudden socialistic pressure.[48]

After a yet more intensive burst of imperialist competition and the Great
War, the 'sudden pressure' appeared as National Socialism. The 'struggle for
existence' that Darwin had made his basic law of natural selection Hitler
would use to back a very literal policy of human selection more unflinching
than ever before conceived. With the help of Darwin's own historically
inspired interventionist leanings, it completed the shift away from the other
basic principle of Darwinism: that there is no plan or intention in natural
selection. The intention of eugenics was to select within nature to plan great
good. The unintended consequence was great evil.

The biological premises of Nazi racism are notorious. Still struggling for
recognition is the extent to which the planting and supplanting example of
colonization powered National Socialist ideology and practice. The most
Darwinian statements came out when the need to be ruthless in colonizing
living space was in the forefront of Hitler's mind. His mealtime conversations
with visitors when the eastern war of conquest was launched make the
connections clear from the very first page of the record. Civilization, race and
nature are bundled together in a familiar combination of superior and inferior:

> By instinct, the Russian does not incline towards a higher form of society. . . .
> If anyone asks us where we obtain the right to extend the Germanic space to the
> east, we reply that, for a nation, the awareness of what she represents carries this
> right with it. It's success that justifies everything. . . .
> There's only one duty: to Germanise this country by the immigration of Germans,
> and to look upon the natives as Redskins. . . .
> If today you do harm to the Russians, it is so as to avoid giving them the
> opportunity of doing harm to us. . . . In this business I shall go ahead cold-
> bloodedly. What others may think about me, at this juncture, is to me a matter of

---

48 Francis Galton, *Hereditary Genius*, facsimile of 2nd edn, London: Macmillan 1892
(Gloucester, MA: Peter Smith 1972), 35.

complete indifference. I don't see why a German who eats a piece of bread should
torment himself with the idea that the soil which produces this bread has been
won by the sword. When we eat wheat from Canada, we don't think about the
despoiled Indians.[49]

The thesis Hitler pressed on his visitors was the right of a superior
population to displace an inferior one. The British rule in India showed
how a small number could impose imperial authority but in the German
East the aim was also colonial settlement. He readied his listeners for
genocide with an already established euphemism.

> If any people has the right to proceed to evacuations, it is we, for we've often had
> to evacuate our own populations. Eight hundred thousand men had to emigrate
> from East Prussia alone. How humanely sensitive we are is shown by the fact that
> we consider it a maximum of brutality to have liberated our country from six
> hundred thousand Jews.[50]

The most radical solutions of population problems were justified by both
history and biology. If the man who loved children was the chief murderer of
children—specifically targeted as children—in the twentieth century, it was
a sad matter of necessity. The years in the trenches had made him hard.
'I saw men falling around me in thousands. Thus I learned that life is a cruel
struggle, and has no other object but the preservation of the species. The
individual can disappear, provided there are other men to replace him.' It
was a far from accurate use of Darwin's language—the terms were in any
case different in German—but for Hitler's purposes it efficiently adopted the
rationality of nature. 'Plainly I belong to another species. I would prefer not
to see anyone suffer, not to do harm to any one. But when I realise that the
species is in danger, then in my case sentiment gives way to the coldest
reason.'[51]

49 Adolf Hitler, *Hitler's Table Talk, 1941–1944*, trans. from the German by Norman
   Cameron and R. H. Stevens, ed. H. R. Trevor-Roper (Oxford: Oxford University Press
   1988), 3, 37–8, 69; see also *Mein Kampf*, ch. 11 ('Nation and race'). For the many
   lineages of the Nazi imperial project, see Enzo Traverso, *The Origins of Nazi Violence*
   (New York: New Press 2003), ch. 2 ('Conquest').
50 Hitler, *Hitler's Table Talk*, 24. Hitler, Himmler and other Nazis certainly saw their resort
   to genocide in terms of a larger historical morality that overcame objections about its
   criminality. For problems associating the Holocaust with other genocides, see A. Dirk
   Moses, 'Conceptual blockages and definitional dilemmas in the "racial century":
   genocides of indigenous peoples and the Holocaust', *Patterns of Prejudice*, vol. 36, no.
   4, 2002, 7–36, and A. D. Moses, 'The Holocaust and genocide', in Dan Stone (ed.), *The
   Historiography of the Holocaust* (New York: Palgrave Macmillan 2004), 533–55.
51 Hitler, *Hitler's Table Talk*, 44. On medical and military reasoning about populations
   conquered by Germany, see Paul Weindling, *Epidemics and Genocide in Eastern Europe
   1890–1945* (Oxford: Oxford University Press 2000).

German historians will know what I mean by the danger of reading Darwin, and all developments after his time, through 'brown lenses'. I have tried not to retroject Nazism into Darwin's science, or to hold science responsible for political distortions. The fact remains that Nazi convictions about ruthless struggle in nature were based on more than slogans. One recent writer believes the passages on eugenics in *Mein Kampf* show 'a good grasp of the science involved',[52] though references to the potent intellectual 'stew' popularized at the time Hitler and others were susceptible to it seem closer to the mark.[53] Who contributed to the 'stew' and with what effect remains contentious; Hitler's own samplings of it indicate no direct encounter with Darwin's writings and they produced a distinctive distortion. Biology for Hitler confirmed violence as the essential means of making history, and the ideology of race as essential to the historic programme of a great civilization asserted over a great living space.[54] Hitler saw himself as willing to face facts without hypocrisy, and to make them. In the Nazi empire the domination and displacement of peoples deemed inferior in culture would mean the physical subjection of all and the physical elimination of some. The images of rats and beetles and fighting stags in Nazi propaganda were designed to evoke Darwinian themes in the most elemental way.[55]

The point of such imagery was to feed into prejudices about human difference, and even into the idea that it was natural to have such prejudices. Darwin was not responsible for 'euthanasia', racial categorization and genocide. But the legacy of Darwin promoted the idea that it is natural for beings with more power to displace others, and to intervene in nature for

52 Brian Appleyard, *Brave New Worlds: Genetics and the Human Experience* (London: HarperCollins 2000), 67. For other signs of the new worlds upon us or possible, see Nicholas Rose, 'The politics of life itself', *Theory, Culture and Society*, vol. 18, no. 6, 2000, 1–30.

53 Burrow, 'Introduction', 44–5. The lineages of biology and politics in imperial Germany and Austria did not all tend to the right; Paul Crook, *Darwinism, War and History: The Debate over the Biology of War from the 'Origin of Species' to the First World War* (Cambridge: Cambridge University Press 1994) is more measured than Alfred Kelly, *The Descent of Darwin: The Popularization of Darwinism in Germany, 1860–1914* (Chapel Hill: University of North Carolina Press 1981). The context of colonialism is specifically addressed in Jan Breman (ed.), *Imperial Monkey Business: Racial Supremacy in Social Darwinist Theory and Colonial Practice* (Amsterdam: VU University Press 1990).

54 The racial and biological interpretations of Nazi imperialism inevitably foregrounded here need to be corrected by the (no less Darwinian) political, military and economic rationale of German policy. On Hitler and the economics of *Lebensraum*, cf. Rainer Zittelmann, *Hitler, the Politics of Seduction* (London: London House 1999), 270–324; Hitler's modern, scientific view of the world is emphasized on 331–7.

55 One of the elemental themes was the naturalness of sexuality. In this the Nazis took a progressive social theme and allied it with the sexual selection that had so preoccupied Darwin in his work on race.

such ends. Darwin did not confront this as directly as he might have in his later work.[56] Significantly, though, his earliest historical reflections saw in organization and reason a grim potential.

> When two races of men meet, they act precisely like two species of animals—they fight, eat each other, bring diseases to each other, but then comes the most deadly struggle, namely which have the best fitted organisation, or instincts (i.e. intellect, in man) to gain the day.[57]

Darwin knew by 1838 that colonies were the testing ground for the 'best-fitted organisation' and the deadly struggle. They were interventions in ecology, biology and human populations on an unprecedented scale. Almost everywhere, they instituted relations of genocide. A century later Hitler had ample precedent to hand. He exploited the rhetoric of nature for an intervention of unparalleled focus and ferocity but it was his ambition to build a colonial empire that gave him the motive and opportunity for his genocidal onslaught against Slavs and Jews. The integration of the Holocaust into this conceptualization is only now being ventured, although the research making it irresistible is well advanced.[58] Russians and Poles were loaded with all the attributes of shiftless 'natives' and 'the Jews' were endowed with the power to manipulate all other powers against Germany's imperial birthright. Ruthless war, he told his soldiers, was 'the unalterable law for the whole of life'.

56 Marx did confront intervention directly, and should be reassessed together with Darwin as a powerful promoter of the global project being carried through by colonization and commerce. Brantlinger does not fail to notice that the *Communist Manifesto* claims all nations are compelled 'on pain of extinction' to adopt the bourgeois mode of production. He adds: 'The elimination of the primitive is not just a tragic side effect of modernization; as this passage suggests, it is its definition and destination'; Brantlinger, *Dark Vanishings*, 203n15.

57 Darwin's Notebook E, December 1838, quoted in Traverso, *Origins of Nazi Violence*, 59, in which it is selected as a passage 'that would not have been out of place in *Mein Kampf'*. I agree with him, not least because here Darwin slips into the confusion between species and race fundamental to Hitler's ideology.

58 For a sample of the best work (and a guide to other references), see Jürgen Zimmerer, 'Colonialism and the Holocaust. Towards an archeology of genocide', in Moses (ed.), *Genocide and Settler Society*, and J. Zimmerer, 'The birth of the *Ostland* out of the spirit of colonialism', in this special issue. Ulrich Herbert (ed.), *National Socialist Extermination Policies: Contemporary German Perspectives and Controversies* (London: Berghahn Books 2001) and Christopher Browning (with Jürgen Matthäus), *The Origins of the Final Solution: The Evolution of Nazi Jewish Policy, September 1939–March 1942* (Lincoln: University of Nebraska Press 2004) show how policy developed as the East was won. Dan Stone, *Constructing the Holocaust* (London: Vallentine Mitchell 2003) points to a continuing gap between research and the search for meaning in the Holocaust, which only the most imaginative historical work on Nazism and its contexts can begin to close.

Nature is always teaching us ... that she is governed by the principle of selection: that victory is to the strong and the weak must go to the wall. ... A people that cannot assert itself must disappear and another must take its place. All creation is subject to this law; no one can avoid it ...[59]

It was not natural selection that gave 'selection' a terrible new meaning after Auschwitz. It was an undertaking of the human will for a rational end. It was the power to demonstrate total domination, a ruthlessness that pretended to mimic nature while making nature count for nothing. The lessons were presented as natural history but derived from human history. History, not nature, would be the court of appeal. There, the unnatural selection Darwin could not resist bested natural selection at every turn. Hitler had seen how it worked. Those armed by a superior civilization would beat the inferior in war; they could take from them anything they liked, and kill any of them they chose.

Tony Barta is an Honorary Associate in the School of Historical and European Studies at La Trobe University, Melbourne.

---

59 Hitler's speech to officer cadets, 22 June 1944, quoted in Helmut Krausnick, 'The persecution of the Jews', in Institut für Zeitgeschichte, *Anatomy of the SS State*, trans. from the German by Richard Barry, Marian Jackson and Dorothy Long (New York: Walker 1968), 13. This appeal to the law of nature, and the equally devastating law of history, is my concern in 'On pain of extinction: laws of nature and history in Darwin, Marx, and Arendt', in Dan Stone and Richard H. King (eds), *Imperialism, Slavery, Race, and Genocide: The Legacy of Hannah Arendt* (forthcoming).

Caribbean genocide: racial war in Haiti, 1802–4

PHILIPPE R. GIRARD

A country born in blood

When Haiti's founding fathers gathered in Gonaïves on 1 January 1804 to declare their country's independence from France, the mood was as vengeful as it was celebratory.[1] Louis Boisrond-Tonnerre complained that the first draft of the declaration of independence was not aggressive enough, saying that 'we should use the skin of a white man as a parchment, his skull as an inkwell, his blood for ink, and a bayonet for a pen'.[2] For all its hyperbole, Boisrond-Tonnerre's outburst was surpassed when Jean-Jacques Dessalines, the head of Haiti's army and the island's dictator, addressed the crowd.

Citizens,

It is not enough to expel from our country the barbarians [the French] that drenched it in blood for two hundred years.... We must by one last act of national sovereignty secure for all eternity the reign of liberty in our motherland....

[Soldiers,] give to all nations a terrible, but just example of the vengeance that must be exacted by a people proud to have found freedom again, and eager to preserve it. Let us frighten all those who would dare to steal our freedom; let us start with the French! May they shudder when they approach our coastline, either because they remember all the exactions they committed, or because of our horrifying pledge to kill every Frenchman who soils the land of freedom with his sacrilegious presence.[3]

The words were not mere rhetoric. Over the following four months, on Dessalines's orders, soldiers rounded up white planters, their families, French soldiers and the urban poor known as *petits blancs*, and killed them. Neither women nor children were spared.

In Cap Français, the island's largest city, some civilians had fled with the departing French navy. Others, lacking means of transportation or trusting Dessalines's promises that they would be treated well, had stayed. 'Those poor Whites who stayed with the rebels all had their throats cut', wrote the bishop of neighbouring San Domingo. With a modesty befitting a man of the cloth, he alluded to, rather than gave lurid details of, the interracial rape that accompanied the massacres. 'And what is even worse, the victims, especially the women, were treated in such a way as to desire death a thousand time before they actually expired.'[4] An American resident of Cap Français was more explicit, reporting that a Haitian-born widow of a white

1 From 1697 to 1804, Haiti was known as Saint-Domingue, and only changed its name after it declared its independence. The article will use the name 'Haiti' for both the colonial and the national period.
2 Quoted in Laurent Dubois, *Avengers of the New World: The Story of the Haitian Revolution* (Cambridge: Harvard University Press 2004), 298.
3 Jean-Jacques Dessalines, 'Proclamation', 1 January 1804: Archives Nationales, Paris (hereafter AN), AB/XIX/3302/15. All translations from the French, unless otherwise stated, are by the author.
4 Letter from Guillaume Mauviel to Portalis, French Council of State, [early 1804]: AN, F/19/6212.

planter, who had stayed in Cap Français with her three daughters, was approached by her former slave who offered to protect the family should she give her elder daughter in marriage. The mother refused and was killed along with two of her daughters. The putative bride, who persisted in refusing her unyielding fiancé, was hanged 'by the throat on an iron hook in the market place, where the lovely, innocent, unfortunate victim slowly expired'.[5]

Contemporary accounts mention thousands of victims, though the exact number is hard to come by. Haiti's white population numbered 30,000 in 1789, the last year when reliable figures are available.[6] Some settlers died during the 1791 slave revolt and the years of upheaval that followed. Others emigrated to Cuba, Louisiana, France and the United States, though many returned with the arrival of a French expedition in 1802.[7] As late as 1803, a French lieutenant counted 1,800 civilians in the small city of Cayes alone.[8] Thousands fled with the departing French troops when the black army took over; those who stayed behind became the victims of Dessalines's wrath. A few non-French veterans and American merchants, along with some useful professionals such as priests and doctors, were spared. Those who failed the triple test of skin colour, citizenship and vocation were simply wiped out.

When the genocide was over, Haiti's white population was virtually non-existent. Dessalines's 1805 constitution allowed a few widows, Poles and Germans to settle in Haiti, then immediately added that all Haitians would officially be known as 'Blacks' (art. 13 and 14).[9] The new nation also abandoned the French tricolour, choosing instead strips of blue and red from which the central white strip was conspicuously absent. For the rest of the century, Haiti remained in western eyes a pariah state born in an orgy of white blood. France did not recognize its former colony's independence until 1825; the United States waited until 1862.

---

5 [Leonora Mary Hassall Sansay], *Secret History; or, The Horrors of St Domingo, in a Series of Letters, Written by a Lady at Cape Francois to Colonel Burr* (Philadelphia: Bradford and Inskeep 1808), 152–3.

6 Moreau de Saint-Méry, *Description topographique, physique, civile, politique et historique de la partie française de l'isle Saint-Domingue*, vol. 1 [1797–8] (Paris: Société de l'histoire des colonies françaises 1958), 86–100.

7 About 10,000 refugees reached Louisiana from 1792 to 1810. Another 10,000 arrived in Cuba from 1801 to 1806. Carl Brasseaux and Glenn Conrad, 'Introduction' and Gabriel Debien, 'The refugees in Cuba', in C. Brasseaux and G. Conrad (eds), *The Road to Louisiana: The Saint-Domingue Refugees, 1792–1809* (Lafayette: Center for Louisiana Studies 1992), vii, 72.

8 Lieutenant Débuour, 'Précis des événements militaires qui se sont passés aux Cayes avant l'évacuation de cette place', 30 Fructidor Year XII [17 September 1804]: AN, CC9A/35.

9 See also Sibylle Fischer, *Modernity Disavowed: Haiti and the Cultures of Slavery in the Age of Revolution* (Durham, NC: Duke University Press 2004).

When Raphaël Lemkin coined the term 'genocide' in 1944, he defined it as the 'criminal intent to destroy or cripple permanently a human group'.[10] To 'cripple' usually means to kill, and the 'human groups' most likely to be targeted are ethnic and religious groups like the Jews; but later definitions have considerably extended the scope of the term. Some scholars have considered the bloodless destruction of a culture (such as the forcible assimilation of Australian Aborigines) to be a form of genocide; others have argued that groups defined by their political beliefs or social status (such as Russia's *kulaks*) can be victims of genocide; some have even claimed that the unintentional wiping out of a people through disease (such as Native Americans in the United States) is genocide.[11] For the purpose of this essay, Lemkin's two basic criteria will be used. First, a genocide is intentional, which distinguishes it from other, accidental demographic catastrophes. Second, it differs from simple massacres because its large-scale, systematic nature is intended to extirpate fully a particular group from a society, thus introducing revolutionary change.

The first criterion—intent—was unmistakably in play in 1804. Unlike the early sixteenth century, when Spanish conquerors unwittingly wiped out the Taino population of Haiti through hard work and European diseases, there was a clearly stated desire to annihilate the enemy race in 1802-4. 'Dessalines', a French spy reported as black troops closed in on Cap Français, 'has declared that if he takes over Cap [Français] he will not leave a single White alive there, he will cut everybody's throat, even that of babies not yet weaned from their mother's milk'.[12] No attempt was made to hide the genocide as it was unfolding. In Port-au-Prince, Frenchmen were dressed as if for a funeral, 'paraded through the streets in great fanfare, then drowned in the port' in full view of British and American ships.[13] A copy of Dessalines's vengeful independence day proclamation was even sent to the *Gazette of Philadelphia*.[14] In April 1804 Dessalines proudly announced that the genocide was then consummated. 'The implacable enemies of the rights of man have finally met a punishment worthy of their crimes.'[15] He then went

10 Raphaël Lemkin, *Axis Rule in Occupied Europe: Laws of Occupation, Analysis of Government, Proposals for Redress* (Washington, D.C.: Carnegie Endowment for International Peace 1944), 80. See also Robert Melson, 'A theoretical inquiry into the Armenian massacres of 1894-1896', *Comparative Studies in Society and History*, vol. 24, no. 3, July 1982, 483.

11 A. Dirk Moses, 'Genocide and settler society in Australian history', in A. D. Moses (ed.), *Genocide and Settler Society: Frontier Violence and Stolen Indigenous Children in Australian Society* (New York: Berghahn Books 2004), 20-8.

12 'Rapport d'espionnage', 23 Messidor Year XI [12 July 1803]: AN, 135AP/3.

13 Letter from Brigadier General Lavalette to Minister of the Navy [Decrès], 2 Ventôse Year XII [22 February 1804]: AN, CC9B/19.

14 Letter from Pichon, French ambassador to the United States, to Minister of the Navy [Decrès], [c. July 1804]: AN, CC9B/18.

15 Jean-Jacques Dessalines, 'Proclamation', 28 April 1804: AN, AB/XIX/3302/15.

on to warn that the inhabitants of neighbouring Santo Domingo would meet the same fate if they refused to submit to his rule.[16] Dessalines's decision to kill all Whites was overt enough that scholarly debates on the chain of command (who ordered what) have much less value in the Haitian case than they do in other genocides.

The second criterion—magnitude—lends itself more easily to scholarly debate. One may argue that the events of early 1804 did not constitute a genocide because they only affected a few thousand settlers (30,000 if one includes previous victims and exiles). Such numbers pale in comparison with French military losses (50,000 in 1802–3 alone) and total civilian losses (estimated at half Haiti's pre-war population of 550,000). In this analysis, 1804 would have turned from massacre to genocide only if there had been more white people for Dessalines to kill. But this argument overlooks the impact 1804 had on Haitian society. Prior to 1791 Haiti had been organized along strict racial lines; even the poorest *petit blanc* considered himself superior to a slave-owning free person of colour. After 1804 Whites were reduced to a token presence, much of it non-French; Blacks and Mulattoes were the new masters of Haiti. The change was nothing short of revolutionary. When one takes into account the percentage of the victimized group that survived the genocide, along with the social transformation it engineered, 1804 was more radical than other, more deadly genocides. A 'little' genocide it was; but it was a world-shattering event in the context of Haiti.

Rationale is another puzzling question. What led Dessalines to commit a crime, genocide, whose systematic nature is considered unique in the annals of human cruelty? Dessalines offered a military explanation (killing all Whites would forever scare away potential invaders) that was far from convincing. The genocide took place *after* the last French troops surrendered. Some battered remnants of the French expeditionary force regrouped in Cuba and Santo Domingo, but they were too small to go on the offensive and the resumption of France's war with England made further reinforcements impossible. If anything, horror at Dessalines's cruelty could have prompted France to summon another expedition to avenge the dead. Economically, the genocide also exterminated planters who, for all their faults, were the most educated and entrepreneurial members of Haiti's population. By the 1820s the large sugar plantations had been divided into small lots cultivated by illiterate subsistence farmers. The shift pleased the former slaves immensely, but it shattered Dessalines's hopes for large-scale agriculture.

Existing documents—letters by French generals Charles Victor Emmanuel Leclerc and Donatien Rochambeau, and speeches by Dessalines—mention four possible justifications. First, the French Revolution had shown that

16 Jean-Jacques Dessalines, 'Proclamation aux habitants de la partie espagnole', 8 May 1804: AN, AB/XIX/3302/15. Dessalines's invasion of Santo Domingo failed.

ideals were worth dying, and killing, for. Second, atrocities committed by French troops in Haiti provoked Dessalines's calls for revenge. Third, after thirteen years of fighting, radical measures seemed the only way finally to secure freedom for the slaves. Fourth, racism led to dehumanization of the other side. To these factors can be added a final one, which only appears as a subtext in existing documents: black generals hoped to take over their victims' plantations.

The question of rationale leads to a more general one. Was the genocide of 1804 a purely local phenomenon, born of the only successful slave revolt in world history, or did it follow a pattern that was replicated elsewhere, from Armenia to Germany, Cambodia and Rwanda? Can one also verify Hannah Arendt's thesis that the great twentieth-century genocides were intellectual heirs to nineteenth-century imperialism, and that Dessalines's use of genocide, however horrific, was a sign that the country had entered the modern era? To answer the questions raised by Dessalines's 1804 proclamation, one must step back fifteen years to analyse the revolutionary turmoil that led to Haiti's bloody independence.

1789 to 1798: in the shadow of the French Revolution

When the French Revolution started, Haiti was France's most valued colony, producing half of Europe's consumption of sugar and coffee. Immense economic wealth, however, was matched by great political tyranny. Whites (about 30,000 of them) complained that they were subjected to the whims of royal governors. Free people of colour (about 20,000 of them) were the victims of an increasingly strict regime of racial discrimination. The brutally oppressed black slaves (more than 500,000 of them) were denied even the limited rights accorded to them under the *Code Noir* regulating slavery.[17] Their attention monopolized by metropolitan turmoil, French revolutionaries failed to decide whether the Rights of Man awarded Frenchmen in August 1789 also applied to black inhabitants of the colonies.[18]

In the absence of leadership from the metropolis, and given the atmosphere of revolutionary turmoil, revolt became the most obvious way to achieve political goals. White settlers threatened governors and routinely disregarded their orders.[19] Vincent Ogé, a free person of colour who had tried unsuccessfully to obtain legal equality in Paris, launched a revolt in

17 Saint-Méry, *Description topographique*, i.86–100; 'Questions sur la population et les productions de Saint Domingue et des isles du vent', [c. 1785]: Centre des Archives d'Outre-Mer, Aix-en-Provence (hereafter CAOM), DFC/XXXIII/Memoires/3/202.
18 Yves Benot, *La Révolution française et la fin des colonies, 1789–1794* (Paris: La Découverte 2004).
19 Letter from Blanchelande to M. De Thevenard, [c. September 1791]: CAOM, F/3/197.

1790 that was quickly crushed. In August 1791 black slaves of northern Haiti launched a general insurrection that marks the official beginning of Haiti's war of independence. Many slaves called for revenge against the planter class, but their leaders were divided. Jeannot, a rebel chief, was known for his great brutality. In Limbé, a white observer wrote that he 'hanged 22 Whites in a day' and went on to describe other alleged atrocities.[20] Two other leaders, Jean-Francois and Biassou, preached moderation and eventually executed the bloodthirsty Jeannot.

There is considerable scholarly debate on the political beliefs of those Blacks who refused to work on plantations, called *marrons* before the abolition of slavery and *rebelles* or *brigands* thereafter. Some, like Gabriel Debien, have concluded that illiterate African peasants had a parochial outlook, reacting to local events (such as a plantation manager's excessive cruelty) rather than more abstract concepts of freedom borrowed from the European Enlightenment.[21] Others, like Carolyn Fick, think that, as early as the Makandal rebellion (1757–8), black slaves were committed to emancipation of all Blacks, or even outright independence from France.[22]

Existing evidence tends to support the latter thesis, particularly among black leaders. Toussaint Louverture claimed to be the 'Black Spartacus' whose coming the Abbé Raynal had predicted.[23] When addressing his troops on the eve of a battle against the British, Louverture invoked freedom, 'the most precious asset a man may possess', and exulted that 'the time to expel the enemies of the Republic from the land of liberty has finally arrived'.[24] The political views of the rank-and-file are more difficult to assess, but black soldiers sang revolutionary songs and fought under the revolutionary tricolour.[25] Blacks could easily draw parallels with the

20 [Moreau de Saint-Méry?], 'Notes de quelques événements particuliers arrivés dans l'insurrection des noirs à Saint-Domingue en 1791', 14 January 1792: CAOM: F/3/197. See also Jeremy Popkin, 'Facing racial revolution: captivity narratives and identity in the Saint-Domingue insurrection', *Eighteenth Century Studies*, vol. 36, no. 4, 2003, 511–33.

21 Gabriel Debien, *Les Esclaves aux Antilles françaises: dix-septième au dix-huitième siècles* (Basse Terre: Société d'Histoire de la Guadeloupe 1974), 424. See also François Girod, *La Vie quotidienne de la société créole: Saint-Domingue au dix-huitième siècle* (Paris: Hachette 1972), 168–9.

22 Carolyn E. Fick, *The Making of Haiti: The Saint Domingue Revolution from Below* (Knoxville: University of Tennessee Press 1990), 6, 60.

23 Pierre Pluchon, *Toussaint Louverture* (Paris: Fayard 1989), 148.

24 Toussaint Louverture, 'Adresse aux officiers, sous-officiers et soldats, composant l'armée en marche', [*c*. January–February 1798]: AN, CC9A/19.

25 Pamphile de Lacroix, *La Révolution de Haïti* [1819] (Paris: Karthala 1995), 333; Jan Pachonski and Reuel K. Wilson, *Poland's Caribbean Tragedy: A Study of Polish Legions in the Haitian War of Independence, 1802–1803* (Boulder, CO: East European Monographs 1986), 203; Dubois, *Avengers of the New World*, 103–5.

ongoing French Revolution. They, like the French serfs, were simply overthrowing an idle class of abusive landowners.

During that period, Haitians also learned that revolutionary change was more effectively secured through violence than debate. The French granted political equality to Mulattoes (1792) and freedom to Blacks (1793–4) only when the military situation required it. In 1802–4, when France reneged on its policy of emancipation, former slaves reminded themselves that during the French Revolution right had amounted to might, and that they would be justified in exterminating their political enemies. Debating with a fellow black officer whether their rebellion was morally acceptable, Brigadier General Cangé argued: 'you know that when it comes to revolutions, the strongest party is always right, and we are stronger.'[26] Dessalines, who typically mixed calls to arms and idealistic statements in his proclamations, could not have agreed more. 'War to the death for tyrants: this is my motto. Liberty, independence: this is our rallying cry.'[27]

In this respect, the Haitian genocide resembles its Communist counterparts of the twentieth century, such as the agricultural collectivization in the Soviet Union. In both cases, the French Revolution was heralded as an example of social change engineered by popular armies. In both cases, ideological fervour made it easier to justify the eradication of those who found themselves on the wrong side of history.

1798 to February 1802: who will own the sugar and coffee plantations?

In 1798 war temporarily abated. French revolutionary authorities, faced with a general uprising, had abolished slavery and enrolled the former slaves in the French army. Thanks to their help, an Anglo-Spanish invasion of Haiti was repulsed. Under the leadership of Toussaint Louverture, a former slave, sugar and coffee production partially recovered. One powerful group, however, was unhappy with the new state of affairs: white planters. Emancipation reduced their investment in human flesh to nothing. Those who had fled the fighting, accused of being *émigrés* implicated in monarchist politics, also saw their plantations confiscated by the state. Planters formed a vocal group in Paris that called on French authorities (Napoleon Bonaparte after 1799, notably) to help them recover their previous wealth.[28] For France to have a powerful navy, the argument went, it needed a large supply of skilled sailors. These could only be found if there was an active trade with

26 Letter from Brigadier General Cangé to Battalion Chief Delpech, 6 Frimaire Year XI [27 November 1802]: AN, CC9B/19.
27 Dessalines, 'Proclamation', 28 April 1804.
28 Colonial Office (Ministry of the Navy), 'Rapport aux Consuls de la République', 12 Frimaire Year VIII [3 December 1799]: AN, CC9B/18.

the colonies in peace-time, and these colonies required slavery to flourish.[29] Bonaparte confessed yielding to 'the forceful advice of *messieurs les habitants de Saint-Domingue*', along with 'the opinion of the Conseil d'Etat and of his ministers, who were pushed by the constant whining [*criailleries*] of the settlers, a powerful party in Paris'.[30]

Echoing theses expounded in Vladimir Lenin's *Imperialism: The Highest Stage of Capitalism* (1916), Hannah Arendt posited that imperialism originated in a small clique of financiers who hijacked a state's foreign policy to further their private greed.[31] The planters' lobbying campaign seems to confirm these views but for one important point: the former slaves were also motivated by financial gain. The *status quo* as it existed in 1798–1802 allowed black generals such as Louverture and Dessalines, who were *de facto* rulers of the island, to take over dozens of plantations, from which they derived a substantial income that was essential in an era of public destitution.[32] Louverture alone owned between eight and ten plantations.[33] He used his control of public lands to ensure the loyalty of his subordinates, and neither he nor his officers were desirous of ceding such advantages.[34] In 1799, when Louverture ordered his mulatto rival André Rigaud to give away some of the land he controlled to a black general, Laplume, Rigaud revolted, starting a bloody civil war known as the War of the South.[35]

29 Gautier, 'Aperçu sur les intérêts du commerce maritime', Frimaire Year X [November–December 1802]: AN, CC9A/28.
30 Toussaint Bréda Louverture, *Mémoires du Général Toussaint l'Ouverture écrits par lui-même* (Paris: Pagnerre 1853), 127–8; Emmanuel de Las Cases, *Mémorial de Sainte Hélène*, 2 vols (Paris: Gallimard–La Pléiade 1956), i.769. See also Barry Edward O'Meara, *Napoléon en exil: relation contenant les opinions et les réflexions de Napoléon sur les événements les plus importants de sa vie, durant trois ans de sa captivité, recueillies*, 2 vols (Paris: Garnier 1897), ii.277.
31 Hannah Arendt, *The Origins of Totalitarianism* [1951] (New York: Meridian Books 1958), 138.
32 Letter from Battalion Chief Saint-Martin to Ministry of the Navy, 22 Messidor Year VII [10 July 1799]: AN, CC9A/21. Louverture's nephew Moïse enjoyed an annual income of £1.2 million. Letter from 'Painty' to Moreau de Saint-Méry, 27 February 1802: CAOM, FM/F/3/202.
33 Pluchon, *Toussaint Louverture*, 369.
34 Colonial Office, Ministry of the Navy, 'Rapport aux Consuls de la République', 7 Vendémiaire Year IX [29 September 1800]: AN, CC9B/18; letter from Leclerc to Minister of the Navy [Decrès], 20 Pluviôse Year X [9 February 1802]: AN, CC9B/19. Even when he was exiled to a French prison, Louverture adamantly demanded that his plantations be given back to him. Letter from Rochambeau to Minister of the Navy [Decrès], 16 Frimaire Year XI [7 December 1802]: AN, CC9B/19.
35 Commandant Delaunay, 'Extrait d'un rapport sur la situation politique de Saint-Domingue', 7 Vendémiaire Year VIII [29 September 1799]: CAOM, FM/F/3/202; [Commissioner Roume?], 'Rapport aux consuls de la république', 1 Nivôse Year VIII [22 December 1799]: AN, CC9A/18.

The arrival of a French army in 1802 dealt a severe blow to the black generals' financial well-being. To deny French soldiers access to resources, Louverture and his officers set their own plantations on fire. White planters returned from exile and recovered their lands. Those plantations still requisitioned by the state were carefully listed, appraised and apportioned between prominent French officers. General Rochambeau, for example, found himself at the head of six coffee plantations, one sugar plantation and one cotton plantation.[36]

For obvious reasons, when he gave the order for the genocide, Dessalines did not mention his own financial interest in doing so. The paucity of documents makes it difficult to make a definitive statement concerning his intentions. Dessalines might have seriously considered the peaceful option: returning to the 1798–1802 model in which the cautious Louverture controlled the Haitian plantations while accepting the presence and expertise of white planters. Or he might have calculated that, as hundreds of planters either fled or died, he and his fellow generals could acquire dozens of plantations and become fabulously wealthy.

February to May 1802: war, atrocities, disease

By late 1801 Louverture had defeated all his rivals. Relying on a network of white planters and black officers, he governed Haiti with an iron hand. The colony, relatively peaceful for the first time in ten years, was slowly drifting towards independence. Meanwhile, after years of prodding by exiled planters, Bonaparte was preparing an expedition to Haiti. Led by his own brother-in-law, General Charles Leclerc, the troops arrived in Haiti in February 1802. In his secret instructions to Leclerc, Bonaparte hoped that his troops would land peacefully, deport troublesome black leaders and reassert French authority in Haiti without having to resort to extreme measures.[37] Bonaparte wrote Louverture that he was merely sending reinforcements, whose commanders were instructed to support, not supplant, black troops. Louverture and his men, rightly afraid that the French had ulterior motives, would have none of it. When Rochambeau's forces landed at Fort Liberté near Cap Français, Leclerc wrote, they were

36 [Government Land Office], 'Etat de divers baux à ferme passés par l'administration des Domaines en vertu des ordres de l'administration supérieure', [c. 1802]: AN, 135 AP/3.
37 Napoleon Bonaparte, 'Notes pour servir aux instructions à donner au Capitaine Général Leclerc', 31 October 1801, reproduced in Gustav Roloff, Die Kolonialpolitik Napoleons I (Munich: Drud und Berlag von R. Didenbourg 1899), 245. See also Paul Roussier (ed.), Lettres du Général Leclerc (Paris: Société de l'histoire des colonies françaises 1937), 28; Ralph Korngold, Citizen Toussaint (Boston: Little, Brown 1945), 246.

attacked by black troops who shot at them, while saying that they did not want white people. Our soldiers continued to land, yelling to the Blacks that they were their brothers, their friends, and that they were bringing them freedom. Black troops continued to shoot. Our forces crushed them.[38]

Blacks burned the cities and retreated to the hills, ushering in a war whose violence was exceptional even by Haitian standards. Less than a month after he landed, and before the first large battle at Crête à Pierrot, Leclerc reported that 600 of his men had already died in combat, that 1,500 were wounded and that 2,000 were suffering from various diseases.[39] Over the following eighteen months, French losses alone (due to both combat and diseases) exceeded 50,000 men.

This brutal conflict, which immediately preceded the 1804 genocide, goes a long way towards explaining Dessalines's decision to kill all Whites. War provides a backdrop against which death is so common and the stakes are so high that normally unacceptable options receive serious consideration, and simmering antipathy turns to crazed hatred. If millions of Germans died in battle, the Nazis reasoned, then why not Jews too? Antisemitism had deep roots in Germany, but the Final Solution was a product of the Second World War. Similarly, the Roman destruction of Carthage occurred at the end of the Third Punic War, the Armenian genocide took place during the First World War, the Cambodian genocide emerged in the shadow of the Vietnam War and the Srebrenica massacre coincided with the Bosnian War.

High casualties on both sides served as a justification for retaliatory massacres, which themselves sparked more atrocities, in a tit-for-tat sequence that eventually culminated in the genocide. A French officer remembered that French troops, upon encountering the bodies of 800 white victims (women and children included) of Dessalines's wrath,

> were so brave that this horrible sight, far from frightening them, only made them more ardently desire to strike their enemy. One of the detachments volunteered to fight while we were still visiting the carnage; never have I seen anything comparable to the ardour they displayed in their task.[40]

'The atrocities that this man [Louverture] ordered in cold blood make one freeze in horror', Rochambeau wrote.

38 Letter from Leclerc to Minister of the Navy [Decrès], 20 Pluviôse Year X [9 February 1802]: AN, CC9B/19.
39 Letter from Leclerc to Minister of the Navy [Decrès], 8 Ventôse Year X [27 February 1802]: AN, CC9B/19. One of Leclerc's officers later wrote that Leclerc exaggerated losses due to diseases in order to divert attention from his losses in combat. Lacroix, *La Révolution de Haïti*, 336.
40 Lacroix, *La Révolution de Haïti*, 328.

All the columns of the army encountered trails, roads covered with half-mutilated corpses, trees loaded with pieces of human flesh.... It is obvious that from this point on the generous disposition of our troops changed into fury and that they swore eternal hatred against their tormentors.[41]

In May, fighting subsided as prominent black leaders (Dessalines among them) switched sides and joined the French. Louverture was captured through trickery and exiled to France. But the grim atmosphere continued as the rainy season brought a powerful epidemic of yellow fever that eventually accounted for nine out of ten French casualties. Losses were so great that Leclerc, when writing to Paris for reinforcements, calculated that 70,000 men had to leave French ports to create a combat-ready group of 12,000 men in Haiti.[42] The epidemic was widely understood to favour the black camp. Having lived for years in Haiti, most Blacks were immune to the disease. White troops, on the other hand, routinely died within days of setting foot in Haiti. The French, who could not afford the losses, buried their dead at night to hide the true extent of the dreadful number.[43] In one letter to his spy in Cap Français, Louverture joked that 'la Providence rushes to our rescue'.[44] Avoid a frontal assault, he had told his men with keen military sense as soon as the French landed in Haiti.

> Don't forget that the only resources we have until the rainy season rids us of our enemies are destruction and fire. Know that the earth that we worked with our own sweat must not provide a single morsel of food to our enemies.... Annihilate and burn everything, so that those that come to put us back in bondage always encounter here a portrait of the hell they all deserve to go to. [45]

In this context, to the French, the yellow fever epidemic was yet another weapon in the enemy's arsenal, and one that the slaves might very well control. Or so Dessalines suggested at war's end, explaining that nature

---

41 Rochambeau estimated that Louverture had killed 10,000 to 12,000 civilians, Leclerc 10,000 and Lacroix 3,000; Rochambeau, 'Précis des opérations de l'expédition de Saint-Domingue de 1802 à 1803', 6 October 1803: AN, CC9A/36. Letter from Leclerc to Minister of the Navy [Decrès], 5 Germinal Year X [26 March 1802]: AN, 416AP/1; Pluchon, *Toussaint Louverture*, 572.
42 Letter from Leclerc to Napoleon Bonaparte, 5 Vendémiaire Year XI [27 September 1802]: AN, CC9B/19.
43 Lacroix, *La Révolution de Haïti*, 351.
44 'Providence' means 'God', but it was also the name of Cap's main hospital. Lacroix, *La Révolution de Haïti*, 352.
45 Letter from Toussaint Louverture to Jean-Jacques Dessalines, 19 Pluviôse Year X [8 February 1802], reproduced in Lacroix, *La Révolution de Haïti*, 319.

obeyed the orders of 'the angry genius [*génie*] of Haiti' and sent 'diseases, plague, devouring hunger, fires and poison'.[46]

Death, whether by the sword or by disease, struck fast and without warning, creating an otherworldly ambiance in which participants did not know if they would be alive the following month, though they could have safely predicted an answer in the negative. In this atmosphere, naked greed, murder and sexual exploits multiplied, indicating a complete breakdown in moral values. The colony's tradition of loose morals combined with the unusual war-time conditions to create 'an extraordinary change in the morality of many men', Rochambeau complained.[47] The colonial prefect warned that Rochambeau himself had been perverted.

> In the midst of such a great and general disaster people devote themselves, as in ancient Capua, to the pleasures of a dissolute life—balls—promenades—every-everything is designed to take people's minds away from a situation that is growing more alarming each day.... Lost women have gained such credit with the central authority [Rochambeau] that they decide on favours and positions, even on military matters.[48]

Dissolute morals and the desperate military situation explain why French soldiers resorted to methods deemed unacceptable in the European theatre, including such tortures as burning and breaking at the wheel that were by then illegal in France.[49] Blacks were gassed in the hold of ships or thrown overboard, a practice one captain referred to as 'mettre de la morue à la trempe' (giving codfish a bath).[50] Rochambeau even imported 200 slave-hunting dogs from Cuba.[51] To test this new weapon, or to fulfil some sadistic fantasy, he ordered an arena built in which the dogs devoured a black man. All the leading members of Cap Français society attended, as if this were a gladiator fight in a decadent Rome.[52]

---

46 Dessalines, 'Proclamation', 28 April 1804. In French, 'génie' can refer to a gifted person or to the spirit of the nation. It is not clear whether Dessalines was referring to himself in his speech, or to the collective will of his people.

47 Letters from Rochambeau to Minister of the Navy [Decrès], 10 Brumaire Year XII [2 November 1803] and 19 Brumaire Year XII [11 November 1803]: AN, CC9B/19.

48 Hector Daure, 'Rapport confidentiel sur l'état de la colonie et de son administration', [*c.* November 1803]: AN, CC9A/36.

49 [Sansay], *Secret History*, 99.

50 Poterat, 'Mémoire sur la colonie de Saint-Domingue', 21 Fructidor Year XI [8 September 1803]: AN, CC9A/35; Pachonski and Wilson, *Poland's Caribbean Tragedy*, 69; Christophe Paulin de la Poix, Chevalier de Fréminville, *Mémoires du Chevalier de Fréminville (1787–1848)* (Paris: Librairie Ancienne Champion 1913), 78.

51 Letter from Brigadier General Louis Noailles to Rochambeau, 9 Nivôse Year XI [30 December 1802]: AN, 416AP/1; Rochambeau, 'Précis des opérations de l'expédition de Saint-Domingue de 1802 à 1803', 6 October 1803: AN, CC9A/36.

52 Pachonski and Wilson, *Poland's Caribbean Tragedy*, 114.

Dessalines, a man usually not remembered for his compassion, noted with alarm that for ten months the French 'had hanged Mulattoes and Blacks with abandon; it would be impossible for me to show you how many men and women they have drowned and that they are still drowning at night.'[53] In his later calls for genocide, he made powerful reference to these French atrocities.

> Indigenous citizens, men, women, daughters and children, look everywhere in the island for your wives, your husbands, your brothers, your sisters—what!—look for your infants, still sucking their mother's breasts. What have they become? I dare not tell you ... they have become the prey of these vultures. Will you die without avenging them? No, in the family tomb, their bones would push yours away.[54]

'Yes!' he exulted after the white population was exterminated. 'We answered these cannibals' war with war, crime with crime, outrage with outrage.'[55] To him, after the horrors of slavery and war, genocide merely amounted to vengeance, even justice.

May to October 1802: slavery

Aside from a few free people of colour, the vast majority of the soldiers that made up Haiti's army were former slaves. The white troops sent from France included few slave owners, but they fought on behalf of white planters, alongside the national guard composed of local white citizens. As months passed, many French officers acquired plantations, further aligning their destiny with that of the master class.[56] The 1804 genocide must thus be understood in a context of class warfare: former slaves killed their would-be masters. To this extent, the 1804 genocide is closely related to twentieth-century genocides inspired by class resentment, such as the rural peasants' war on the urban bourgeoisie in 1970s Cambodia.[57]

The 1791 revolt forced the French to emancipate Haiti's slaves in 1793, but Haiti's Blacks only benefitted from a regime of limited freedom. Louverture, a former slave but also a plantation owner and a statesman, understood that slaves dreamed of carving out plantations, acquiring a small plot and living off subsistence farming. This would have resulted in the complete ruin of an economy based on sugar and coffee, so he instituted rules that tied the slaves to the plantations. *Cultivateurs*, as the slaves were now called, received one-

53 'Dessalines aux hommes de couleur habitant la partie ci-devant espagnole', 6 Nivôse Year XI [27 December 1802]: AN, CC9A/32.
54 Dessalines, 'Proclamation', 1 January 1804.
55 Dessalines, 'Proclamation', 28 April 1804.
56 [Government Land Office], 'Etat de divers baux à ferme'.
57 One survivor labelled the Khmer Rouger 'Kum-munists', after the Khmer word for 'revenge'. Haing Nor and Roger Warner, *Survival in the Killing Fields* [1987] (New York: Carroll and Graf 2003), 171.

fourth of the crop, but working conditions changed surprisingly little.[58] In 1799, when French commissioner Roume de St Laurent drafted an elaborate plan to send a Haitian army to Jamaica to free that island's slaves, Louverture co-operated half-heartedly in public.[59] In private, he warned the British of Roume's plans. One French agent in Jamaica was arrested and hanged, and the project foundered.[60]

When the Leclerc expedition landed in February 1802, the French adamantly denied that they had come to restore slavery. 'Whatever your origins and your skin colour might be, you are all French, you are all free and equal in the eyes of God and the Republic', Bonaparte explained. 'If anyone tells you: "this army is here to take our freedom away", answer: "the Republic gave us our freedom, it will not take it away."'[61] Many black generals joined the French army under a solemn promise that slavery would not be restored. Bonaparte did not specifically mention the restoration of slavery in his secret instructions to Leclerc, which makes it difficult to assess whether his public reassurances were sincere or not. Leclerc seems to have intended to keep Louverture's system of *cultivateurs* ('it is so strict that I would never have dared to draft such a text in the current circumstances'); Rochambeau wanted to restore slavery, but never did.[62]

Louverture nevertheless urged his officers to resist the French invasion, explaining that promises of freedom were clever lies on Bonaparte's part. 'The Whites of France and Saint-Domingue all want to take our freedom away.... Be suspicious of the Whites for they will betray you if they can. Their most manifest desire is the restoration of slavery.'[63] According to a French eyewitness account, Dessalines, upon hearing of the arrival of the French expedition, told his men that the French had come 'to steal this freedom that cost us so many sacrifices and to push us back into a shameful

58 Letter from Toussaint Louverture to General Hédouville, 23 Thermidor Year VI [10 August 1798]: AN, CC9B/6; Colonial Office (Ministry of the Navy), 'Rapport aux Consuls de la République', 27 Fructidor Year VIII [14 September 1800]: AN, CC9B/18.
59 Letters from Commissioner Roume to Sieyès, 19 Fructidor Year VII [5 September 1799] and 9 Vendémiaire Year VIII [1 October 1799]: AN, 284AP/13/6.
60 Colonial Office (Ministry of the Navy), 'Rapport aux consuls de la république sur la colonie de Saint-Domingue', Vendémiaire Year IX [September–October 1800]: AN, CC9B/18.
61 Napoleon Bonaparte, 'Proclamation du consul à tous les habitants de Saint-Domingue', 17 Brumaire Year X [8 November 1801]: CAOM, FM/F/3/202.
62 Letter from Leclerc to Minister of the Navy [Decrès], 16 Floréal Year X [6 May 1802]: AN, CC9B/19; Colonial Office (Ministry of the Navy), 'Extrait de différentes lettres écrites par le Général Rochambeau', 3 Floréal Year XI [23 April 1803]: AN, CC9A/34. See also Marcel Dorigny and Yves Benot, *1802: Rétablissement de l'esclavage dans les colonies françaises* (Paris: Maisonneuve et Larose 2003).
63 Letter from Toussaint Louverture to Brigadier General Domage, 20 Pluviôse Year X [9 February 1802]: AN, CC9B/19. See also General Rigaud, 'Réflexions du Gén. Rigaud sur les événements survenus à Saint-Domingue depuis le départ du Gén. Hédouville', [c. 1799]: AN, 284AP/13/6.

slavery. You know that in 1792 Blacks had no weapons to defend their freedom. Today, you have weapons.' The report noted that 'Blacks screamed and asked for the death of all Whites'.[64]

Initial fighting was fierce, but the French prevailed, and by June 1802 combat operations had seemingly come to an end. Contrary to all expectations, Louverture's capture and exile did not spark a general uprising, a possible consequence of his oppressive labour laws.[65] The situation changed dramatically over the summer, partly because yellow fever decimated French ranks, but mostly because a series of political *faux pas* convinced the black population that the French were about to restore slavery.

Upon recovering Martinique and St Lucia (which had been under English occupation during the French Revolution), Bonaparte could have decided to extend the emancipation decrees of 1793–4 to these islands, but he decided otherwise.[66] Worse, General Richepanse, sent to occupy Guadeloupe (where the slaves had been freed in 1794), decided in May 1802 that he would restore slavery. 'Gen. Richepanse's decrees are well known here, and they hurt us a lot', Leclerc complained.

> The one restoring slavery . . . will cost the lives of many soldiers and civilians in Saint-Domingue. . . . [In Gros Morne,] 50 prisoners were hanged. Men die with incredible fanaticism. They laugh at death. The same with women. . . . This fury is the direct product of Gen. Richepanse's proclamation and of the planter's inconsiderate declarations.[67]

After the arrival of French forces, the planters Leclerc alluded to in his letter boasted in public that slavery would soon be reinstituted in Haiti. Near Jérémie, a *cultivateur* who had been flogged by a rural policeman started 'spreading dangerous rumours, and said while touching his wounds that *Whites cut up niggers and will restore slavery*'.[68] In the same district, townspeople complained that a young man named Collet, who managed his mother's plantation, was acting 'with excessive injustice and cruelty against

64 Commandant Figeat, 'Mémoire', 14 Vendémiaire Year XI [6 October 1802]: AN, CC9A/32.

65 Letter from Leclerc to Minister of the Navy [Decrès], 26 Prairial Year X [15 June 1802]: AN, CC9B/19. See also Fick, *The Making of Haiti*, 213–14, which demonstrates that Blacks found the theoretical difference between *cultivateurs* and *esclaves* negligible.

66 Admiral Villeret Joyeuse, 'Proclamation aux habitants de la Martinique et de Ste Lucie', [c. 1802]: AN, CC9B/19.

67 Letter from Leclerc to Minister of the Navy [Decrès], 21 Thermidor Year X [9 August 1802]: AN, CC9B/19.

68 Letter from Brigadier General d'Arbois to Général de Division Desbureaux, 23 Thermidor Year X [11 August 1802]: AN, 135AP/1 (emphasis in original): the term 'nigger' (*nègre*), used commonly in Haiti, is not as pejorative in the local French as in modern English.

his own workers'; everyone's safety was 'imperiled by such revolting conduct'.[69]

The French incorporated some black soldiers into their army, but their general policy was to disarm Blacks. The only rational goal of such a policy, Blacks reasoned, was to pave the way for the restoration of slavery. When the disarmament campaign intensified in the summer of 1802, uprisings broke out all over Haiti.[70] The French only seized 30,000 guns, leaving 80,000 functioning weapons, or two for each adult black male. The Blacks refused steadfastly to give up their weapons, not trusting French promises of everlasting freedom. Spreading apart their children's legs, some women told a French officer that they 'would rather dismember them than see them enslaved'.[71] The intensity of the Blacks' feelings regarding slavery cannot be overestimated. A French officer, talking to a black general whose loyalty to France was undimmed, was 'very touched' by what the aptly named Paul Lafrance had to say.

> He took me aside, crossed his hands on his chest and spoke to me in tears: 'my general, you look honest, so tell me the truth: are you here to restore slavery? . . . Whatever happens, the old Paul Lafrance would never do you any harm . . . But my daughters, my poor daughters . . . slaves . . . Oh! I would die of grief.'[72]

Allegations that the French intended to restore slavery featured prominently in Dessalines's 1804 speeches. He spoke of the 'frightening despotism . . . imposed on Martinique', of 'Guadeloupe, devastated and destroyed'.[73] Most importantly, he told Haitians that, as long as a planter class survived in Haiti, France and other European nations would send expeditions, as they had done for thirteen years. For slavery to be eliminated permanently, slave owners themselves had to be eliminated.

> It was not enough to expel from our country the barbarians that have bloodied it for the past two centuries. . . . We must, by a last act of national authority, protect forever the country of our birth as an empire of freedom. We must take away from this inhuman government . . . every hope of enslaving us. We must live *independent or die* . . . . Let us frighten all those who would dare to steal our freedom; let us start with the French![74]

69 Letter from the Council of Notables of Jérémie to Brigadier General d'Arbois, 8 Brumaire Year XI [30 October 1802]: AN, 135AP/1. The term 'revolting' was obviously chosen with great care.
70 Letter from Leclerc to Minister of the Navy [Decrès], 4 Thermidor Year X [23 July 1802]: AN, CC9B/19.
71 Letter from Chef de Brigade Naverrez to Ministry of the Navy, 2 Ventôse Year XI [21 February 1803]: AN, CC9A/30.
72 Quoted in Lacroix, *La Révolution de Haïti*, 306.
73 Dessalines, 'Proclamation', 28 April 1804.
74 Dessalines, 'Proclamation', 1 January 1804 (emphasis in original).

November 1802 to April 1804: the race war

Haiti's brutal journey through colonial exploitation, slave revolt, revolutionary turmoil, foreign invasion, war-time atrocities and revenge was not yet over. By the end of 1802, the war became a racial one, in which the colour of one's skin, regardless of one's social status, military role or political opinions, was sufficient to warrant execution. This last step on the path to genocide, ironically, was the result of France's own policies.

Sexual intercourse between white planters and their female slaves was common in eighteenth-century Haiti, so to divide the Haitian population into two, hermetically closed groups (Blacks and Whites) would grossly oversimplify racial divisions. With a 'scientific' precision exceeding that of the Nazis' Nuremberg laws, Haitian historian Moreau de Saint-Méry listed 128 distinct racial categories in Haiti, based on the amount of white and black blood in a person's veins.[75] Because they were often manumitted by their biological father, Mulattoes constituted a privileged class, wealthy enough to own land, plantations, even black slaves. Mulattoes and Blacks often found themselves at odds with each other, the War of the South being the classic example.[76]

In his instructions, Bonaparte advised Leclerc to play on these racial differences and side with Mulattoes against the Blacks. Leclerc failed to implement these orders, exiled mulatto generals such as Rigaud, and hired black generals such as Dessalines, whose loyalty proved illusory. But the true shift took place in November 1802, when Leclerc died of yellow fever and Rochambeau took over as Lieutenant-General of Haiti. Rochambeau's hatred of the Mulattoes verged on the obsessional. In a bizarre party held in Port-au-Prince, he led mulatto women into a room decorated with candles and crêpe. He frightened them with the macabre atmosphere and chants, then told them that they had just attended the funeral of their brothers, and that the bodies were in the adjoining room.[77]

Arbitrary arrests of prominent mulatto citizens, massacres of black and mulatto troops suspected of disloyalty, and exactions by French soldiers convinced most Mulattoes to join ranks with the black rebels for whom they initially had little love.[78] In the autumn of 1802, when over 1,000 black troops were drowned in Cap Français, the officers who had briefly collaborated with the French (Henry Christophe, Dessalines, André Pétion) defected and joined the rebels. 'Cassé zé, quitté jaunes, mangé blan': the simplicity of

75 Saint-Méry, *Description topographique*, i.86–100.
76 An alternative to the prevalent, race-based interpretation of the war is that Generals Rigaud and Louverture merely used racism to justify a highly personal power struggle for control of Haiti. Dubois, *Avengers of the New World*, 230–3.
77 Lacroix, *La Révolution de Haïti*, 347; A. J. B. Bouvet de Cressé (ed.), *Histoire de la catastrophe de Saint Domingue* (Paris: Peytieux 1824), 58.
78 Lacroix, *La Révolution de Haïti*, 360, 364.

Dessalines's slogan befitted the stark reality now prevalent in Saint-Domingue. Break the eggs, take out of the yoke (a pun on the word 'yellow', which means both yoke and Mulatto) and eat the white.[79] By December, the French only counted four officers of colour in their ranks.[80] Skin colour was now the dividing line in Haiti.[81]

In her *Origins of Totalitarianism* (1951), Arendt explained that European racism helped rationalize the brutal treatment of Africans in the colonial era, and provided a powerful tool to enlist the help of 'armed Bohemians' (violent, lower-class mobs) in colonial ventures; racism and antisemitism later justified the Holocaust by placing victims of genocide in a subhuman category to which normal standards of guilt did not apply.[82] Applying a racial framework is indeed useful in order to conceptualize the extreme, random violence that characterized the end of the Haitian conflict, with one caveat: the *petits blancs* were not the only ones to succumb to the racist virus. French officers, planters and black slaves also did. This reservation aside, racism facilitated the last, fateful step to genocide by dehumanizing the enemy, whether they were the black 'savage beasts' of French accounts or the white 'tigers' of Dessalinian proclamations, and by simplifying existing political divisions. There no longer were slave-owning Mulattoes, faithful black maids acting as informants for Louverture, black officers of dubious loyalty or *cultivateurs* moonlighting as rebels: any person with a dark skin was a rebel. There no longer were French officers enamored of revolutionary ideals, white planters who had collaborated with Toussaint, metropolitan troops forced to serve in Haiti or *bons maîtres* who treated their slaves well: all Whites had to leave or die. Systematic suspicion warranted systematic death.

Despite his reputation as a moderate, Leclerc was the first one to understand that the war was heading towards a bloody, fateful denouement. 'Here is my opinion on this country', he wrote Bonaparte.

> We must destroy all the Negroes in the mountains, men and women, keeping only infants less than twelve years old; we must also destroy half those of the plain, and leave in the colony not a single man of color who has worn an epaulette. Without this the colony will never be quiet.[83]

79 Quoted in Pachonski and Wilson, *Poland's Caribbean Tragedy*, 121.
80 Letter from Rochambeau to Minister of the Navy [Decrès], 23 Frimaire Year XI [14 December 1802]: AN, CC9B/19.
81 The rebel army kept a few white priests, enlisted some Polish deserters and received the support of the British navy and US merchants. 'Extrait du journal du lieutenant de vaisseau Babron, embarqué sur la *Surveillante*', Brumaire Year XII [October–November 1803]: AN, CC9A/36.
82 Arendt, *Origins of Totalitarianism*, 185–91, 317, 447–9.
83 Letter from Leclerc to Napoleon Bonaparte, 7 October 1802, quoted in English translation in Henry Adams, *History of the United States of America during the Administrations of Thomas Jefferson*, ed. Earl N. Harbert (New York: Library of America 1986), 280. See also Lacroix, *La Révolution de Haïti*, 360.

After Leclerc died in November 1802, Donatien Rochambeau replaced him and acquired a reputation for killing coloured Haitians on a massive scale. Within a month of taking over, he wrote Paris that an essential step was 'the destruction, or deportation, of black and mulatto generals, of officers, of soldiers, and of farm labourers, all of them'.[84] He returned to this theme repeatedly over the following months, dropping the alternative (deportation) and referring to 'extermination' instead of 'destruction'.[85]

Parisian officials never addressed these demands,[86] but they complained of French troops' excessive brutality in putting down the revolt.[87] Indeed, it might seem counter-intuitive to exterminate the entire black population when slaves were the backbone of Haiti's plantation economy. But, Leclerc argued, Blacks were so corrupted by freedom that they could never be re-enslaved. It was safer, despite the human and financial cost, to kill them all and import a new batch of slaves from Africa.

> To control the mountains after I defeat the rebels, I will have to destroy all the crops and a large part of the *cultivateurs* that have been accustomed to living like brigands for 10 years, and will never get used to working again. I will have to fight a war of extermination.[88]

Should the French stop short of extermination, Rochambeau later wrote, 'we will have to start [this war] all over again every two or three years'.[89]

> Commercial interests may argue that we are destroying all the Blacks: but one must understand that we must exterminate all the armed Blacks, the farm labourers and their chiefs and, to use a metaphor, cut the legs of everyone else: without this we will lose our colonies, and any hope of ever having any.[90]

84 Letter from Rochambeau to Minister of the Navy [Decrès], 16 Frimaire Year XI [7 December 1802]: AN, CC9B/19.
85 Colonial Office (Ministry of the Navy), 'Extrait de différentes lettres écrites par le Général Rochambeau'; letters from Rochambeau to Minister of Navy [Decrès], 25 Nivôse Year XI [15 January 1803] and 2 Ventôse Year XI [21 February 1803]: AN, CC9B/19; letter from Rochambeau to Ministry of the Navy, 8 Floréal Year XI [28 April 1803]: AN, CC9A/34.
86 For example, see Colonial Office (Ministry of the Navy), 'Extrait de différentes lettres écrites par le Général Rochambeau', in which Rochambeau's letters are transcribed and annotated, and the status of each of his demands is listed in the margin, apart from those referring to the immediate restoration of slavery and the extermination of the rebels.
87 Letters from Rochambeau to Ministry of the Navy, 25 Floréal Year XI [15 May 1803] and 23 Frimaire Year XI [14 December 1803]: AN, CC9B/19.
88 Letter from Leclerc to Ministry of the Navy, 30 Fructidor Year XI [17 September 1803]: AN, CC9B/19.
89 Letter from Rochambeau to Ministry of the Navy, 8 Floréal Year XI [28 April 1803]: AN, CC9A/34.
90 Letter from Rochambeau to Ministry of the Navy, 29 Frimaire Year XI [20 December 1802]: AN, CC9B/19.

During the debates that preceded the departure of Leclerc's expedition, various opponents of slavery had foreseen that genocide and slavery were intertwined in Haiti. To restore slavery, one of them wrote, France 'would have to resort to the atrocious method of destruction, until there would not be a single nigger alive in the islands where emancipation has taken place'.[91] A French victory, another one concurred, 'could only be obtained by reducing the country to ashes, and immolating the *cultivateurs*. The colony, without farmers, would then cost money rather than benefit the metropolis.'[92]

The French unwittingly sealed their own fate by deporting Louverture. Louverture governed with the help of white secretaries and white planters whose expertise he viewed as essential to the island's economic well-being. He also restrained the more murderous inclinations of those of his subordinates who talked of killing all Whites.[93] His exile brought to the fore leaders who, like Dessalines, were racists. 'What do we have in common with this people of executioners?', Dessalines asked. 'Its cruelty, which contrasts with our patient moderation, its colour, so different from ours, the vast seas that separate us, our vengeful climate: all of these are testimony to the fact that they are not our brothers, and that they will never be.'[94] Leclerc and Rochambeau's planned genocide never took place: they were defeated before they could implement it. Dessalines reached a similar conclusion; he won the war and carried it out.

The Haitian genocide and its historical counterparts

The 1802–4 period remains little studied, perhaps because it lacks the moral clarity typically associated with genocide. The perpetrators were murderers and rapists, but they were also former slaves fighting to preserve their freedom. The victims were unarmed civilians and wounded soldiers, but they were also members of the planter class that had abused the slaves for decades and would have carried out their own genocide had they won the war. For this reason, one may speak of a 'co-genocide' or 'counter-genocide'. Haitian society was ethnically black and white, but morally far from Manichaean.

In the popular psyche, 'genocide' is virtually equated with the Jewish Holocaust of the Second World War. Those who use the term in a colonial

91 Letter from Alliot-Vauneuf to Lescalier, Council of State, 3 Prairial Year VIII [23 May 1800]: AN, CC9A/27.
92 General Lavaux, 'Rapport', 20 Brumaire Year VII [10 November 1798]: AN, CC9A/20.
93 Letter from Adjutant General Devaux to Ministry of the Navy, 11 Frimaire Year VIII [2 December 1799]: AN, CC9A/23; Toussaint Louverture, 'Adresse faite par le général en chef aux généraux de brigade et aux chefs de colonne', 24 Ventôse Year VI [14 March 1798]: AN, CC9A/19.
94 Dessalines, 'Proclamation', 1 January 1804.

context generally study genocides carried out by Whites against so-called inferior races (such as Native Americans, Jews and Hottentots).[95] The 1804 Haitian genocide, in contrast, was a form of revenge exacted by an oppressed group against those who dominated it, much like the Rwandan and Cambodian genocides. It differs from the Holocaust not least in the fact that each side tried to annihilate the other, a policy that even Warsaw ghetto Jews never even imagined.

In many cases of genocide, responsibility is diffused. Low-level executioners claim that they are merely carrying out orders, while senior officials argue that they never kill anyone personally, or even that they never give a written order. The result is collective guilt (as in the German–Jewish case) or no guilt at all (as in the Turkish–Armenian case). The protagonists of the Haitian tragedy may have been murderers, but they were no hypocrites. Leclerc, Rochambeau and Dessalines explained their motives, gave specific orders and personally oversaw their execution. Only French officials in Paris (Bonaparte included), who left dispatches from Haiti unanswered, and Louverture, who kept the brutal Dessalines on his staff, emerge as ambiguous figures.

The overt nature of the Haitian genocide also differs from the Holocaust. There has been considerable debate over whether Germans knew that Jews were being exterminated in the death camps; the Nazis went to great lengths, in Western Europe at least, to carry out the killings out of the public eye (the same was true in Cambodia).[96] In Haiti, both Whites and Blacks massacred their opponents in the market squares; the French, who buried victims of the yellow fever at night, were more anxious to hide their own corpses than those of their victims. The reason for this transparency is two-fold. First, the killings were intended as a warning to the white (or black) population that those who dared fight would endure unspeakable hardships. Second, documents suggest that there was little popular opposition to each side's genocidal plans. Stories of faithful Blacks protecting their former masters, numerous in 1791, are rare in 1804. There is only one account of a French captain who refused to drown black prisoners as ordered.[97]

The road to genocide followed a path that in some regards was uniquely Haitian. Dessalines killed the Whites, he said, because this was the only way to defeat slavery (and, he could proudly add today, Haitian slaves were indeed the only ones whose revolt was successful). The genocide was also a

95 A. Dirk Moses, 'Conceptual blockages and definitional dilemmas in the "racial century": genocides of indigenous peoples and the Holocaust', *Patterns of Prejudice*, vol. 36, no. 4, 2002, 16; Jürgen Zimmerer, 'Colonialism and the Holocaust: towards an archeology of genocide', in Moses (ed.), *Genocide and Settler Society*, 51.

96 Jean-Louis Margolin, 'Cambodia: the country of disconcerting crimes', in Stéphane Courtois (ed.), *The Black Book of Communism: Crimes, Terror, Repression* (Cambridge, MA: Harvard University Press 1999), 577–635.

97 Christophe Paulin de la Poix, *Mémoires du Chevalier de Fréminville*, 78.

response to a specific list of crimes committed by the French in Haiti, both during the days of slavery and during the 1802–3 war. That Haiti was a French colony probably explains why these slaves (and those of Guadeloupe) revolted in 1791, and not those of Jamaica, who had been traditionally more restless. The ideals of the French Revolution, when contrasted with the reality of colonial society, created an explosive mix that consumed an estimated 300,000 Haitians of all races from 1791 to 1804. That Louverture and, to a lesser extent, Leclerc were replaced by the sadistic Dessalines and Rochambeau was another accident of history with fateful consequences.

Other factors were of a more universal nature. Killing Jews to appropriate their wealth was a recurrent feature of mediaeval pogroms. Aryans, Hutus, ethnic Khmers and Turks would have seen nothing wrong with condemning a person on the basis of their ethnic ancestry. Communists and Jacobins would have agreed with Dessalines that the sanctity of human life paled in comparison with the success of a revolution. Frantz Fanon's violent anti-colonial rhetoric echoed Dessalines's earlier calls for an independence secured in blood. 'Decolonization is quite simply the replacing of a certain "species" of men by another "species" of men', Fanon wrote in *The Wretched of the Earth* (1961). 'For if the last shall be first, this will only come to pass after a murderous and decisive struggle between the two protagonists.'[98]

What is more difficult, however, is to establish a direct link between the Haitian genocide's more 'modern' features—political extremism, racism—and its later counterparts. The event did not spark a string of successful slave revolts the way the US War of Independence served as a template for nineteenth-century Latin American wars of independence. Human, political, economic or intellectual connections between 1804 Haiti and, say, 1943 Germany are non-existent. The central assumption in Arendt's *Origins of Totalitarianism*—that antisemitism and imperialism were precursors of totalitarianism—thus cannot be verified in the Haitian case.[99] One should speak of similarities that are coincidental, not intentional; of succession, not causation. This disconnection mirrors revolutionary Haiti's status as a society at the juncture of two periods. It was an *ancien régime* society, with sharp social and racial boundaries, mercantilist trade rules, a dictatorial government, forced labour and an agricultural economy; but it was also the richest colony of its time, a marvel of capitalism, in the middle

98 Frantz Fanon, *The Wretched of the Earth* [1961] (New York: Grove Press 1968), 35, 37.
99 Arendt barely referred to the Caribbean at all, selecting instead the English experience in South Africa as a precursor of the death camps; Arendt, *Origins of Totalitarianism*, 440. Arendt herself was less than categorical about imperialism–genocide links in some passages of her book; Roy T. Tsao, 'The three phases of Arendt's theory of totalitarianism', *Social Research*, vol. 69, no. 2, Summer 2002.

of extensive trade routes, influenced by revolutionary ideals, as well as being a society with a distinctively modern capacity for evil.

Philippe R. Girard is Assistant Professor of Caribbean History at McNeese State University, Lake Charles, Louisiana, and the author of *Paradise Lost: Haiti's Tumultuous Journey from Pearl of the Caribbean to Third World Hot Spot* (forthcoming from Palgrave Macmillan).

Raphaël Lemkin's 'Tasmania': an introduction[1]

ANN CURTHOYS

In the late 1940s and into the 1950s, in his spare time between lobbying United Nations representatives—initially to support the Genocide Convention passed in 1948 and later to ratify it—Raphaël Lemkin was writing a major study of genocide: its nature, history, psychology and sociology. During these years, and with financial support from the Yale Law School and other bodies, he researched and wrote several chapters. The book (or books) remained unfinished when he died from a heart attack in New York in 1959, and was never published. In Lemkin's thinking, the two projects—the UN Convention and the book—were connected. His aims were not only to establish a new crime and the mechanisms for its prevention, but also to reinterpret the course of human history in light of the new concept. Lemkin was very clear about the relationship between the present and the past: the

1 My thanks to the following for their assistance: James Fussell, Dirk Moses, John Docker, Steven L. Jacobs, the American Jewish Historical Society, the New York Public Library and the Library of Congress.

experience of the Nazi campaign to exterminate the Jews should lead us not only to a determination that such a thing should never happen again but also to a broader understanding of genocide, as a recurring (though variable) theme throughout human history. He hoped that his notion of 'genocide' would be used to help better comprehend past instances of the attempt by one people to annihilate another people, whether by mass murder or by removing the foundations of life through a wide range of strategies, including land seizure, the importation of diseases, the prevention of births and the stealing of children.

After his death, Lemkin's papers were deposited in at least three major libraries: the New York Public Library (NYPL),[2] the American Jewish Historical Society (AJHS) in New York City,[3] and the American Jewish Archives at the Jacob Rader Marcus Center in Cincinnati, Ohio.[4] The NYPL collection, in particular, includes a number of typescripts of chapters for Lemkin's book on genocide. For many years they attracted little notice; by the 1990s, however, some genocide scholars were becoming aware of their existence. Rabbi Steven L. Jacobs worked with Lemkin's papers extensively, and drew them to the attention of genocide scholar Helen Fein. In her book, *Genocide: A Sociological Perspective* (1993), Fein referred to the NYPL collection very briefly and listed twelve of Lemkin's case studies in the history of genocide as being among its contents.[5] Yet these studies are still not widely known and have been subject to little scholarly scrutiny. The chapter on Tasmania has been mostly unknown to historians specializing in Tasmanian history, although Henry Reynolds used Helen Fein's inclusion of Tasmania in her list of Lemkin's case studies in the NYPL as grounds for writing in his book *An Indelible Stain?* (2001) that 'Raphael Lemkin considered Tasmania the site of one of the world's clear cases of genocide'.[6] Reynolds argued that Tasmania did not constitute a case of genocide, although 'genocidal moments' occurred in other parts of Australia, notably in Queensland. The revisionist Australian historian Keith Windschuttle also noticed Fein's reference and, in *The Fabrication of Aboriginal History* (2002), drew from it the conclusion that Lemkin rated the events in Tasmania as 'on a par with those of the Belgian Congo, the Huguenots

---

2 The Raphaël Lemkin Papers are held in the Manuscripts and Archives Division, New York Public Library; the entire collection has been microfilmed.

3 Raphael Lemkin Collection P-154, American Jewish Historical Society, Newton Centre, MA and New York, NY. A description of the collection is available online at www.cjh.org/academic/findingaids/AJHS/nhprc/Lemkinf.html (viewed 29 January 2005).

4 A complete inventory of the Raphaël Lemkin Papers in the American Jewish Archive is available online at www.americanjewisharchives.org/aja/collections/01_l.html (viewed 29 January 2005).

5 Helen Fein, *Genocide: A Sociological Perspective* (London: Sage Publications 1993), 11.

6 Henry Reynolds, *The Indelible Stain? The Question of Genocide in Australia's History* (Ringwood, Victoria and Harmondsworth: Viking 2001), 50.

of France, the Incas of Peru and Ukrainians under the Soviet Union'.[7] But neither of these Australian historians had actually seen Lemkin's essay on Tasmania.

When my colleague John Docker and I visited the two New York libraries to look at the Lemkin papers in 2003, we found much more than we had expected. Not only were there many notes, outlines and prospectuses for Lemkin's book on genocide in both libraries,[8] but in the NYPL there were also a number of chapters intended for that book, including the one on Tasmania published here for the first time. Although Lemkin may not have considered the text represented by the typescript to be ready for publication, the 'Tasmania' chapter seems to me to warrant publication for the benefit of both genocide scholars and historians of Tasmania. Despite any limitations it may have, it clearly shows the subtlety of Lemkin's understanding of genocide, and the care he took over the vexed question of intention.

In this chapter, we see Lemkin applying his own analytical methodology to Tasmania. For his projected book on genocide, he developed a framework for looking at a range of historical cases. In each case, he thought it important to look at the following aspects: background, conditions leading to genocide, methods and techniques of genocide, the genocidists, propaganda, responses of victim group, responses of outside groups, and aftermath. Among papers related to the planned book of case studies is the following typescript headed 'Revised Outline for Genocide Cases', in which Lemkin describes these eight categories.

REVISED OUTLINE FOR GENOCIDE CASES[9]

1. Background—historical

2. Conditions leading to genocide—Fanaticism (religious, racial)
Irredentism (national aspirations)
Social or political crisis and change

7 Keith Windschuttle, *The Fabrication of Aboriginal History. Volume 1: Van Diemen's Land, 1803–1847* (Sydney: Macleay Press 2002), 14. Windschuttle is mistaken in assuming that Lemkin attributed some kind of parity to different cases of genocide; indeed, one of his aims in the unpublished studies is to investigate the variety of genocides.
8 These materials at the AJHS are included in Series III: History of Genocide, n.d., Boxes 7–9.
9 The two-page typescript, revised by Lemkin in pen and pencil, is here reproduced as faithfully as is practicable from the original in the Lemkin papers at the AJHS (Series III: History of Genocide, Box 8, Folder 10). I am grateful to the AJHS for permission to publish this document. Text added by Lemkin in pen or pencil is here given in angle brackets < >, cancelled text is given in brace brackets { }, and editorial interventions in square brackets [ ].

Economic exploitation (e.g. slavery)
Colonial expansion or milit. conquest
Accessability [*sic*] of victim group
evolution of genocidal values in genocidist group
(contempt for the alien, etc.)
<factors weakening victim group>

3. Methods and techniques of genocide—Physical:
massacre and mutilation
deprivation of livelihood (starvation,
exposure, etc.—often by deportation)
<slavery—exposure to death>

Biological:
separation of families
sterilization
destruction of foetus

Cultural:
<desecration and> destruction of cultural
symbols (books, objects of art, religious
relics, etc.)
loot
destruction of cultural leadership
destruction of cultural centers (cities,
churches, monasteries, schools, libraries)
prohibition of cultural activities or codes of
behavior
forceful conversion
demoralization

4. The Genocidists—responsibility
intent
motivation
feelings of guilt
demoralization
attitude towards victim group
<opposition to genocide within genocidist group>

5. Propaganda—rationalization of crime
appeal to popular beliefs and intolerance; <sowing discord (divide
and rule)>
misrepresentation and deceit
intimidation

6. Responses of victim group—active:
submission
({panic and flight} <suicide, hiding, etc.>) escape
disguise
<(planned)> emigration
polit. subordination (divide & rule)
assimilation
resistance
demoralization

6. Responses of victim group (cont.)—passive (emotional, mental)
terror
{beliefs regarding} <conceptions of>
genocidist and his crimes

7. Responses of outside groups—opposition to genocide
                                  indifference to "
                                  condonement of "
                                  collaboration in "
                                  demoralization (exploitation of genocide situation)
                                  <Fear as potential victims>

8. Aftermath—cultural losses
                    population changes
                    economic dislocations
                    material and moral {destitution} deterioration
                    political consequences
                    <social and cult. Changes>

With the aid of assistants, Lemkin researched each of his cases extensively. His method was to rely largely on secondary sources but he also made use of primary sources whenever possible. (He looked, for example, at an original manuscript in the British Library that provides evidence for the story that General Jeffrey Amherst in 1763 supported the deliberate spreading of smallpox among the Indian nations; a research assistant had found a memorandum by Amherst that reads as follows: 'Could it not be Contrived to Send the Small Pox among those Disaffected Tribes of Indians? We must on this occasion, use every Stratagem in our power to Reduce them. JA'[10])

Lemkin studied a large number of cases, perhaps too many for his purpose, possibly one reason he never completed the task. One of his contents lists for the book in the NYPL collection (there are several, drawn up for various grant and fellowship applications) includes forty-one chapters. The proposed volumes were to include case studies from antiquity, with chapters on the early Christians, the Pagans, Carthage, Gaul, the Celts, Egypt and Ancient Greece. Then, there would be a section on the Middle Ages, with chapters on genocides committed by groups such as the Goths, Huns, Mongols, Vikings, French and Spanish against peoples and groups like the Albigensians, Jews, Valdenses, Moors and Moriscos. In the section on 'Modern Times', chapters on a large number of cases were envisaged, including the forced deportation of the Cherokee, the Herero in South-west Africa, the Gypsies, the Armenian genocide and genocides against Polish Jews, Russian Jews, Romanian Jews and others. Towards the end of the very long typed list of chapters we find 'chapter 38: Tasmanians' (annotated by hand 'good and duplicate'), which seems to refer to the chapter reproduced here. Chapter 39 on the list is 'Armenians', chapter 40 is 'S. W. Africa'; at the very end of the list is the handwritten additional item '41. Natives of Australia', which is also annotated 'good with duplicate'. This suggests another Australian chapter, although there isn't one among Lemkin's papers in either the New York Public Library or the American Jewish Historical Society, and it may no longer exist.

10 Amherst's original memorandum is in the British Library (Add. MS 21634, f. 243); a copy is among Lemkin's papers in the AJHS (Box 7, Folder 10 'Miscellaneous').

For the Tasmanian chapter, Lemkin relied very largely on James Bonwick's *The Last of the Tasmanians* (1870).[11] Although published almost eighty years earlier, this was still the most detailed historical study available at the time. In addition, there was James Calder's 'Some Account of the Wars, Extirpation, Habits, & c., of the Native Tribes of Tasmania', a paper originally delivered to the Anthropological Institute of Great Britain and Ireland in 1874,[12] and rather limited discussions in James Fenton's *History of Tasmania* (1884), J. B. Walker's *Early Tasmania* (1902) and R. W. Giblin's *Early History of Tasmania* (1939), all of which Lemkin used.[13] Indeed, Lemkin seems to have found most of the available published literature. He could not, however, have known of a well-researched new book that was just appearing in Australia at around the same time as he was writing, Clive Turnbull's *Black War: The Extermination of the Tasmanian Aborigines* (1948).[14] Interestingly, the two men, working on opposite sides of the world in ignorance of each other, shared a similar concern regarding the morality of the British colonization of Tasmania, seemingly prompted, in different ways, by the then recent genocidal events in Europe.

Faced with a meagre secondary literature, Lemkin tracked down some published primary documents as well, such as the notable and very telling despatch of 5 November 1830 from Sir George Murray, the Secretary of State for the Colonies, to Governor Arthur, expressing fear that the Aboriginal Tasmanians would 'at no distant period, become extinct';[15] the highly critical 'Report from the Select Committee on Aborigines (British Settlements)', published as part of the *British Parliamentary Papers* of 1836 and 1837;[16] the indictment of settler cruelty by Dr Nixon (afterwards Bishop of Tasmania

11 James Bonwick, *The Last of the Tasmanians; or, The Black War of Van Diemen's Land* (London: Sampson Low 1870).

12 J. E. Calder, 'Some account of the wars, extirpation, habits etc. of the native tribes of Tasmania', *Journal of the Anthropological Institute of Great Britain and Ireland*, vol. 3, 1874, 7–29.

13 James Fenton, *A History of Tasmania from Its Discovery in 1642 to the Present Time* (Hobart: J. Walch 1884); James Backhouse Walker, *Early Tasmania: Papers Read before the Royal Society of Tasmania during the Years 1888 to 1899* (Hobart: J. Vail 1902); R. W. Giblin, *The Early History of Tasmania*, vol. 2 (1804–28) (Melbourne: Melbourne University Press 1939). Lemkin also refers to the work of Henry Melville, cited in a footnote to 'Tasmania' (see note 47 to Lemkin's 'Tasmania') as 'Henry Melville—Australasia and Immigration, London 1857' but probably meant to be Henry Melville, *Australasia and Prison Discipline* (London: Charles Cox 1851).

14 Clive Turnbull, *Black War: The Extermination of the Tasmanian Aborigines* (Melbourne and London: F. W. Cheshire 1948).

15 Copies of All Correspondence between Lieutenant-Governor Arthur and His Majesty's Secretary of State for the Colonies, *British Parliamentary Papers*, 1831 (259), XIX, 56.

16 Report from the Select Committee on Aborigines (British Settlements;) Together with the Minutes of Evidence, Appendix and Index, *British Parliamentary Papers*, 1836 (538), VII; Report from the Select Committee on Aborigines (British Settlements); With the Minutes of Evidence, Appendix and Index, *British Parliamentary Papers*, 1837 (425), VII.

from 1842–63);[17] and Herman Merivale's condemnation of the 'destruction of native races by the uncontrolled violence of individuals and colonial authorities' in his well-known eighteenth lecture in the series published as *Colonization and Colonies*.[18] Yet Lemkin's major source was unquestionably Bonwick's detailed and sympathetic account of the destruction of Tasmanian Aboriginal society.

Using his analytical framework and these materials, then, Lemkin wrote his own account of what happened in Tasmania. To provide the background, he outlines the discovery of Tasmania by Dutch sailors, and its establishment as a British colony from 1803. He recounts the infamous Risdon Cove massacre of 1804, and outlines the increasing conflict between settlers and indigenous peoples, as well as the series of proclamations by governing authorities from 1810 to 1830 that were attempts to control or prevent it. He tells the story of the notorious 'Black Line', which involved a military 'sweeping' of the eastern side of the island to capture the remaining Aboriginal people in order to relocate them on an offshore island away from the settlers. The Black Line seemed to fail in that very few Aboriginal people were captured, but it probably did weaken the remaining Aboriginal resistance. Its aim was actually achieved shortly afterwards through conciliation and negotiation by government agent George Augustus Robinson. Lemkin goes on to describe the removal of the Aboriginal people to Gun Carriage Island, Bruny Island and, finally, Flinders Island, where most of them died. He ends the story with the death of Truganina in 1876, seeing this as representing the extinction of the Aboriginal people.

Having given the bare bones of the story, Lemkin's chapter considers the question of intent, under the subheading 'Intent to destroy—who is guilty/ Government or individuals?' His answer is both, especially individuals. He places the blame for the destruction of Tasmanian society first on the settlers and convicts who attacked the Aboriginal people, provoking them to retaliation, and second on the governing authorities who, while neither planning nor conducting genocide, failed in their basic duty of protection.

Lemkin's interest then shifts to the means and techniques whereby genocide in Tasmania had occurred. It was characteristic of him to pay considerable attention to the brutal treatment, kidnapping, prostitution and economic exploitation of the women, seeing these as forms of genocide in that they eventually destroyed the ability of Tasmanian Aborigines to reproduce. He discusses at some length the rapid decline in the birth rate,

17 Francis Russell Nixon, *The Cruise of the Beacon: A Narrative of a Visit to the Islands in Bass's Straits* (London: Bell and Daldy 1857).
18 Herman Merivale, *Lectures on Colonization and Colonies, Delivered before the University of Oxford in 1839, 1840, and 1841* (London: Longman, Orme, Brown, Green and Longmans 1841).

the result of conditions of warfare, the loss of land and the loss of women to sealers and others. He had a particular interest in the stealing of children as a way of destroying a human group, and saw this as especially evident in the Tasmanian case. He describes the loss of children through tribal killing of half-caste children, and the killing and stealing of children by settlers. There follow sections on cruelty, legal status and the effects of liquor and disease. Lemkin pays particular attention to the effects of confinement on Gun Carriage, Bruny and Flinders Islands, which left the people 'lifeless and dispirited'.

The final section, the seemingly least complete of all, considers public opinion. Part of Lemkin's methodology was always to consider the ways in which genocide was understood, justified or criticized at the time. In the Tasmanian case, he noted that, while the settlers felt justified in their behaviour, the Tasmanian press and commentators in both Tasmania and England were horrified. The chapter does not cover the remaining aspects of Lemkin's analytical framework—victim responses, outside group responses and the consequences—and it is impossible to know whether or not he would have extended the essay before publication.

Though Lemkin is constrained here by the available sources and the chapter may be incomplete, it nevertheless provides us with a glimpse into the way Lemkin thought about genocide historically: how he dealt with the difficult question of intent and the importance he attached both to direct killing and the myriad other means whereby one group can destroy another. His account has, of course, been superseded by extensive historical research published since the mid-1970s;[19] it retains, however, a distinctive analytical flavour all its own. While Lemkin's is by no means an authoritative or unblemished text, it is a thoughtful and thought-provoking one. It is interesting to ponder how international genocide scholarship and Australian historiography might have been changed had his book been completed and published as originally intended.

Ann Curthoys is Manning Clark Professor of History at the Australian National University, Canberra.

---

19 Some of the key works on this aspect of Tasmanian history are: Lyndall Ryan, *The Aboriginal Tasmanians* [1981], 2nd edn (Sydney: Allen and Unwin 1996); L. L. Robson, *A History of Tasmania*, vol. 1 (Melbourne: Oxford University Press 1983); N. J. B. Plomley, *The Aboriginal/Settler Clash in Van Diemen's Land, 1803–1831* (Launceston: Queens Victoria Museum and Art Gallery 1992); Henry Reynolds, *The Fate of a Free People* (Melbourne: Penguin 1995); Windschuttle, *Fabrication of Aboriginal History*; and Robert Manne, *Whitewash: On Keith Windschuttle's Fabrication of Aboriginal History* (Melbourne: Black Inc. Agenda 2003).

Tasmania[1]

RAPHAËL LEMKIN

edited by Ann Curthoys

Background

Tasmania was discovered in 1642 by a Dutch sea captain named Abel Janzen. Tasman who named the country Van Diemen's land in honor of the daughter of the Governor of Java. It was not until late in the nineteenth century that the island became known as Tasmania.

In his journal Captain Tasman describes the natives as a peaceable if shy race, and his dealings with them were on the whole friendly.[2] They were[3] of negroid stock with black skins and fuzzy hair.

The island was visited in the succeeding years by many navigators of different races, including Marion du Fresne and Captain Cook, and according to all their accounts the natives showed no great hostility and generally welcomed the travelers after their first fear and timidity had been overcome.

The real history of Tasmania as an English colony begins in 1803 with the establishment of Risdon, on the Derwent River by Captain Collins. This settlement was largely composed of convicts who, in the words of James Bonwick, 'having been indifferent about the virtues when with their

---

1 [Raphaël Lemkin Papers, Manuscript and Archives Division, The New York Public Library, Astor, Lenox and Tilden Foundations. I am grateful to the NYPL for permission to publish this original typescript, which is transcribed here as faithfully as is practicable. Underlined words are here given in italics and double quotation marks have been altered to single quotation marks, as per the journal's house style. The original is for the most part a fair copy but there are occasional cancellations and revisions, both typed and added later by hand. Only those revisions that can be construed as substantive are given here in footnotes. Obvious typographical errors and spelling mistakes have been silently corrected. Editorial interventions are given in square brackets. If Lemkin typed quoted material as a separate paragraph, it is set here as a displayed quotation; if he included it within a paragraph, his typescript has been followed. Lemkin's own footnotes have been cited *not* as they appear in the typescript but in the journal's house style, and are numbered consecutively throughout the text (rather than beginning with '1' on each page as in the typescript). All additional material in the footnotes is in square brackets.]

2 [Tasman did not actually see or meet any Aboriginal people during his time in Tasmania. His comments were based on what he thought they might be like.]

3 [Lemkin originally wrote 'They are of negroid stock . . .' but, later, revised it by hand to 'They were of negroid stock'.]

countrymen at home, were not likely to be more courteous and conscientious in dealing with savages abroad.'[4]

The aboriginal population of Tasmania at that time was estimated at between 5000 and 7000.

Captain Collins received the following instructions from Lord Hobart, Secretary for the Colonies: 'You are to endeavour, by every means in your power, to open an intercourse with the Natives and to conciliate their good-will, enjoining all parties under your government to live in amity and kindness with them; and if any person shall exercise any acts of violence against them, or shall wantonly give them any interruption in the exercise of their several occupations, you are to cause such offender to be brought to punishment according to the degree of the offense.'

At Risdon, early in 1804 occurred the unfortunate event which began the 'Black War' leading to the extermination of the Tasmanian aborigines in less than half a century.

A large group of Aborigines including women and children appeared on the heights above the town. They were not armed, carrying with them only waddies[5] and driving before them a large number of kangaroos, so they were apparently preparing to hold a corrobory.[6] The officer in command of Risdon ordered the soldiers with him to fire upon the hunters, and numbers were killed. One of the settlers who was present asserted that the officer was drunk and that before this event there had been nothing but good feeling between the whites and the blacks.

Edward White, who was hoeing at the time, stated before the Aborigines Committee which investigated the attack, that he saw about three hundred natives with a flock of kangaroos between them: 'They looked at me with all their eyes. I went down to the creek, and reported them to some soldiers, and then went back to my work. The natives did not threaten me. I was not afraid of them. ... The natives did not attack the soldiers. They could not have molested them. The firing commenced about eleven o'clock. There were many of the Natives slaughtered and wounded. I don't know how many. ... This was three or four months after we landed. They never came so close again afterwards. ...'[7]

The attitude of the natives changed after the attack upon them and soon after began their attacks upon the settlers, which grew in frequency and ferocity. Mr. W. C. Wentworth, a colonial barrister and statesman, wrote in 1823: 'Their deep-rooted animosity, however, did not arise so much from the ferocious nature of these savages, as from the inconsiderate and unpardonable attacks of our countrymen, shortly after the foundation of the settlement

4 James Bonwick, *The Last of the Tasmanians; or, The Black War of Van Diemen's Land* (London: Sampson Low 1870), 30.
5 [Waddies: man-made tools for hunting small animals and birds.]
6 [Corrobory: ceremony, usually now 'corroboree'.]
7 Bonwick, *Last of the Tasmanians*, 34.

on the river Derwent. At first the Natives evinced the most friendly disposition toward the newcomers; and would, probably, have been actuated by the same amicable feelings to this day, had not the military officer entrusted with the command directed a discharge of grape and cannister-shot to be made among a large body, who were approaching, as he imagined, with hostile designs; but as it has since been believed with much greater probability, merely from motives of curiosity and friendship. The havoc occasioned among them by this murderous discharge was dreadful, and since then all communication with them has ceased; and the spirit of animosity and revenge which this unmerited and atrocious act of barbarity engendered, has been fostered and aggravated to the highest pitch by the incessant encounters that have subsequently taken place between them and the whites.'[8]

The authorities attempted to protect the settlers but at the same time understood the cause of the native violence and wished to spare the aborigines from the cruel treatment of the whites. For this purpose the following Government Order was issued on January 29, 1810: 'There being great reason to fear that William Russell and George Gelley will be added to the number of unfortunate men who have been put to death by the Natives, in revenge for the murders and abominable cruelties which have been practiced upon them by the white people, the Lieutenant-Governor, aware of the evil consequences that must result to the settlement, if such cruelties are continued, and abhorring the conduct of those miscreants who perpetrate them, hereby declares that any person whomsoever who shall offer violence to a native, or who shall in cool blood murder, or cause any of them to be murdered, shall, on proof being made of the same, be dealt with and proceeded against as if such violence had been offered, or murder committed on, a civilized person.'[9]

The deadly feud between settlers and natives continued to rage, the whites perpetrating acts of great injustice on the natives, stealing their women and children, and murdering their men, while the natives retaliated by burning the houses of settlers in remote places and murdering entire families.

Colonel Arthur, the new Governor of Tasmania, on June 23, 1824, published a Proclamation on behalf of the natives which was full of justice and benevolence, but useless for all practical purposes: 'The Natives of this Island being under the protection of the same laws, which protect the Settlers, any Violation of those Laws, on the Persons or Property of Natives, shall be visited with the same Punishment as though committed on the Person and Property of any other.'

8 Ibid.
9 [Lemkin's footnote was 'Muster Book of 1810 &c.', which was quoted in Bonwick, *Last of the Tasmanians*, 40.]

Finally two years later, when settlers were killed almost daily and the life of no white man in the bush was safe, the following Government Notice appeared in the *Gazette* of Nov. 29, 1826:

> The series of outrages which have of late been perpetrated by the Aborigines of the Colony, and the wanton barbarity in which they have indulged by the commission of murder, in return for the kindness, in numerous instances, shown to them by the Settlers and their Servants, have occasioned the greatest pain to the Lieut. Governor, and called for His most anxious Consideration of the Means to be applied for preventing the Repetition of these treacherous and sanguinary Acts.
>
> His Excellency has uniformly been anxious to inculcate a spirit of Forbearance toward the Aborigines, in the hope that confidence and cordiality might subsist, and be conducive to their Improvement and the security of the Colonists; but it is with extreme regret that He perceives a result so contrary to His hope and expectation.
>
> An impression, however, still remains that these savages are stimulated to acts of Atrocity by one or more Leaders, who from their previous Intercourse with Europeans may have acquired sufficient intelligence to draw them into Crime and Danger. The capture of these Individuals, therefore, becomes an Object of the first Importance, and to this Point the Lieut-. Governor would particularly direct the Attention of those who may be called to Aid the Civil Power in the Execution of the justifiable measures to which they may have recourse: and His Excellency deems it necessary to promulgate, for general Information, but especially for the guidance of the Magistrates, Constables, and Military:—
>
> 1. If it shall be apparent that there is a Determination on the Part of one or more of the Native Tribes to attack, rob, or murder the white Inhabitants generally, any Persons may arm, and joining themselves to the military, drive them by force to a safe distance, treating them as open enemies.
> 2. If they are found actually attempting to commit a felony they may be resisted by any Persons in like manner.
> 3. When they appear assembled in unusual Numbers, or with unusual Arms, or although neither be unusual, if they evidently indicate such Intention of employing Force as is calculated to excite Fear, for the purpose of doing any Harm, short of Felony, to the Persons of Property of any one, they may be treated as Rioters, and resisted, if they persist in their attempt. . . .
> 4. When a Felony has been committed, any Person who witnesses it may immediately raise his Neighbours and pursue the Felons, and the Pursuers may justify the Use of all such Means as a Constable might use. If they overtake the Parties, they should bid, or otherwise signify to them, to surrender; if they resist, or attempt to resist, the Persons Pursuing may use such Force as is necessary: and if the Pursued fly, and cannot otherwise be taken, the Pursuers then may use similar means. . . .[10]

10 [Quoted in Bonwick, *Last of the Tasmanians*, 73–5. Lemkin did not provide a footnote for this quotation.]

This Government Notice, advising the settlers to attack the natives, was the beginning of the Great Black War.

It was suggested that the aborigines be isolated to certain areas of Tasmania where they would be removed enough from the white settlers as to be no menace to them and would also be protected from attacks by them. Colonel Arthur explained why this suggestion was impracticable: 'My intention was to have given up one district to the Natives, but such a spirit of dissension exists among the tribes themselves, that it cannot possibly be accomplished.' He also felt that it was 'painful and distressing to banish the Natives from their private haunts.'[11]

In spite of the difficulties, however, it was felt that isolation was the only remedy[12] and the Demarkation order was proclaimed on April 15, 1828, ordering that the Natives be prevented from entering the settled districts—the central and eastern portions—and confining them to the Western area which consisted of swamps, vast mountains, dreary morasses, and almost lifeless solitudes, practically devoid of game.[13]

This proclamation brought no results whatever, the uncivilized aborigines on the whole never hearing of the pronouncement, and disregarding it if they did. They continued to roam all over the territory and murder and pillage on both sides continued unabated. Another proclamation was then issued on November 1, 1828, prefaced by the false announcement that 'every practicable measure has been resorted to for the purpose of removing the aborigines from the settled districts of the colony; and for the putting a stop to the repetition of such atrocities,' and declaring Martial Law for all but certain stipulated areas, to be reserved for the Blacks.

This was followed by the Order offering five pounds for the capture of an adult native, and two pounds for that of a child. Capture parties were organized to bring in the natives but many more were killed than were captured alive.

Whether because of the activities of settlers engaged in hunting the natives or for other reasons the situation became more peaceful and for a time few outrages were committed. The Governor felt greatly encouraged and produced Government Notice 160, on August 19, 1830:

> It is with much satisfaction that the Lieut. Governor is at length enabled to announce that a less hostile disposition toward the European inhabitants has been manifested by some of the Aboriginal Natives of this island. . . .
>
> As it is the most anxious desire of the Government that the good understanding which has thus happily commenced, should be fostered and encouraged by every possible means, His Excellency earnestly requests, that all settlers and others will

---

11 Bonwick, *Last of the Tasmanians*, 77–8.
12 [Lemkin originally wrote '. . . it was felt that perhaps isolation was the only remedy', but later deleted 'perhaps' by hand.]
13 Bonwick, *Last of the Tasmanians*, 77–8.

strictly enjoin their servants cautiously to abstain from acts of aggression against these benighted beings, and that they will themselves personally endeavour to conciliate them, wherever it may be practicable; and whenever the Aborigines appear without evincing a hostile feeling, that no attempt should be made either to capture or to restrain them; but, on the contrary, after being fed and kindly treated, that they should be suffered to depart whenever they may desire it.

The colony, which but a short time before had been urged to capture the blacks and offered rewards for so doing, was astonished. Some thought the Governor weak of purpose while other [sic] believed he was trying to put the Aborigines off their guard so as to lure them into some net he was preparing.

The settlers replied in an address from the Clyde District stating that they 'altogether despaired' of eventual friendly relations with the hostile savages who regarded them as intruders, and requesting more Government assistance and the removal of the tax on dogs, which were essential to the very life of farmers in remote sections who depended on the bark of their dogs to warn them if natives were come to attack.

The Proclamation of October 1, 1830 sealed the fate of the natives. A new and harsher Martial Law was proclaimed and it was directed that the natives be hunted down by concerted action and driven forth from all their places of refuge on the island.

Governor Arthur established what was known as the 'The Line' composed of military units placed in certain centres of settled districts, to be reinforced by volunteers among the settlers. These units were all to make 'one great and engrossing pursuit', sweeping the island from north to south, 'with the view of converging on the Oyster Bay and Big River tribes, and driving them into the *cul de sac* of Tasman's Peninsula.'[14] On October 7, 1830, about 3000 men took to the field and the Line advanced to the south. The Neck was gained, and every precaution was taken to prevent the blacks from slipping through the line. The Line stretched for a distance of thirty miles with a space of 45 yards between the men. The Neck was crossed and the Peninsula entered and the search for the blacks, believed to have been driven before the Line, was begun but not a single black was there. One black only had been captured in the long march down the peninsula, the sole prize gained at the cost of 30,000 pounds.

The army was dismissed with the Government Order No. 13, on November 26, 1830.

After the failure of the Line the blacks made increasingly violent attacks on the settlers. Parties of military and civilians scoured the bush and by the end of 1832, 236 had been captured but many had been killed. The sufferings of the natives were severe, children and old people dying of fatigue and hunger.

14 James Backhouse Walker, *Early Tasmania: Papers Read before the Royal Society of Tasmania during the Years 1888 to 1899* (Hobart: J. Vail 1902), 234.

When the first natives were captured it was decided that they be removed from Tasmania and settled on some nearby island. George Austus [*sic*] Robinson[15] was appointed to the position advertised in the Gazette of March 1829:

> In furtherance of the Lieutenant Governor's anxious desire to ameliorate the condition of the aboriginal inhabitants of this territory, His Excellency will allow a salary of 50 pounds per annum together with rations, to a steady man of good character, that can be well recommended, who will take an interest in effecting an intercourse with this unfortunate race, to reside on Bruni Island taking charge of the provisions supplied for the use of the Natives at that place.[16]

Bruni Island was generally unfit for cultivation and had little vegetation. Its rocky coast was exposed to the southern ocean and sudden storms. The natives were given rations of bread and potatoes, but these were poor in quality and deficient in quantity. The natives grew ill and homesick and longed for the free hunting of the mainland and many escaped.

Meanwhile war continued on Tasmania. Robinson, with the support of the Aborigines' Protection Society Committee proposed to go unarmed into the wilderness and persuade the aboriginal tribes to surrender peaceably. With the aid of native women he was extremely successful and finished his work in 1833, having brought in 159 natives in four years.

By the end of 1830 some 56 natives had been captured and it became necessary to remove them to a place of safety where they would be under the care of the Government, and powerless to molest the settlers further. The settlement on Bruni Island had proved unsatisfactory and the natives were placed temporarily on Swan Island in Bass Strait. It had little in its favour, as its water was brackish, the soil was barren, and it was only a mile and a half long. The Bishop of Tasmania described it in 1854 as 'little more than a succession of sand-heaps, covered here and there with tussock and stunted shrubs.'

The natives were soon removed to Gun Carriage, or Vansittart Island, which was equally unsatisfactory, being almost devoid of game and 'the unfortunate creatures, having no motive for exercise ... used to sit day after day on the beach, casting tearful glances across the stormy sea towards the mountains of their native land.'

This Island too was abandoned and the final choice rested on Great Island, afterwards called Flinders Island, which for 15 years was the home of the miserable remnant of the native tribes of Tasmania, and for the majority of them it became their grave.

15 [Lemkin is referring to George Augustus Robinson.]
16 [Quoted in Bonwick, *Last of the Tasmanians*, 212. Lemkin did not provide a footnote for this quotation.]

The terrible mortality of the natives on Flinders Island finally aroused the interest of their friends in Hobart Town. The remaining blacks longed to return to their own country but although there were only twelve Tasmanian men left alive in 1847, the white settlers feared a renewal of native attacks if they returned. However in October forty four aborigines, 12 men, 22 women, and 10 children were removed to Oyster Cove. Some of the children were half castes; six were placed in the Orphan School where they died.

The condition of the natives was no better on the mainland than it had been on Flinders Island; many sickened and died, and the rest lost heart and fell into a state of apathy.

The last male aborigine, William Lanne, died on March 5, 1869. The Hobart Town Mercury of March 5 contains this notice of his death:

> He had an unfortunate propensity for beer and rum, and was seldom sober when on shore. . . . died from a severe attack of English cholera . . . His body was removed to the Colonial Hospital on Wednesday night, March 3d, where it awaits burial, and tomorrow the grave will close over the last male aboriginal of Tasmania.

Truganina, the last aboriginal woman to survive, died in 1877.[17] In 1899 Mr. Jas. Barnard read a paper before the Royal Society of Tasmania asserting that a Mrs. Fanny Cochrane Smith, an old resident at Irishtown, near Port Cygnet, was a pure blood Tasmanian aborigine, but investigation proved with a fair amount of certainty that she was a half-caste.[18]

Intent to destroy—who is guilty

Government or individuals?

The Government policy in Tasmania was one of benevolence toward the aborigines. From the earliest days of settlement, Government proclamations were issued ordering kind and lenient treatment of natives, threatening penalties for unjust actions and cruelty, and the declaring the right of the natives to the same treatment as the whites. Unfortunately the Government was unable to cope with the situation created by the very character of the white people overrunning the land.

Tasmania was settled as a penal colony and the riffraff of Britain, convicted criminals and felons, were sent by the thousands to the island. Many convicts escaped and took to the bush where they attacked the natives without mercy, killing them out of savage cruelty, or to the sea where they

17 [The correct date is 1876.]
18 H. Ling Roth, 'Is Mrs F. C. Smith a "last living Aboriginal of Tasmania"?', *Journal of the Anthropological Institute of Great Britain and Ireland*, vol. 27, 1898, 451–4 (451).

preyed on the coastal tribes, stealing their women and selling their young men and children into slavery.

Had the Government devised some plan at the time of colonization for establishing the aborigines in one part of Tasmania and protecting them from the attacks of the whites, the race might have been spared, but with all the good will in the world, once open warfare between black and white had begun, the Government was powerless to persuade them to live in peaceful proximity and was forced to resort to the drastic measures which led to the eventual extermination of the race.

The *Derwent Star* wrote in 1810: 'The Natives, who have been rendered desperate by the cruelties they have experienced from our people, have now begun to distress us by attacking our cattle.'

This led to severe retaliations on the part of the settlers. Jorge Jorgenson, the Dane, wrote in his Autobiography in 1830 that he 'saw traces in numerous places . . . where (natives) had been wantonly shot by spiteful and vindictive stock-keepers,' and the editor of a Wellington paper wrote 'We have ourselves heard "old hands" declare to the common practice of shooting them to supply food for dogs.'[19]

Captain Stokes declared: 'Such is the perversion of feeling among the colonists, that they cannot conceive that anyone can sympathize with the black race as their fellow-men.'[20]

On Dec. 1, 1826, the *Colonial Times* counselled the Government to send the natives to Kings Island: 'We make no pompous display of philanthropy; we say unequivocally "self-defence is the first law of nature." The Government must remove the Natives; if not, they will be hunted down like wild beasts and destroyed.'

Mr. Chief Justice Pedder declared this an unchristian attempt to destroy the whole race, as the natives would die once they were taken from their ancient haunts. This prophecy proved to be true but the Government felt there was no alternative.

The Governor in a speech declared 'It is undeniable that they (the natives) were lamentably neglected in the early colonization of the country and have been treated with cruelty and oppression by the stock keepers, and other convicts in the interior, and by the sealers on the coast; and from the want of due discernment, their vengeance has been indiscriminately wreaked upon the unoffending settlers of the present time. This fact continues to disarm us of every particle of resentment.'

The settlers on outlying farms lived in constant danger of attack and daily reports of massacred families and burned farms reached the authorities. What good to place the blame on the cruelty of the whites when innocent farmers were suffering along with the rest? The Governor had no choice and issued his orders to capture all natives for deportation. The situation had got

19 Bonwick, *Last of the Tasmanians*, 58.
20 Ibid., 59.

completely out of hand, and although the roving bands ostensibly went out to bring the natives in alive, many more were killed than captured.

The few poor remnants of the Tasmanian race were eventually lodged on an island in the Straits and placed under the benevolent care of Mr. Robinson, who did everything in his power to see to their material and spiritual welfare, often in the face of great odds, as the authorities were often remiss in sending him supplies and the colony suffered at times from malnutrition.

Despite the tender ministrations of Mr. Robinson, in the space of a few years most of the natives succumbed to disease, and apathy. Mr. Robinson was activated by the highest and most charitable motives and often gave of his own small income to help his charges, but unfortunately he possessed little understanding of the nature of the aborigines.

The Committee of the Aborigines Society reported in 1839 that they regretted that 'from the first a system had not been applied more suitable to the habits of a roving people, instead of the highly artificial one (referred to in one of Mr. Robinson's reports).'

Mr. Robinson had no conception of the impossibility of suddenly uprooting an uncivilized nomadic people and forcing upon them the ways of civilization. He managed to give them the outward semblance of civilization but in so doing destroyed their interest in life and their zest for living. They became cleaner in their personal habits, learned to read and write, attended church and sang psalms, but their spirit was gone. The days stretched endlessly before them, days in which to perform the tasks laid out for them by their captors, and to dream of the past when they had been free to roam through the forests of Tasmania and hunt at will.

With the will to live destroyed, the natives succumbed rapidly to disease and vice and within a few decades the entire race was wiped out. The blame for this destruction of a race lies on the cruelty and lack of understanding of human beings, on the cruelty of the selfish, grasping settlers and convicts who attacked and aroused the spirit of revenge of the originally peaceable natives, and on the lack of understanding of the men who in the end strove to protect them and make them conform to the standard of an alien civilization, and killed them with misguided kindness.

Prostitution and treatment of women

Tasmania was settled as a convict colony and many of the convicts escaped and took to the bush where they became known as bushrangers. Many of them joined together in groups as outlaws and became a threat to black and white alike. They were the natural foes of the Aborigines, from innate cruelty and also from fear that the Aborigines would divulge their hiding places.

One of the bushrangers called Leon, and his companions, when in a merry mood, bound captured natives to trees and used them as targets for rifle practice. An ex-bushranger confessed to Mr. Bonwick that he would 'as leave shoot them as so many sparrows.'[21]

One bushranger boasted about his cleverness in killing the natives, declaring that he would lay down his musket to induce the blacks to come toward him, but that on their approach he would fire at them from his retreat, pulling the trigger with his toes. The Bushranger Dunn carried off native women to his lair, and cruelly abused them. Mr. Melville, in his sketch of Tasmania recounts that 'The Bushranger Carrots killed a black fellow, and seized his gin; then cutting off the man's head, the brute fastened it round the wife's neck, and drove the weeping victim to his den.'[22]

It was not only the bushrangers, outlaws and convicts, from whom one could expect brutality, but the settlers as well who perpetrated great acts of cruelty on the women. Unfortunately there was a great preponderance of men in Tasmania and native women became the natural objects of their lust. Settlers often enticed the women away from their tribes with offers of food and adornments, bought them from their husbands for liquor or tobacco, or stole them. Their ill-treatment of the women was so abominable that the native men retaliated by killing them. Mr. Backhouse wrote that the settlers 'were of such a character, as to remove any wonder at the determination of these injured people to try to drive from their land a race of men, among whom were persons guilty of such deeds.'[23]

> It was not alone that these unfortunates were the victims of their lust, but the objects of their barbarity. If perchance a woman was decoyed to the shepherd's hut, no gentleness of usage was employed to win her regard, and secure her stay; threatening language, the lash, and the chain were the harsher expedients of his savage love. A story is told by Dr. Ross: 'We met one of Mr. Lord's men sitting on the stump of a tree, nearly starved to death. He told us that three days before a black woman whom he had caught, and had chained to a log with a bullock-chain, and whom he had dressed with a fine linen shirt (the only one he had), in hopes, as he said, to tame her, had contrived somehow to slip the chain from her leg, and ran away, shirt and all.'...
> We hear of another who, having caught an unhappy girl, sought to relieve her fears, or subdue her sulks, as it was termed, by first giving her a morning's flogging with a bullock-whip, and then fastening her to a tree near his hut until he returned in the evening.[24]

21 Ibid., 61.
22 Ibid.
23 James Backhouse, *Extracts from the Letters of James Backhouse, Now Engaged in a Religious Visit to Van Diemen's Land, and New South Wales, Accompanied by George Washington Walker* (London: Harvey and Darton 1838–41). [Lemkin's note cites Backhouse, which he misdates 1878, but the passage is quoted in Bonwick, *Last of the Tasmanians*, 61.]
24 Bonwick, *Last of the Tasmanians*, 60.

Mr. Shoobridge, a Tasmanian colonist, related that two white men were out shooting birds. 'Some natives seeing them approach hastily fled. A woman, far advanced in pregnancy, unable to run with the rest, climbed up a tree, and broke down the branches around her for concealment. But she had been observed by the sportsmen. One of these proposed to shoot her, but the other objected. The first, however, dropped behind, and fired at the unfortunate creature. A fearful scream was heard, and then a new-born infant fell out of the tree.[25]

Mr. Bonwick states that a man boasted to him that he had thrown an old woman upon the fire and burnt her to death, and one convict assured him that he liked to kill a black fellow better than smoke his pipe; adding 'and I am a rare one at that too.'

The sealers

The sealers were run-away convicts, of the same class as the bush-rangers but living their lawless lives on the sea, catching the seals which abounded in the neighbourhood of Van Diemen's Land, and preying on the settlers and natives alike. They captured many natives whom they sold in other lands as slaves.

A Mr. Windsor Earle declared that 'runaway convicts from Van Diemen's Land, who resided on an island near the coast ... were in the habit of visiting the mainland for the purpose of carrying off the native women, and of shooting the men who endeavoured to defend them.'[26]

The unfortunate natives when trying to escape from the bushmen in the interior often fell into the hands of the sealers on the coast, and the acts of violence committed by the natives were often incited by the cruelty of the sealers. Major Lockyer, who was sent to establish a convict settlement at King George's Sound in 1827, wrote:

> It is but too certain that they were driven to it by acts of cruelty committed on them by some gang or gangs of sealers, who have lately visited this place. The fact of these miscreants having left four Natives on Michaelmas Island, who must have inevitably perished if they had not been taken off the boat sent by the Amity, that brought them to this harbour, when one of them exhibited three deep scars on his neck and back that had been inflicted by some sharp instrument, sufficiently proves that they have suffered injuries from white men; and it is not to be wondered at that they should, as people in a state of nature, seek revenge.

The aboriginal women kept by the sealers lived like slaves and were forced to perform the hardest labor. Some sealers boasted of shooting their

25 Ibid., 65.
26 Ibid., 288, 289.

women. 'A poor creature was being beaten when, by struggling, she released herself from her tormentor, and fled. The fellow coolly took up his gun and shot her. Being afterwards asked why he beat her in the first instance, he simply replied: "Because she wouldn't clean the mutton-birds."'[27]

According to Mr. Robinson, a man named Harrington stole a dozen women whom he put on different islands to work for him. If he found they had not accomplished enough in his absence he would tie them to trees for twenty four hours in succession, flogging them from time to time. He also asserted that he had been known to kill them in cold blood when they were too stubborn.

Captain Stokes, in his autobiography, tells of a sealer who 'confessed that he kept the poor creature (a native woman) chained up like a wild beast, and whenever he wanted her to do anything, applied a burning stick, a firebrand from the hearth, to her skin.'

Lieutenant Darling assured the Governor that native women 'instead of being in any degree civilized or enlightened by the sealers, rather became corrupted and depraved. They were made to dance naked, and encouraged in many of their savage propensities.' In an official letter dated May 20, 1832, from Flinders Island, he wrote: 'There are several women here who have lived with them (sealers) for years, and yet there is not one, though I have frequently questioned them upon the subject who wishes to go back again. On the contrary, they express abhorrence at the thought, and have frequently told me that the sealers are in the habit of beating them severely, and otherwise ill-treating them.'

George Washington Walker, the Quaker, who visited Van Diemen's Land in the company of James Backhouse, recorded the following in his Journal: 'We cannot regard the situation of the aboriginal females ... as differing materially from slavery. The object of these men in retaining the women, most of whom, it is asserted, were originally stolen, is obviously from the gratification of their lust, and for the sake of the labour they can exact from them.'[28]

At Mr. Walker's request a native woman, who was called Boatswain by the sealers, described by words and gestures how the women were beaten: 'She then made signs of being stripped, stretched her hands up against the wall, in the attitude of a prisoner tied up to be flogged, making at the same time a doleful cry, and personating a flagellator in the exercise of his duty. After this she described a different scene. She represented a person striking another over the backs and legs, and then herself as sinking down on the ground, while she repeatedly exclaimed, in a piteous tone, "Oh, I will clean the mutton-birds better," until at last her voice seemed to fail through exhaustion. She said the men beat them with great sticks. When asked if

27 Ibid., 298.
28 Journal of George Washington Walker. [This passage is quoted in Bonwick, *Last of the Tasmanians*, 304.]

certain men beat their women, she excepted four, the woman of one of whom was weakly, and would have died if he had beaten her. On her observing of one of the men that "he beat his woman," it was remarked with surprise that she had an infant. To this she replied, "Yes, he beat her when the child was in her."'[29]

Decline in birth rate and child mortality

After the settlement of Tasmania by the British a rapid decline began in the birth rate of the aborigines. The natives led a precarious existence, driven away from the hunting lands of their people, often engaged in inter-tribal warfare, and harassed by the settlers.

Many of the women were stolen by bushrangers, sealers, convicts, and settlers, and contracted venereal diseases from them. Although many of these women did produce half-caste children, a great number became worn out by excesses and were unable to reproduce.

Half-caste children seldom lived long in the tribe. The women often got rid of them by abortion before birth or destroyed them as soon as they were born. If for some reason she spared the life of her child it was generally killed by some male relative. In later years when the birth rate had dropped alarmingly the half-caste children were sometimes allowed to live to the age of puberty but seldom longer.

The Government made an attempt to save the half-castes by granting land to their reputed parents, subject to the life of the child in some cases, and in others dependent upon the marriage of the mother to the child's father, but members of the tribe frequently lured such children away and murdered them.

> Mr. G. A. Murray, Police Magistrate on the river Murrumbidgee was officially informed that eleven half-caste boys had been decoyed, murdered, and afterwards their bodies consumed to ashes in separate fires. He rode to the spot, saw the remains of the fires, and in raking about the ashes, discovered fragments of human bones. In his evidence he averred that, though female half-castes were sometimes permitted to live, the males were invariably destroyed in his district. Even the former were tolerated only as ministering to the lustful appetites of the tribe, and an additional means of obtaining supplies from lascivious white men.[30]

During the movements of the Line and the activities of the Roving parties, attempting to capture the natives for transportation to Flinders Island, many children died of cold and starvation. The fleeing natives were afraid to light

29 Ibid.
30 Bonwick, *Last of the Tasmanians*, 311.

fires which would reveal their hiding places and so were unable to cook their food or warm themselves.

The soldiers and settlers felt no more compunction about killing infants and children than about killing native men, and many a child was bayoneted or thrown into a fire, or had its brains dashed out on the rocks when falling into the hands of an attacking party.

When all the natives were finally captured and deported to the Straits, their children, with a few exceptions, were placed in the Orphan School, near Hobart Town. This school had been established for the care and education of the neglected and orphan children of convicts and housed hundreds of children up to the age of fourteen. The native children grew sickly and depressed in this environment, and died in great numbers.

Very few children were produced on Flinders Island and mortality was very high among them.

Stealing of children

In the early days of Tasmanian settlement the colonists frequently stole native children, whom they kept in a state of semi-slavery and used as laborers on their farms or stock ranges.

The first chaplain in Tasmania entertained many natives at his home, sometimes as many as twenty at a time, and was on extremely friendly relations with them. After 1814 the numbers diminished and finally none came at all. He was told by the natives that they would not go to town again because bad men stole their picaninnies.[31]

On June 26, 1813, the following Government Proclamation was issued: 'The resentment of these poor uncultivated beings has been just provoked by a most barbarous and inhuman mode of proceeding acted toward them, viz. the robbing of their children ... Let any man put his hand to his heart and ask which is the savage—the white man who robs the parent of his children, or the black man who boldly steps forward to resent the injury, and recover his stolen offspring; the conclusion, alas! is too obvious.' The end of the proclamation promises punishment for all offenders.

Unfortunately this proclamation failed to put an end to the practice and we hear of another mass kidnapping which occurred in 1814. A number of natives who were accustomed to visit the Camp at Hobart Town were invited to a feast where they were regaled with rationed flour. During the festivities their children were enticed away and stolen. The kidnappers were deaf to the pleas of the natives for the return of their children, whereupon

31 R. W. Giblin, *The Early History of Tasmania*, vol. 2 (1804–28) (Melbourne: Melbourne University Press 1939), 162.

the natives left Hobart Town in rage and sorrow and no aborigines appeared in the town again for several years.[32]

Colonel Sorell, issued a Government order on March 13, 1819, pointing out the blame of the white people for the attacks of natives, in which he refers to the stealing of children as follow [*sic*]: 'From information received by his Honor the Lieutenant-Governor, there seems reason to apprehend that outrages have been recently perpetrated against some of the Native people in the remote country adjoining the River Plenty, though the result of the enquiries instituted upon these reports has not established the facts alleged, further than that two native children have remained in the hands of a person resident above the falls:—Upon this subject, which the Lieutenant Governor considers of the highest importance, as well to humanity as to the peace and security of the settlement, His Honor cannot omit addressing the settlers. . . . The impressions received from earlier injuries are kept up by the occasional outrages of miscreants whose scene of crime is so remote as to render detection difficult, and who sometimes wantonly set fire to and kill the men, and at others pursue the women for the purpose of compelling them to abandon their children. . . . ' He then ordered that in the future magistrates and district constables are to take a census of all native children brought into the district, and discover under what conditions the children have been obtained. No children were to be retained without the permission of their parents unless it could be proved that they had been found in a state to require shelter and protection. The proclamation ends 'All native youths and children who shall be known to be with any of the settlers or stock-keepers unless so accounted for, will be removed to Hobart Town, where they will be supported and instructed at the Charge and under the direction of the government.'[33]

Cruelties of soldiers and settlers

The retaliatory measures of the settlers and soldiers were harsh and cruel. A single murder committed by a native often resulted in the slaughter of his whole tribe by the aroused whites. A Tasmanian Magistrate gave an account of the death of a shepherd near the Macquarie River. As soon as his death was discovered a company of soldiers went in pursuit of the supposed murderers. Falling in with a tribe around their night fires, in a gully at the back of the river, they shot indiscriminately at the group and killed a great number. An eye-witness of a similar night attack described it thus: 'One man was shot, he sprang up, turned round like a whipping top, and fell dead. The party then went up to the

---

32 Bonwick, *Last of the Tasmanians*, 59.
33 Giblin, *Early History of Tasmania*, Appendix A.

fires and found a great number of waddies and spears, and an infant sprawled on the ground, which one of the party pitched into the fire.'[34]

A party of Richmond police passing though the bush in 1827 were stoned by natives from a hill. The police fired and charged them with bayonets. Mr. G. A. Robinson continues: a 'party of military and constables got a number of Natives between two perpendicular rocks, on a sort of shelf, and killed seventy of them, dragging the women and children from the crevices of the rocks and dashing out their brains.'[35]

There were repeated cases reported of stock-keepers and shepherds emasculating the males of tribes when they stole their women.

At one time seventeen natives were shot at one time in cold blood. They had been bathing on a hot day in a deep pool of a river when they were suddenly surprised by a party of armed colonists who had secured the passes. Not a single native escaped with his life.

During the rounding up of natives under what was known as the 'Five Pounds' Proclamation' large parties of military and civilians scoured the bush, and according to Mr. Carr, the manager of the Van Diemen's Land Agricultural Company: 'The Proclamation as usual will enjoin the sparing of the defenceless, and that the people are not to be killed, but taken alive, and the way in which it will be acted upon will be by killing nine for one taken.' Mr. Carr was proven right in his forecast and a ruthless slaughter of natives took place. At one time a corporal with a party of the 40th atrociously massacred a large number of men, women, and children, upon whose campfires they came suddenly.[36]

Soon after the settlement of Flinders Island, a rebellion broke out among the natives and the Sergeant in command, with the assistance of the sealers, seized fifteen of the men whom he put upon a granite rock in the ocean, without food, water, or wood. They were rescued by Captain Bateman who found them in an almost dying state, having been exposed to the storms for five days without food or shelter. The natives declared that they had been carried off so that the soldiers would not be interrupted in their criminal intercourse with the women.[37]

Legal status

The civil position of the Aborigines is thus pointed out by Judge Willis: 'As a British subject, he is presumed to know the laws, for the infraction of which he is held accountable, and he is shut out from the advantage

34 Bonwick, *Last of the Tasmanians*, 62.
35 Ibid., 64.
36 Ibid., 184.
37 Ibid., 248.

of its protection when brought to the test of responsibility. As a British subject, he is entitled to be tried by his peers. Who are the peers of the Black man?'

Mr. Robinson felt the need of a code suited to the aborigines and in 1843 asserted that 'the destruction of the aboriginal native has been accelerated from the known fact of his being incapacitated to give evidence in our courts of law. I have frequently had to deplore when appealed to by the Aborigines for justice in cases of aggression committed on them by white men, or by those of their own race, my inability to do so in consequence of their legal incapacity to give evidence.'[38]

An attempt was made to judge the natives according to their own code of ethics and several blacks known to be murderers of parties in Van Diemen's Land, were not tried for their crimes when captured and were instead removed to Flinders Island. It was felt, although not declared, that the crime was not murder in our accepted sense of the word. Unfortunately this lenient view-point was not often accepted and the natives were frequently punished for crimes which they did not consider as such, although white men were acquitted of far worse crimes, as in the case of three white men who were charged with shooting three native women and child at Port Fairy and afterwards burning their bodies. Although all the evidence pointed to their guilt these men were exonerated.

In May 1836 two aborigines, Jack and Dick, charged with committing a murder on the evidence of convict stock-keepers who were thought by some to have been the guilty ones, were tried in Hobart Town. The aborigines were found guilty and hung. The Reverend Mr. West described their execution, writing that they were launched into eternity, 'there, to discover whether a warfare in defending their soil from the spoilers, and their females and children from outrage and destruction, were or were not crimes in the estimation of the Almighty Creator of all men.'

Liquor

Liquor was one of the evils introduced to the Tasmanian natives by the whites. Like most natives the Tasmanian aborigines became easily addicted to its use and it was frequently used by the whites to buy native women from their men.

As early as November 7, 1818 there was a Government order against giving the natives 'Bull' or spirits, 'whereby the said Natives have become riotous and offensive by their fighting in the streets, and committing wanton barbarities on each other.'

Mr. G. Robertson, the leader of a roving party, says of them: 'You must not judge of their capability by what you have seen of these who have been

---

38 Ibid., 333.

caught and trained to rum-drinking, smoking, and swearing among the most abandoned of our prisoner population.'[39]

Liquor continued to undermine the morals and health of the natives after their banishment to Flinders Island. Their high mortality rate on the island was partly due to their physical condition induced by drinking the liquor supplied them illicitly by the soldiers. When finally in 1847, forty four aborigines were returned to Oyster Cove on the mainland, many died and the survivors lived in miserable conditions. When drink was brought secretly to the camp they often got drunk and traded their belongings to obtain liquor.

One native, Mathinna, who had been brought up at Government House, enjoying the privileges and education of a daughter of the family, was returned to the native camp when Sir John Franklin returned to England. One night she was missing from Oyster Cove, and was found the next morning in the river into which she had fallen and drowned while drunk.

Disease

Many natives died of the white men's diseases. A great many deaths may be laid to the door of the civilizing process which clothed these people of the outdoors who had grown hardy and strong living a life in the open and were suddenly deprived of their physical exercise, and made to live in houses. In their native state, the aborigines had gone practically naked, covering their bodies with grease off which the water ran easily in the rainy spells. When clothed the natives became soaking wet in rainstorms and often stayed in their wet clothing until it dried, catching colds and frequently succumbing to pulmonary diseases.

> Of their rapid mortality when under the immediate observation of the protector at Bruny, Flinders, and Hunter's Islands ... it may not be improper to add that at the last-named asylum, sickness was sometimes induced by the neglect of the Government, which persisted for some months in supplying them with salt provisions (in spite of the repeated and strenuous remonstrances of Robinson), which they hated the very name of, and only ate from necessity, but to which they were too long restricted. ... the consequence of restricting the natives to salt provisions was to bring on scorbutic complaints, which terminated fatally in some instances.[40]

39 Ibid., 347.
40 J. E. Calder, 'Some account of the wars, extirpation, and habits etc. of the native tribes of Tasmania', *Journal of the Anthropological Institute of Great Britain and Ireland*, vol. 3, 1874, 7–29.

The mortality, which is frequently mentioned elsewhere in this paper, was extremely high. Mr. Robinson wrote in 1861: 'The most serious drawback to the success of the establishment was the great mortality among them, which has continued to so lamentable extent [sic], that at the present time there are but a small remnant living. Had the poor creatures survived to have become a numerous people, I am convinced that they would have formed a contented and useful community.'[41]

Natives in captivity

The whole history of the Tasmanian aborigines after their capture and virtual imprisonment on various islands is a tragic one of mismanagement and misunderstanding. The islands chosen were generally barren and inhospitable, and those selected in the first instances were too small and had a poor and inadequate supply of water. Used to woods and forests the natives were surrounded by nothing but pounding surf.

The settlement on Bruni island was a miserable failure. The rations given the poor blacks persuaded to live at the Station consisted of biscuits made from the refuse of the flour bins and a few potatoes a day. Robinson shared his own rations with the sickening natives and requested better provisions and a small amount of tobacco to solace the natives who had learned smoking from the whites. The tobacco was prohibited as a luxury. Sickness increased and many deaths occurred.

The avowed intention in placing the natives on the island was to civilize them but on Bruni they were in close proximity to some of the worst characters of the colony. The women were frequently cruelly assaulted by convict woodcutters and enticed away to the lodgings of the whalers where they contracted diseases and created dissension in the camp.

It was eventually conceded that the island was too small and the colony was moved to Van Sittart or Gun Carriage Island. Here the Government provided such inadequate rations that the whole colony would have died of starvation if a sealer's boat loaded with potatoes had not sheltered there in a storm and given some of its cargo to the hungry natives.

The final choice of a resting place for the homeless Tasmanians was Flinders Island, which is forty miles long and from twelve to eighteen broad. It has no rivers but is covered with vast morasses, and over-run with scrub and thickets. The interior is a waste land of rock, sand and swamp and there are no forests such as the natives were used to in their original homeland. The island is assailed by cold penetrating winds and drenched with frequent rains. Many natives contracted consumption and rheumatism to which they succumbed.

41 Bonwick, *Last of the Tasmanians*, 254.

Inter-tribal quarrels occurred and chaos reigned. New shipments of natives were constantly being sent from the mainland as they were rounded up in the bush and captured by roving parties, and the supplies were inadequate. The natives brought in toward the last were in a pitiable condition. 'At one place on the west coast where sixteen were collected, their appearance was so wretched as to resemble ourang-outangs rather than human beings. One poor old man had had his eyes shot out by some *Christian* pursuer.'[42]

Most of the children captured were placed in the Orphan School, near Hobart Town where their numbers dwindled rapidly.

Conditions on the island were so bad that eventually a rebellion broke out, with the one good result that the Governor sent a suitable officer to rule there in 1832. He found the conditions terrible, and reported that although apparently adequate supplies had been sent to the settlement these had been pilfered by the soldiers. Under this officer, Lieutenant Darling, the civilizing process, which eventually succeeded in bringing about their deaths, began for the natives.

Mr. Robinson was appointed to take charge of Flinders Island and took command in 1835, continuing the civilizing process begun by Lieut. Darling.

Unfortunately the more civilized the blacks became the more they grew to depend on their protectors and the less they were to exert themselves. They became good and listless, and lacked the energy to hunt, looking to their keepers for their food.

A colonial writer of the period commented on the system in 1836: 'The commandant has an establishment of thirty-two convicts to wait on the Aborigines, and supply the deficiency of their own labour, and is rewarded by a great deal of reading, writing, singing, rehearsal of the Catechism, tailoring, submission, attachment, decorum, tranquility—everything, in a word, which gratifies superficial examination; and he persuades himself that he is eminently successful with them, but they have no free agency, are mere children at school, and they cannot escape from their prison. They cannot subsist at a distance from it; they must not break its rules; it must be a place of extensive *ennui* to them: as moral agents now, they are lower than when they were savages, and they die, I fear, the faster for this kindness. The Commandant imputes the mortality among them to the situation and climate, and wishes to transport them to the south coast of New Holland; but in six months, I am persuaded, they would be on this place happy savages in the Bush.'[43]

The last years on Flinders Island is [sic] a story of death. By 1835 the number of aborigines had been reduced to 100. Surgeon Allen officially reported on Sept. 20, 1837: 'On my arrival I found one-fourth of the Natives on the sick list, and since then more than one-half have been ill. Dr. Story

42 Ibid., 232.
43 Ibid., 256.

was of the opinion that "the deaths at Flinders Island and the attempt at civilizing the Natives were consequent on each other [*sic* no closing quotation mark].

The natives, consisting of twelve men, twenty-two women and ten children, were finally returned to Oyster Cove on the mainland in October 1847. For a time the settlement prospered but at the end of 1854 there remained of the original forty four, only three men, eleven women, and two boys at the station.

Mr. Bonwick visited the camp at Oyster Cove in 1859 and described the sad spectacle which met his eyes. The buildings were in ruins and swarming with fleas, and the roofs were full of holes and leaked in the rains, the windows were broken and the doors would not close. The furniture was gone, and the few bedclothes were filthy and torn. The few remaining natives sold everything they could in order to get money for liquor, the only solace remaining to them.

The authorities began the civilizing process and then at the end left the aborigines, lifeless and dispirited, without even the solace of civilized ways. The moral condition of the station was described by a half-caste woman: 'We had souls in Flinders, but we have none here. There we were looked after, and the bad Whites were kept from annoying us. Here we are thrown upon the scum of society. They have brought us among the off-scouring of the earth (convict population). Here are bad of all sorts. We should be a great deal better if some one would read and pray to us. We are tempted to drink, and all bad practices, but there is neither reading nor prayer. While they give us food for the body, they might give us food for the soul. They might think of the remnant of us poor creatures, and make us happy. Nobody cares for us.'[44]

The end of the Tasmanians came in 1877[45] with the death of Truganina, an aboriginal woman. Civilization had done its work well and in seventy four years had wiped out a race consisting of several thousands of human beings.

Reactions of public opinion[46]

The settlers of Tasmania felt on the whole completely justified in their treatment of the aborigines but the Tasmanian press and public figures both in Tasmania and in England were horrified at the unfairness and cruelty practiced in the vanquished country.

44 Ibid., 277.
45 [Actually 1876.]
46 [There are two versions of this section. One has been constructed by cutting and pasting and is, therefore, taken to be the version representing Lemkin's later intentions. This is the text reproduced here; differences from the first, presumably earlier, version are given in footnotes.]

Mr. Howitt's report of the Colonization Commissions in 1840 to the House of Commons contains the following: 'We have actually turned out the inhabitants of Van Diemen's Land because we saw that it was a "goodly heritage," and have comfortably sate down in it ourselves; and the best justification that we can set up is, that if we did not pass one general sentence of transportation upon them, we must burn them up with our liquid fire, poison them with the diseases with which our vices and gluttony have covered us, thick as the quills on a porcupine, or knock them down with our bullets, or the axes of our woodcutters.'

In 1813 Governor Davey was so strongly incensed over the treatment of the natives that he wrote: 'That he could not have believed that British subjects would have so ignominiously stained the honour of their country and themselves, as to have acted in the manner they did toward the Aborigines.'

In an early proclamation Governor Sorell condemns the whites as follows: 'Cruelties have been perpetrated upon the Aborigines repugnant to humanity, and disgraceful to the British character; whilst few attempts can be traced on the part of the colonist, to conciliate the Natives, or to make them sensible that peace and forbearance were the objects desired.'

Mr. Melville, horrified by the treatment of the natives wrote: 'In this riot of wildness, favourable in its very existence to the display of our worst attributes, or to the concealment of our better ones; how have they been treated? Worse than dogs, or even beasts of prey; hunted from place to place; shot; their families torn from them. The mother snatched from her children, to become the victim of the lust and cruelty of their civilized Christian neighbours![47]

Dr. Nixon (afterwards Bishop of Tasmania) declared: 'There are many such cases (cruelty to the blacks) on record, which make us blush for humanity when we read them, and forbid us to wonder that the maddened savage's indiscriminate fury should not only have refused to recognise the distinction between friend and foe, but have taught him to regard each white man as an intruding enemy who must be got rid of at any cost.'[48]

Herman Merivale, Professor of Political Economy at Oxford, 1837–1841, and afterwards Permanent Under-Secretary of State for the Colonies, 1847–1859, in one of his lectures stated:

> I shall not detain you over the wretched details of the ferocity and treachery which
> have marked the conduct of civilized men, too often of civilized governments, in
> their relations with savages, either in past times, or during the present age, rich

47 [Lemkin's note was 'Henry Melville—Australasia and Immigration, London 1857' but he was probably citing Henry Melville, *Australasia and Prison Discipline* (London: Charles Cox 1851).]

48 Francis Russell Nixon, *The Cruise of the Beacon: A Narrative of a Visit to the Islands in Bass's Straits* (London: Bell and Daldy 1857).

almost beyond precedent in such enormities. They have been of late the s
much attention and of much indignant commentary. You may study them in
accounts of travellers and missionaries, in the reports of our own legislature, in the
language of philanthropic orators and writers. You will there read of . . . the nation
of Van Diemen's Land reduced to a few families by long maltreatment, and those
few transported, six years ago, to a small island in the vicinity, almost as a measure
of precaution, to save them from the settlers who shot them down in the woods, or
laid poisoned food within their reach. . . . The history of the European settlements
in America, Africa, and Australia, presents everywhere the same general feature: a
wide and sweeping destruction of native races by the uncontrolled violence of
individuals and colonial authorities, followed by tardy attempts on the part of
government to repair the acknowledged crime.[49]

The *Hobart Town Times* criticized the Government for issuing
paternal proclamations but making very little effort to punish the crimes
committed against the aborigines: 'They have been murdered in cold blood.
They have been shot in the woods, and hunted down as beasts of prey. Their
women have been contaminated, and then had their throats cut, or been
shot, by the British residents, who would fain call themselves civilized
people. The Government, too, by the common hangman, sacrificed the lives
of such of the Aborigines as in retaliation destroyed their wholesale
murderers, and the Government, to its shame be it recorded, in no one
instance, on no single occasion, ever punished, or threatened to punish, the
acknowledged murderers of the aboriginal inhabitants.' (Hobart Town
Times, April, 1836)[50]

The Rev. Mr. West wrote: 'The wounded were brained, the infant cast into
the flames; the musket was driven into the quivering flesh; and the social
fire, around which the Natives gathered to slumber, became, before morning
their funeral pile.'[51]

Sir G. Murray wrote: 'The great decrease which has of late years taken
place in the amount of the aboriginal population, render it not unreason-
able to apprehend that the whole race of these people may, at no distant

49 Herman Merivale, *Lectures on Colonization and Colonies, Delivered before the University of
Oxford in 1839, 1840, and 1841* (London: Longman, Orme, Brown, Green and
Longmans 1841), Lecture 18. [Both versions of this section are identical to this point.
The next two paragraphs do not appear in the earlier version, which has instead the
following paragraph: 'In a report to the Aborigines Committee, Sir John Franklin, the
Governor of Van Dieman's Land and My Lord Glenelg, strongly recommended . . . "That any asylum should be given to them (the natives) at Port Philip, on the
coast of New Holland, the expense of their maintenance to be paid by Van Dieman's
Land. But even this miserable boon, my Lord, has been refused them, on the ground
of their not being sufficiently civilized and Christianized yet. . . . [*sic* no closing
quotation mark]'.]
50 [The correct title of the paper is *Colonial Times*.]
51 John West, *The History of Tasmania*, 2 vols (Launceston: Henry Dowling 1852).

Butwithwhateverfeelingssuchaneventmaybe...oseofthesettlerswhohavebeensufferersbythe...akenplace,itisimpossiblenottocontemplatesuch...cupationoftheislandasoneverydifficulttobe...eelingsofhumanity,orevenwithprinciplesofjustice...cy;andtheadoptionofanylineofconduct,havingforits

But with whatever feelings such an event may be ...ose of the settlers who have been sufferers by the ...aken place, it is impossible not to contemplate such ...cupation of the island as one very difficult to be ...eelings of humanity, or even with principles of justice ...cy; and the adoption of any line of conduct, having for its a...... ...ecret object the extinction of the native race, could not fail to leave an indelible stain upon the British Government.[52]

The establishment of the 'Black Line' for the purpose of driving the natives to the point of the peninsula for capture was scathingly commented upon by the Sydney *Australian* of October, 1830: 'We call the present warfare against a handful of poor, naked, despicable savages, a HUMBUG in every sense of the word. Every man in the island is in motion, from the Governor downwards to the meanest convict. The mercer dons his helmet, and deserts his counter, to measure the dimensions of the butchers' beef, or the longitude of his own tapes with his broadsword. The farmer's scythe and reaping-hook are transmuted to the coat of mail and bayonet. The blacksmith, from forging shoes for the settler's nag, now forges the chain to enslave, and whets the instruments of death! These are against savages whose territory in point of fact this very armed host has usurped!! Savages who have been straitened in their means of subsistence by that very usurpation!!.! Savages who knew not the language, nor the meditations of their foes, save from the indiscriminate slaughter of their own people.'[53]

The reaction to banishment to Flinders Island was very strong. The following was reported at the Aborigines' protection Society: 'Van-Diemen's Land has hitherto been reported as a British colony, from which its Aboriginal population had been swept off, a remnant being transported to Flinders Island, where an almost unprecedented rate of mortality has prevailed.

> Within a few months, seven natives have been drawn out of a place of concealment and security in Van-Diemen's Land, where they must have regarded themselves as the Reliquias Christianorum et immitis Britanni, and have been conveyed, untried, perhaps without accusation, to Flinders Island; which, until some convulsion of nature shall have recalled it to the depths of the ocean, must remain to be the mausoleum of the Tasmanian race.[54]

52 Despatch from Sir George Murray, Secretary of State for the Colonies, to Governor Arthur, 5 November 1830; Copies of All Correspondence between Lieutenant-Governor Arthur and His Majesty's Secretary of State for the Colonies, *British Parliamentary Papers*, 1831 (259), XIX, 56.
53 [This paragraph, in the earlier version, did not sit here but followed the final paragraph (beginning 'The *Penny Cyclopaedia* ...'); it was, in other words, the last paragraph of the essay.]
54 *Report of the Sixth Annual Meeting of Aborigines' Protection Society*, 22 May 1843.

The civilizing process practiced at Flinders Island came in for a lot of criticism. The *Melbourne Argus* wrote in a leading article:

> Look at the means had recourse to in the case of the remnant of the Aboriginals of Tasmania! They were beguiled to the number of some hundreds from their native haunts, and transferred to an island in Bass's Straits, where a system of restraint and plodding methodised daily pursuits was imposed upon them, which would be perfectly unbearable to our own people, and has terminated in those savages pining away, and dying *en masse*. They were, in the most literal sense, 'civilized off the face of the earth' by that process of vegetable existence' [*sic* no opening quotation mark] which the European finds too irksome to subscribe to himself, but which he thinks quite good enough to be the preliminary step for introducing and reconciling the wild denizen of the woods to the new condition proffered to him—proffered in so uncongenial, or rather absolutely revolting, a manner that it is impossible of acceptance.[55]

The *Penny Cyclopaedia* also criticizes the civilization of Flinders Island as follows: 'It would be tedious to detail the features of the "civilizing" system pursued there. It is sufficient to mention that every habit and amusement peculiar to the Aborigines has been discouraged; the cumbrous and uncongenial forms and incidents of advanced civilization have been enforced in everyday life; the native language has been as much as possible suppressed; native names have been made to yield to those of the Caesars, the Hannibals, and the Scipios; a disposition to indulge in the pleasures of the chase has been recorded as a delinquency; and the verbal repetition of the Commandments and the Catechism is alleged as the evidence of religious progress, and a confutation of all disbelief as to the capacity of uncivilized races to appreciate the doctrines of Christianity.'[56]

Bibliography

Early History of Tasmania, Vol II, 1804–1828, R. W. Giblin, Melbourne University Press[57]
Early Tasmania, J. B. Walker, John Vail, Government Printer, 1902[58]
The Last of the Tasmanians, James Bonwick, Sampson Low and Co., London, 1870[59]

55 Bonwick, *Last of the Tasmanians*, 351.
56 Ibid.
57 [See note 31.]
58 [See note 14.]
59 [See note 4. Bonwick was Lemkin's principal source.]

Aboriginal Tribes Report, London, 1837[60]
Letters, James Backhouse, Harvey and Darton, London, 1888 [*sic*][61]
History of Tasmania, James Fenton, MacMillan & Co., London, 1884[62]
Anthropological Institute of Great Britain and Ireland, Vols. III and 27.[63]

60 [Report from the Select Committee on Aborigines (British Settlements); With the Minutes of Evidence, Appendix and Index, *British Parliamentary Papers*, 1837 (425), VII.]
61 [See note 23.]
62 [James Fenton, *A History of Tasmania from Its Discovery in 1642 to the Present Time* (Hobart: J. Walch 1884). No publication of this text by Macmillan has been traced.]
63 [See notes 18 and 40.]

The birth of the *Ostland* out of the spirit of colonialism: a postcolonial perspective on the Nazi policy of conquest and extermination[1]

JÜRGEN ZIMMERER

The Third Reich's policy for the occupation of territories in 'the East' involved, in essence, the complete reorganization of the economy, politics and demography of those territories.[2] This policy was heralded by Ewald Liedecke, the Nazis' official planner for East Prussia, who made the following announcement on 1 September 1939, the day on which Germany invaded Poland.

1 This article is a revised English version of Jürgen Zimmerer, 'Die Geburt des "Ostlandes" aus dem Geiste des Kolonialismus. Die nationalsozialistische Eroberungs- und Beherrschungspolitik in (post-)kolonialer Perspektive', *Sozial.Geschichte*, vol. 19, no. 1, 2004, 10–43.
2 For an excellent overview of current research, see Ulrich Herbert (ed.), *National Socialist Extermination Policies: Contemporary German Perspectives and Controversies* (New York and Oxford: Berghahn Books 2000).

There is of course the temptation, and the danger, of trying to expand the economy in accordance with German requirements. This can be done through partial measures, such as factory estates and amalgamations or the occasional new settlement, which is the way the farming community is being restructured throughout the entire area at present. But the result would be dubious and culturally worthless because, if we are to transform the German countryside, we cannot follow in Polish footsteps and allow Polish forms of settlement and land distribution to become the basis of German settlement. What is required in place of this partial policy is an act of total colonization, which takes in the entire area, turns it round and resettles it according to German ideas. And, where necessary, so-called economic assets, such as may have been invested in buildings and farm installations, will have to be sacrificed in the higher interests of a definitive German design for the area.[3]

This utopian plan, alongside the brutal exploitation of the local population and, of course, the Holocaust, was a chief cause of the catastrophic destruction in 'the East'. During the four years of German occupation in Belorussia alone, a quarter of the population died and 30 per cent lost their homes. The number of factories was cut by 85 per cent and industrial capacity by 90 per cent. Herds of livestock were reduced by 80 per cent, and the amount of fertile land was halved. As Christian Gerlach has noted: 'White Russia's [Belorussia] economic development was set back decades, and the region would be marked by the war for a very long time.'[4] Understandably, these statistics and the suffering of millions that they represent have led many to regard the war conducted by the Germans on its eastern front as unprecedented in the history of humankind, with regard to the size of the army on both sides, the extent of the territories that were occupied and the brutality of the battles.[5]

There are intellectual costs associated with this perspective. An insistence on the uniqueness of Nazi brutality views it as a singular event that can be isolated, excised from German history like a cancerous growth without any deeper roots in national traditions. Also left untroubled by such a

3 Ewald Liedecke, quoted in Michael A. Hartenstein, *Neue Dorflandschaften. Nationalso- zialistische Siedlungsplanung in den 'eingegliederten Ostgebieten' 1939 bis 1944* (Berlin: Köster 1998), 79 (English translation by Stanley Mitchell).
4 Christian Gerlach, *Kalkulierte Morde. Die deutsche Wirtschafts- und Vernichtungspolitik in Weißrußland 1941–1944* (Hamburg: Hamburger Edition 1999), 11. All translations from the German, unless otherwise stated, are by the author in consultation with the editors.
5 For an overview of the literature on the war against the Soviet Union, see Rolf-Dieter Müller and Gerd Überschär, *Hitlers Krieg im Osten 1941–1945. Ein Forschungsbericht* (Darmstadt: Wissenschaftliche Buchgesellschaft 2000).

perspective is the 'grand narrative' of Enlightenment modernity.[6] Indeed, the question arises as to how 'ordinary men' could develop into mass murderers capable of overcoming well-established taboos.[7] But did average Germans experience the Third Reich's way of waging war and its occupation policy as the breaking of a taboo, or did they believe it was 'normal' behaviour?

The aim here is not to equate German war crimes with those of earlier generations and other countries or to weigh them against each other. It is to make the case that Nazi atrocities required prior mental preparation: German military strategies and tactics, as well as the administration of the occupied territories, had precursors. Exposing these does not exculpate the guilty. It clarifies how such events could have happened, and why so many Germans condoned, accepted or voiced no opposition to them.

(Post)colonial perspectives

Where one stands is the deciding factor in the identification of precursors and the sources of ideas and traditions. And, in this regard, a Eurocentric perspective has blocked the view. The commonly used term 'occupation' already enforces certain restrictions in that it makes unavailable a term that far better describes National Socialist aims and intentions, namely, 'colonialism'. 'Occupation' generally means the appropriation of conquered territories by foreign troops during military conflict. In order to secure the territory, the occupying forces establish an administration above, next to or instead of the local administration, which is more or less thoroughly restructured to meet the occupiers' needs. The occupiers as well as the occupied generally regard the foreign administration as a temporary phenomenon.

Next to the term 'occupation' is the term 'colonialism'. Not always in tandem with military conflict, colonial rule shares with occupation the institution of a foreign administration. The difference is that colonial rule exists in an unlimited time-frame or at least sets its own end very far in the future. The long-term aims of colonial rule result generally—intentionally or unintentionally—in a profound political, economic and social restructuring of the subjugated society. According to current paradigms, the difference between colonial rule and military occupation is clearly defined. Whereas, for the former, a civilizing mission, often connected with racial hubris,

6 See Zygmunt Bauman, *Modernity and the Holocaust* (Ithaca, NY: Cornell University Press 1989); Z. Bauman, *Modernity and Ambivalence* (Cambridge: Polity 1991); A. Dirk Moses, 'Structure and agency in the Holocaust: Daniel J. Goldhagen and his critics', *History and Theory*, vol. 37, 1998, 194–219; and Omer Bartov, *Murder in Our Midst. The Holocaust, Industrial Killing, and Representation* (New York and Oxford: Oxford University Press 1996), 53–70.
7 Christopher R. Browning, *Ordinary Men: Reserve Police Battalion 101 and the Final Solution in Poland* (London: Penguin 2001).

constitutes the ideological basis, the latter is based—at least officially—on military necessity and outcomes. Unfortunately, this not only perpetuates a distinction between European and non-European development, but also hinders a useful perspective on both European military history and the history of foreign occupation during the Second World War.

In considering the envisaged or realized restructuring of areas of 'the East' by the Nazis mentioned above, it becomes blatantly obvious that their occupation was a form of colonial rule. Wolfgang Reinhard defined the latter as 'the control of one nation over another foreign nation, exploiting the differences between them in economic, political and ideological development'.[8] If this definition is expanded to include also the deliberate creation of developmental differences, that is, the conscious underdevelopment of certain territories and their inhabitants, it begins to embrace the Nazi policy in Eastern Europe.

The project of investigating the colonial elements of Nazi rule is well-suited to the fundamental questions posed by 'postcolonial studies', whose researchers argue that colonial history should not be regarded as a one-way street in which the non-European world was created according to European models and ideas. Instead, developments inside and outside Europe should be examined for evidence that they influenced, drove and radicalized each other. This approach connects non-European with European history in revealing ways.

In this article, I draw parallels between the Nazi concept of 'occupation' and European colonial rule in their ideological, administrative and military aspects, and analyse the National Socialist regime in Eastern Europe using the tools of colonial historiography. I am not concerned with a detailed reconstruction of the politics of German occupation in specific areas. Instead, I wish to uncover fundamental structures of dominance, exploitation and murder. Examples are therefore chosen from diverse places and times, with a focus on the German administration in Eastern Europe, Poland and parts of the Soviet Union in particular. (The German occupation of Western Europe is not part of this study as its practices differed greatly from those in the East. Whether colonial structures might also be seen to be at work in the German occupation of Western Europe would need a separate investigation.[9]) The German occupation of Eastern Europe was not static. It evolved and presented a different face at the beginning of the war than it did, say, after the battle of Stalingrad, to name but two random dates. In order to unearth

---

8 Wolfgang Reinhard, *Kleine Geschichte des Kolonialismus* (Stuttgart: Kröner 1996), 1. Reinhard himself, it should be noted, did not think about Nazi policies in Eastern Europe in this way.

9 Peter Schöttler emphasized recently that plans for large-scale resettlements in Western Europe also existed; Peter Schöttler, 'Eine Art "Generalplan West". Die Stuckart-Denkschrift vom 14. Juni 1940 und die Planungen für eine neue deutsch-französische Grenze im Zweiten Weltkrieg', *Sozial.Geschichte*, vol. 18, no. 3, 2003, 83–131.

the similarities between colonialism and National Socialism, I analyse the utopian fantasies of dominance that mobilized and legitimized both projects,[10] as well as the structural similarities between the two historical phenomena.

Surprisingly, to this day, no systematic research has been undertaken into the relationship between colonialism and National Socialism,[11] although Hannah Arendt had already raised the topic fifty years ago.[12] At best, some publications comment on Hitler's 'colonial' plans for the East, but the notion of 'colonialism' is here mostly used as a synonym for 'settlement'.[13] However, people at the time understood that 'colonialism' meant more than just the arrival of German settlers, and they were well aware of the

10 I have used this concept in Jürgen Zimmerer, *Deutsche Herrschaft über Afrikaner. Staatlicher Machtanspruch und Wirklichkeit im kolonialen Namibia* (Hamburg: LIT 2001).
11 See Jürgen Zimmerer, 'Colonialism and the Holocaust. Towards an archeology of genocide', in A. Dirk Moses (ed.), *Genocide and Settler Society: Frontier Violence and Stolen Indigenous Children in Australian History* (New York: Berghahn 2004), 49–76, and J. Zimmerer, 'Kolonialer Genozid? Möglichkeiten und Grenzen einer historischen Kategorie für eine Globalgeschichte des Völkermordes', in Dominik J. Schaller, Boyadjian Rupen, Hanno Scholtz and Vivianne Berg (eds), *Enteignet—Vertrieben—Ermordet. Beiträge zur Genozidforschung* (Zurich: Chronos 2004), 109–28. The best-known consideration of the connection between colonial mass murders and the Holocaust is Sven Lindqvist, *'Exterminate all the brutes'*, trans. from the Swedish by Joan Tate (London: Granta 1997). As Lindqvist's understanding of European colonialism and the German policy of annihilation in the East does not go beyond simplistic descriptions, the questions he poses are more significant than his answers. Much the same applies to Ward Churchill, who speaks of the National Socialists imitating the colonial conquest of North America, in *A Little Matter of Genocide: Holocaust and Denial in the Americas, 1492 to the Present* (San Francisco: City Lights 1997). Some recent books that acknowledge the importance of the colonial experience for a history of European violence, at least in a few sentences, demonstrate that this neglect is about to end: see Dan Diner, *Das Jahrhundert verstehen. Eine universalhistorische Deutung* (Munich: Luchterhand 1999); Volker Berghahn, *Europa im Zeitalter der Weltkriege. Die Entfesselung und Entgrenzung der Gewalt* (Frankfurt: Fischer 2002); and Enzo Traverso, *The Origins of Nazi Violence*, trans. from the French by Janet Lloyd (New York and London: The New Press 2003).
12 Hannah Arendt, *The Origins of Totalitarianism* (New York: Harcourt, Brace 1951). David Furber has shown in his doctoral thesis how interesting the use of postcolonial concepts can be for understanding Nazi occupation policy; D. Furber, 'Going East. Colonialism and German Life in Nazi-occupied Poland', Ph.D. thesis, State University of New York at Buffalo, 2003. His methodology and results are summarized in D. Furber, 'Near as far in the colonies: the Nazi occupation of Poland', *International Historical Review*, vol. 26, no. 3, 2004, 541–79. With his account of the daily life of German occupation and its personnel, especially at the lower and middle levels, Furber demonstrates that the strategies of legitimation were indeed very similar to colonial justifications in other parts of the world.
13 Andreas Hillgruber, for example, wrote that the Nazis intended to transform large parts of Eastern Europe into a colonial entity for the purpose of exploitation and settlement; A. Hillgruber, *Hitlers Strategie. Politik und Kriegführung 1940–1941*, 2nd edn (Munich: Bernard and Graefem 1982), 567.

parallels between German plans and the colonial empires of history. To Hitler, the parallels were obvious.

> The struggle for the hegemony of the world will be decided in favour of Europe by the possession of the Russian space. Thus Europe will be an impregnable fortress, safe from all the threat of blockade.... The Slavs are a mass of born slaves, who feel the need of a master.... The Russian space is our India. Like the English, we shall rule this Empire with a handful of men.... We'll supply the Ukrainians with scarves, glass beads and everything that colonial peoples like.... In any case, my demands are not exorbitant. I'm only interested, when all is said, in territories where Germans (*Germanen*) have lived before. The German people will raise itself to the level of this empire.[14]

Obviously, Hitler's use of the word 'colonial' does not in itself provide sufficient grounds for proving Nazism's structural similarity to colonialism. Nevertheless, the quotation highlights the two concepts at the centre of both National Socialism and colonialism, namely, 'race' and 'space'.

The new ordering of the world

The several aspects of the Nazi regime in Eastern Europe—the military campaign, the occupation and genocide—are bound together by the two concepts 'space' and 'race'. According to the National Socialists' view of history and society, the preservation and expansion of the *Volk*, an organic entity, had to be secured by any means. *Lebensraum* (living space) was needed to preserve the numbers of this 'racially pure *Volk*'. Thus the concept of space was connected directly to racial ideology, and it encompassed economic autarky and settlement of the occupied areas by *Volksgenossen* (members of the German 'race').[15]

Both concepts also stand at the centre of colonialism. Colonial empires —sometimes even individual colonies—formed economic systems stretching over vast areas (*Grossraumökonomie*). Fundamental to their control was the model on which the relationship with the local inhabitants was based, not one of equal partnership, but one of subjugation, at times extending even to extermination. Racism motivated and justified the policies that divided

---

14 Adolf Hitler, *Hitler's Table Talk, 1941–1944*, trans. from the German by Norman Cameron and R. H. Stevens, ed. Hugh Trevor-Roper (Oxford: Oxford University Press 1988), 32–5.
15 See Michael Burleigh and Wolfgang Wippermann, *The Racial State. Germany 1933–1945* (Cambridge: Cambridge University Press 1991); Götz Aly and Susanne Heim, '*Vordenker der Vernichtung': Auschwitz und die deutschen Pläne für eine neue europäische Ordnung* (Hamburg: Hoffmann und Campe 1991); and G. Aly, '*Final Solution': Nazi Population Policy and the Murder of the European Jews* (London and New York: Arnold 1999).

humankind into superior beings, destined to rule, and lower races, destined to be subjugated. The lowest in this hierarchy were those destined for extinction, even by means of deliberate murder.[16]

Of course, in its 500 years, European colonialism experienced different stages of development and assumed different forms. Justifications changed for European expansion and rule over indigenous people in the newly 'discovered' and conquered regions.[17] Yet belief in one's own righteousness or destiny was always the ideological prerequisite for the expansion of power, whether it was represented by the White Man's Burden or by Manifest Destiny. Genuine equality seldom existed between Europeans and the indigenous population. It is true that the content and meaning of these notions varied, but it is in this context important to acknowledge the underlying asymmetry of the relationships, as Reinhart Koselleck, for example, has pointed out: ancient Greeks–barbarians, Christians–heathens, superman–subhuman, human–inhuman, and culminating in the formal distinction of friend–enemy, as formulated by Carl Schmitt.[18] Postcolonial theorists have emphasized that this binary encoding of the world is the central prerequisite for colonial rule.[19] It homogenizes the disparate group of rulers as well as the ruled, and at the same time creates a distance between the two groups, a distance that is necessary for colonial supremacy.

During the nineteenth century, the influence of social Darwinism became more widespread and, with it, notions of hierarchy and competition between nations, not only between colonial masters and colonized, but also between powerful colonial empires. This 'biologistic' interpretation of world history, the belief in the need to secure space for one's own people's survival, is the most important parallel between colonialism and Nazi expansionist policies.[20] The 'discovered' or conquered colonial regions, thought to be wild,

16 See Zimmerer, 'Colonialism and the Holocaust'. Tzvetan Todorov also emphasized the importance of the construction of inequality between colonizers and colonized in order to kill them on a large scale; T. Todorov, *Die Eroberung Amerikas. Das Problem des Anderen* (Frankfurt: Suhrkamp 1985), 177.
17 The use of terms like 'Europeans', 'colonizers' etc. must not give the impression that they refer to homogeneous groups of people, all with the same aims and interests; see the enlightening article by Ann Laura Stoler, 'Rethinking colonial categories: European communities and the boundaries of rule', *Comparative Studies in Society and History*, vol. 31, 1989, 134–61.
18 See Reinhart Koselleck, 'Zur historisch-politischen Semantik asymmetrischer Gegen-begriffe', in Reinhart Koselleck, *Vergangene Zukunft. Zur Semantik geschichtlicher Zeiten* (Frankfurt: Suhrkamp 1989), 211–59.
19 See the article on 'binarism' in Bill Ashcroft, Gareth Griffith and Helen Tiffin, *Key Concepts in Post-Colonial Studies* (London: Routledge 1998), 23–7.
20 Similar conclusions can be found in Woodruff D. Smith, *The Ideological Origins of Nazi Imperialism* (Oxford: Oxford University Press 1986); see also Charles Reynolds, *Modes of Imperialism* (Oxford: Robertson 1981), 124–71. Annegret Ehmann has pointed to the close connection between colonial and Nazi racism; A. Ehmann, 'Rassistische und antisemitische Traditionslinien in der deutschen Geschichte des 19. und 20.

chaotic and dangerous,[21] had to be opened up and 'civilized'. In the settler colonies especially, whole areas were imagined to be uninhabited. In these places, space was to be organized according to the colonial rulers' ideas, disregarding indigenous settlements and economic structures, 'order' was to replace 'chaos', cities were to be founded and streets—later also railways—to be built, and the land was to be surveyed and entered in land registries.

National Socialists, too, saw the East as a huge *tabula rasa* that had to be developed according to their ideas, an ideal field of operation for regional developers, demographers, engineers and business economists. One only has to think of the gigantic plan for the Autobahn network, reaching far into Asia, with the Reich's capital Germania at the hub of the wheel. When German conquerors described what they found in the East, they used colonial history as a reference point. For example, a member of the 12th Luftwaffe regiment wrote a few weeks after the invasion of the Soviet Union: 'the successes were fantastic, the advances victorious . . . but Russia is on the whole a great disappointment. Nothing of culture, nothing of paradise . . . the bottom of the barrel, a filthy place, a species of inhabitant, all of which make clear our great colonial task.'[22]

The perception that many areas of Belorussia were 'primitive, desolate and backward', as Christian Gerlach has noted,[23] resulted in the total reorganization and modernization of the whole country, ignoring existing

---

Jahrhunderts', in Sportmuseum Berlin (ed.), *Sportstadt Berlin in Geschichte und Gegenwart. Jahrbuch 1993 des Sportmuseums Berlin* (Berlin: Sportmuseum 1993), 131–45. Birthe Kundrus tried recently to refute any relation between colonial and Nazi racial policy in B. Kundrus, 'Von Windhoek nach Nürnberg? Koloniale "Mischehenverbote" und die nationalsozialistische Rassengesetzgebung', in B. Kundrus (ed.), *Phantasiereiche. Zur Kulturgeschichte des deutschen Kolonialismus* (Frankfurt: Campus 2003), 110–31. This attempt was not wholly convincing because the alleged openness and heterogeneity of the colonial discourse in imperial Germany, on which she bases her argument, is contradicted by the praxis of colonial rule. Being an African woman or man in German South-west Africa, for example, meant, at least after 1907, that you were subject to extremely discriminatory racial laws. See the early results of my current project, on the similarities and continuities between the racially privileged society in German South-west Africa and the post-1933 racial state, in Jürgen Zimmerer, 'Von Windhuk nach Warschau. Die rassische Privilegiengesellschaft in Deutsch-Südwestafrika—ein Modell mit Zukunft?', in Frank Becker (ed.), *Rassenmischehen—Mischlinge—Rassentrennung. Zur Politik der Rasse im deutschen Kaiserreich* (Stuttgart: Steiner 2004), 97–123.

21 See, for example, Albert Wirz, 'Missionare im Urwald, verängstigt und hilflos. Zur symbolischen Topografie des kolonialen Christentums', in Wilfried Wagner (ed.), *Kolonien und Missionen* (Münster: LIT 1994), 39–56; and Johannes Fabian, *Out of Our Minds. Reason and Madness in the Exploration of Central Africa* (Berkeley: University of California Press 2000).

22 Quoted in Gerlach, *Kalkulierte Morde*, 102.

23 Ibid.

social, political and economic structures. It was precisely this comprehensive redesign that was understood as colonization. The justification for ruling the occupied territory lay not only in its underdevelopment, but also in its perceived backwardness and in the immaturity of its inhabitants. According to Hitler one needed only to see 'this primitive world (*Urwelt*)' to know 'that nothing will drag it out of its indolence unless one compels the people to work. The Slavs are a mass of born slaves, who feel the need of a master.'[24] Himmler's Secretary Hanns Johst, who travelled with the Reichsführer of the SS through Poland during the winter of 1939–40, shared his superior's opinions.

> The Poles are not a state-building nation. They lack even the most elementary preconditions for it. I drove alongside the *Reichsführer-SS* up and down that country. A country which has so little feeling for systematic settlement, that is not even up to dealing with the style of a village, has no claim to any sort of independent political status within the European area. It is a colonial country![25]

Similarly, African and American 'natives' were said to lack all capability for state-building and, thus, for having their own history. Hegel's description reflected the popular view in the 1930s and 1940s:

> The Negro, as already observed, exhibits the natural man in his completely wild and untamed state.... From these various traits it is manifest that want of self-control distinguishes the character of the Negroes. This condition is capable of no development or culture, and as we see them at this day, such have they always been.... it [Africa] is no historical part of the world; it has no movement or development to exhibit.... What we properly understand by Africa, is the Unhistorical, Undeveloped Spirit, still involved in the conditions of mere nature, and ... on the threshold of the World's History.[26]

The ideology of the European civilizing mission justified not only conquest and colonization, but also the exploitation of the indigenous population. Accordingly, the French, in taking over Togo from the Germans who had introduced 'tax labour', that is, forced labour as payment of taxes, regarded these measures as positive ones, as the Africans needed a strong hand:

> Tax labour is necessary, even indispensable.... Besides material advantages it offers significant moral benefits. The native ... needs the protection of capable and sensible people as well as a just and benevolent administration to look after

24 Hitler, *Hitler's Table Talk*, 33.
25 Hanns Johst, translated and quoted in Michael Burleigh, *The Third Reich: A New History* (London: Macmillan 2000), 447.
26 Georg Wilhelm Friedrich Hegel, *The Philosophy of History*, trans. from the German by J. Sibree (New York: Dover Publications 1956), 93, 98–9.

him and his people and protect him from 'rogues' and 'villains'; the moral and political benefits of tax labour come precisely from the opportunity it gives the administrators to impress the natives with their authority and to make contact at least once a year with those population groups still living in remote areas.[27]

Parallels with colonialism are not limited to ideological justifications of rule and conquest, but are also evident in the methods employed by rulers. In the colonies, a small elite of colonial administrators and officers ruled over a much larger indigenous population that barely participated in governance.[28] The colonizers and the colonized belonged to different, racialized legal systems.[29] The influence of colonial images on Nazi occupation policy is demonstrated by the fact that the Ostministerium (Ministry for the East) in Berlin was explicitly said to be modelled on the British India Office.[30]

Preferential treatment within this 'racially privileged society' was not solely the result of the formal colonial legal system.[31] A *situation coloniale* was evident in all social interactions between colonizers and colonized. Europeans enjoyed privileges generally; they had their own schools and kindergartens as well as their own counters at post offices and other establishments. In German South-west Africa, for example, Africans were not allowed to ride horses, forced to salute all Whites and forbidden to use the footpath. Under occupation, Poles had to display appropriate humility before the Germans by making way for them on footpaths, removing their hats and saluting. They were banned from attending cinemas, concerts, exhibitions, libraries, museums and theatres, and not permitted to own bicycles, cameras or radios.[32] The ideal of the 'racially privileged society' underpins the following statement by Hitler: 'The Germans—this is essential—will have to constitute amongst themselves a closed society, like a fortress. The least of our stable-lads must be superior to any native.'[33]

The 'natives' of Eastern Europe were socially and legally separate from the Germans. However, their contributions as workers integrated them into the Third Reich's economy and guaranteed their right to life.[34] Here, too, there are colonial precedents. The slave trade involving millions of Africans being

27 Captain Sicre, 29 September 1918, quoted in Trutz von Trotha, *Koloniale Herrschaft: zur soziologischen Theorie der Staatsentstehung am Beispiel des 'Schutzgebietes Togo'* (Tübingen: J. C. B. Mohr 1994), 358.
28 The settler colonies are an exception, since more and more 'white' settlers changed the numerical relations.
29 See Rüdiger Voigt (ed.), *Das deutsche Kolonialrecht als Vorstufe einer globalen 'Kolonialisierung' von Recht und Verwaltung* (Baden-Baden: Nomos 2001).
30 See Gerlach, *Kalkulierte Morde*, 157.
31 I explain this concept in Zimmerer, *Deutsche Herrschaft über Afrikaner*, 94–109.
32 Burleigh, *Third Reich*, 450f. On the *situation coloniale*, see Furber, 'Going East'.
33 Hitler, *Hitler's Table Talk*, 34.
34 See the classic study by Ulrich Herbert, *Hitler's Foreign Workers: Enforced Foreign Labor in Germany under the Third Reich* (Cambridge: Cambridge University Press 1997).

taken to America and the Caribbean islands is the most blatant precursor to the National Socialists' forced labour scheme. Various forms of exploitation of the indigenous labour force developed during colonialism. An economy based on forced labour was paramount in the German colonization of South-west Africa, the paradigmatic case linking colonialism and National Socialism.[35] At times, colonial recruitment procedures were highly formalized and, in any event, the complexity of the Nazi bureaucracy that mobilized resources for the workforce should not be over-emphasized.[36] In Russia, during the Second World War, workers were procured by being actually hunted down in ways commonly associated with the Congo.[37]

Space was a similarly protean concept in both the colonialism of the nineteenth century and that of the Nazis. The idea of a vacant land waiting to be developed corresponded with the deprivation of indigenous peoples' rights and their degradation, right down to the level of becoming disposable items to be used in the interest of the colonizer.[38] If the 'natives' could not be useful in their original places of settlement, colonial rulers readily resettled them on to reserves or simply evicted them from their homes, according to what was needed. The reserves for indigenous peoples in North America and South-west Africa testify to the fact that the 'natives' had become strangers in the new—now colonized—society: they were removed from their homelands to usually barren and useless land. German plans for resettling millions of people in Eastern Europe, especially the placing of Jews in 'reserves', stands in this tradition, albeit on a much larger scale. In any case, the fact that this sort of behaviour was seen as more or less 'normal' in dealing with 'natives' might have contributed to the inability to register fully the scale of the atrocities that would be committed several decades later.[39]

35 See Zimmerer, *Deutsche Herrschaft über Afrikaner*, 126–75. Various aspects of the link between German colonialism in South-west Africa and the Third Reich have been touched on in Henning Melber, 'Kontinuitäten totaler Herrschaft. Völkermord und Apartheid in Deutsch-Südwestafrika', *Jahrbuch für Antisemitismusforschung*, vol. 1, 1992, 91–116.

36 In German South-west Africa, a system of total control and mobilization was planned that was probably unique in the history of colonialism, one based on the idea of a complete deployment of the indigenous population for the benefit of the colonial state; see Jürgen Zimmerer, 'Der totale Überwachungsstaat? Recht und Verwaltung in Deutsch-Südwestafrika', in Voigt (ed.), *Das deutsche Kolonialrecht*, 175–98.

37 For examples of this sort of forced recruitment, see Burleigh, *Third Reich*, 551–4. Adam Hochschild, *Schatten über dem Kongo. Die Geschichte eines der großen fast vergessenen Menschheitsverbrechen* (Stuttgart: Klett-Cotta 2000), 165–99.

38 With regard to German South-west Africa, see Jürgen Zimmerer, 'Der Wahn der Planbarkeit: Vertreibung, unfreie Arbeit und Völkermord als Elemente der Bevölkerungsökonomie in Deutsch-Südwestafrika', in Michael Mann (ed.), *Menschenhandel und unfreie Arbeit*, a special issue of *Comparativ*, vol. 4, 2003.

39 Similarly, Gerlach argues that the so-called territorial plans made the break with civilization a gradual one; see Christian Gerlach, *Krieg, Ernährung, Völkermord. Forschungen zur deutschen Vernichtungspolitik im Zweiten Weltkrieg* (Hamburg: Hamburger Edition 1998), 262.

Military traditions of exterminatory wars

Parallels with colonialism, especially the German, are not only to be found in the 'civil' sphere of the Nazi occupation of the East. They are also evident in the military sphere. If one looks at the tactics behind modern warfare, one sees that the war fought by the German army reveals similarities with colonial wars. The war against the Soviet Union was officially a 'normal' war between two European powers. However, from the beginning, Germany's war was predatory (*Raubkrieg*) and, by ignoring international law, became ever more similar to colonial wars than those customarily fought in Europe. The similarities include denying the enemy the status of a legitimate and equal opponent who, even when captured or defeated, has certain rights, and leaving prisoners of war to perish on racial grounds or even murdering them.[40] Summary executions of prisoners and mass murder through hunger, disease and dehydration also occurred during colonial wars. In German South-west Africa, Herero and Nama prisoners of war, including women and children, were incarcerated in purpose-built concentration camps, as they were called at the time, in which the mortality rate was 30–50 per cent. They were deliberately left to die from lack of food and inadequate shelter.[41] 'Extermination through deliberate neglect' was the term for a similar practice, although much larger in scale, with regard to the murder of millions of Russian prisoners of war during the Second World War.

Massacres and the destruction of all essentials for life were common practices in both colonial wars and the German war in the East. In the campaigns against the Wahehe in German East Africa in the 1890s, burning villages and fields and 'devouring the Mkwawa [leader of the Wahehe] land', as Governor Eduard von Liebert called it, were already seen as valuable tactics.[42] It was also common practice during the Maji-Maji war in German East Africa (1905–6) and the war against the Herero and Nama in South-west Africa (1904–8) for the colonial forces to 'take over the property of the enemy (livestock, provisions) and ravage villages and fields'.[43] The aim was to deny the guerrillas the civilian population's support by destroying infrastructure and all means of subsistence. During the Second

---

40 For the treatment of Soviet POWs in general, see the classic study by Christian Streit, *Keine Kameraden. Die Wehrmacht und die sowjetischen Kriegsgefangenen 1941–1945* (Stuttgart: Deutsche Verlagst-Anstalt 1978).

41 This is analysed in detail in Jürgen Zimmerer, 'Kriegsgefangene im Kolonialkrieg. Der Krieg gegen die Herero und Nama in Deutsch-Südwestafrika (1904–1907)', in Rüdiger Overmans (ed.), *In der Hand des Feindes. Kriegsgefangenschaft von der Antike bis zum Zweiten Weltkrieg* (Cologne: Böhlau 1999), 277–94.

42 Eduard von Liebert, quoted in Martin Baer and Olaf Schröter, *Eine Kopfjagd. Deutsche in Ostafrika* (Berlin: Ch. Links 2001), 57.

43 Detlef Bald, 'Afrikanischer Kampf gegen koloniale Herrschaft. Der Maji-Maji-Aufstand in Ostafrika', *Militärgeschichtlichen Mitteilungen*, vol. 19, no. 1, 1976, 23–50 (40).

World War, the German army designated 'dead areas' in order to combat resistance fighters. These areas were encircled by large armies who systematically destroyed villages, infrastructure and sources of food and shelter.[44]

Colonial tactics for fighting partisans that included the destruction of the means of subsistence and the deliberate neglect of prisoners were part of these wars against whole populations, including women and children. They were part of the racial war (*Rassenkrieg*) that General Lothar von Trotha, a protégé of General von Schlieffen, chief of staff of the German army, waged against the Herero and later the Nama, and that he thought would only come to an end with the extermination of those peoples. For this reason, it can be seen as paradigmatic for the Nazi military campaign (*Vernichtungskrieg*).[45] As the Africans would 'only give in to force', Trotha set out to fight using 'extreme terror and even cruelty' and to annihilate 'the rebellious tribes in streams of blood'.[46] After all, as he wrote later, a war in Africa could not be fought under the statutes of the Geneva Convention.[47] The notorious order to shoot of 2 October 1904 is the most blatant example of von Trotha's genocidal policy. After the battle of the Waterberg, when the Hereros attempted to flee into the Omaheke desert, he sealed off the area:

> They have murdered and stolen, they have cut off the ears, noses and other body parts of wounded soldiers, now out of cowardice they no longer wish to fight. I say to the people anyone who delivers a captain will receive 1000 Mark, whoever delivers Samuel will receive 5000 Mark. The Herero people must however leave the land. If the populace does not do this, I will force them out with the *Groote Rohr* [cannon]. Within the German borders every Herero, with or without a gun, with or without cattle, will be shot. I will no longer accept women and children, I will drive them back to their people or I will let them be shot at.[48]

44 Gerlach, *Kalkulierte Morde*, 859–1055. On German anti-partisan warfare, see also Philip Warren Blood, 'Bandenbekämpfung: Nazi Occupation Security in Eastern Europe and Soviet Russia 1942–4', Ph.D. thesis, Cranfield University, UK, 2001.

45 See Jürgen Zimmerer, 'Krieg, KZ & Völkermord. Der erste deutsche Genozid', in Jürgen Zimmerer and Joachim Zeller (eds), *Völkermord in Deutsch-Südwestafrika. Der Kolonialkrieg (1904–1908) in Namibia und seine Folgen* (Berlin: Ch. Links 2003), 45–63; and Jürgen Zimmerer, 'Das Deutsche Reich und der Genozid. Überlegungen zum historischen Ort des Völkermordes an den Herero und Nama', in Larissa Förster, Dag Henrichsen and Michael Bollig (eds), *Namibia–Deutschland: Eine geteilte Geschichte. Widerstand—Gewalt—Erinnerung*, vol. 24 of *Ethnologia* (Cologne: Minerva 2004), 106–21.

46 Letter from von Trotha to Leutwein, 5 November 1904, original quoted in Horst Drechsler, *Südwestafrika unter deutscher Kolonialherrschaft. Der Kampf der Herero und Nama gegen den deutschen Imperialismus 1884–1915*, 2nd edn (Berlin: Akademie-Verlag 1984), 156.

47 Von Trotha in *Der deutschen Zeitung*, 3 February 1909, original quoted in Gerhard Pool, *Samuel Maharero* (Windhoek: Gamsberg Macmillan 1991), 293.

48 Lothar von Trotha, 'Proklamation', 2 October 1904, translated and quoted in Jan-Bart Gewald, *Herero Heroes: A Socio-Political History of the Herero of Namibia 1890–1923* (Oxford: James Currey 1999), 172–3.

In an order of the day, he clarified that, for the maintenance of the good reputation of German soldiers, the instruction to 'shoot at women and children' meant 'that shots are to be fired above them, to force them to run'. He said that he assumed that his decree would lead to 'no more male prisoners [being] taken, but not to cruelty against women and children'. They would 'run away when shots [are] twice fired above them'.[49] The only place, however, to which they could run was the desert where, due to his orders, thousands died of thirst. The official war history reads as follows:

> Like a wild animal hunted half to death the enemy was driven from one source of water to the next, until, his will gone, he finally became a victim of the nature of his own land. Thus the waterless Omaheke would complete what German weapons had begun: the destruction of the Herero people.[50]

The intention to destroy an entire people and the official acknowledgement of its execution can hardly be expressed more clearly.[51]

Von Trotha's strategy 'to drive them into the desert' became proverbial. In October 1941, for instance, Hitler answered those who objected to his hard-line stand by commenting: 'Let nobody tell me that we can't drive them into the marshes of Russia.'[52] Von Trotha's order to shoot can be found replicated in one of Himmler's orders dated 1 August 1941, in which he ordered the massacres of the Pripjet swamps: 'All Jews must be shot, Jewish women must be driven into the marshes.'[53] There they would die—like the Herero women and children in the Omaheke desert—without one German soldier having to raise his gun.

It has often been argued that, due to the role of the state, the Holocaust differs from all other mass murders in history. This is a rather reductive and ahistorical view. The state certainly played a different role during genocides in the colonies than it did during the Holocaust.[54] This is unsurprising since the state in North America and Australia was far 'weaker' than in Germany between 1933 and 1945. If one historicizes the notion of 'the state' then the differences between colonial and Nazi genocides do not appear so great. Although the extermination procedures vary, depending on the level of bureaucracy within the state that commits or orders the murders, the common factor still remains: the 'perpetrator' is prepared to eliminate a

49 Ibid.
50 Großer Generalstab, Kriegsgeschichtlichen Abteilung I (ed.), *Die Kämpfe der deutschen Truppen in Südwestafrika*, 2 vols (Berlin: Ernst Siegfried Mittler 1906–8), i.211.
51 See Zimmerer and Zeller, *Völkermord in Deutsch-Südwestafrika*; Zimmerer, 'Das Deutsche Reich und der Genozid'; Zimmerer, 'Colonialism and the Holocaust'; and Zimmerer, 'Kolonialer Genozid?'.
52 Adolf Hitler, *Monologe im Führerhauptquartier*, ed. Werner Jochmann (Hamburg: Knaus 1980), 106.
53 Gerlach, *Deutsche Wirtschaftsinteressen*, 278.
54 See Zimmerer, 'Colonialism and the Holocaust' and Zimmerer, 'Kolonialer Genozid?'.

distinct group of people. This ultimate breaking of a taboo—not only contemplating the extermination of whole ethnic communities but actually executing such a plan—was first committed in the colonies. This fact contributed to making the Holocaust thinkable and executable, even if the motives for killing Jews, Sinti and Roma, homosexuals and the handicapped were vastly different. Even the murder of Jews, which differs from other genocides in terms of motive—namely, the fear of a supposed Jewish world conspiracy—would not have been possible without the earlier breaking of the taboo. The Holocaust represents therefore an extreme, radical form of behaviour that was not unfamiliar in the history of colonialism.

A historicized notion of the state also helps to explain the different forms of mass murder in the colonies and in Eastern Europe under German occupation. A bureaucratized form of murder, for which Auschwitz is the universally recognizable symbol, needs the administrative apparatus of a well-organized central government as a precondition. There was no such administrative organization in the colonies. As the example of German South-west Africa shows, as the level of organization increased, the first beginnings of a bureaucratic form of extermination can be seen. However, actual 'industrial' killings, as practised after 1941 in the Nazi extermination camps, had no precursor. But, even during the Third Reich, execution and starvation killed more people than industrial gas chambers; some 40 per cent of all Jewish victims of the Nazis died from other causes.[55]

Transmission channels

Telling structural similarities between colonialism and National Socialism allow the expansionist policies of the Third Reich to be seen as part of colonial history. This connection immediately raises the question of the transmission of colonial ideas and experiences to the decision-makers and planners in Nazi Germany. Although research here is in its infancy, three channels—first-hand experience, institutional history and collective memory—can be perceived.

First-hand experience is the most obvious source, although the most difficult one to trace, as no prosopographical study has been undertaken, with regard to either the German colonial administrators and military personnel or the settlers. Nonetheless, some individuals were in possession of such experience:[56] for example, Herero fighter Hermann Ehrhardt (Marinebrigade),[57] Ludwig Maercker (Frei-

55 See Herbert (ed.), *National Socialist Extermination Policies*.
56 'Colonial revisionists', who were fighting for the re-establishment of a German empire in Africa, are not mentioned here; their inclusion would considerably swell the numbers.
57 Hagen Schulze, *Freikorps und Republik, 1918–1920* (Boppard am Rhein: Boldt 1969), 257.

korps),[58] Wilhelm Faupel (Freikorps),[59] Franz Ritter von Epp (Freikorps and the Imperial Colonial Office),[60] Paul von Lettow-Vorbeck ('Hero of East Africa', participant in the Kapp Putsch, and the settlement commissioner for South-west Africa), Paul Rohrbach (journalist),[61] and Friedrich von Lindequist (Governor of South-west Africa and later head of the Third Reich's Colonial Office). During the Nazi regime, von Lettow-Vorbeck, Rohrbach and von Lindequist contributed mainly as propagandists. Directly involved in the administration of the occupied districts was Dr Viktor Boettcher, district president (Regierungspräsident) of Posen in the Warthegau, who had been Deputy Governor in Cameroon before the First World War.[62]

It would be wrong to think that enthusiasm for the colonial project necessarily went hand-in-hand with enthusiasm for National Socialism on the part of individuals with experience of both. After 1918, their colonial engagement led many to demand the re-establishment of the colonies; this group overlapped in many respects with but was not identical to the *völkisch* movement,[63] although a fundamental belief in territorial expansion was the prerequisite for the Nazi policies of conquest. Furthermore, a rejection of the restrictions on expansion, as set out in the Versailles treaty,[64] was entrenched on the left as well as in Catholic circles, which were both critics of National Socialism. Others became opponents of colonialism and even developed into

58 Ehmann, 'Rassistische und antisemitische Traditionslinien', 143.
59 Oliver Gliech, 'Wilhelm Faupel. Generalstabsoffizier, Militärberater, Präsident des Ibero-Amerikanischen Instituts', in Reinhard Liehr, Günther Maihold and Günter Vollmer (eds), *Ein Institut und sein General. Wilhelm Faupel und das Ibero-Amerikanische Institut in der Zeit des Nationalsozialismus* (Frankfurt: Vervuert 2003), 131–279 (176–94). Faupel later worked with Rudolf Böhmer (former district officer of Lüderitzbuch in German South-west Africa) and Lübbert (former head of the mining board there) in the Volksbund für Arbeitsdienst (People's Society for Compulsory Labour) and the Gesellschaft zum Studium des Faschismus (Society for the Study of Fascism), the latter of which aimed to foster Nazi ideology and to increase support for Italian Fascism in Germany.
60 Katja Wächter, *Die Macht der Ohnmacht. Leben und Politik des Franz Xaver Ritter von Epp (1868–1946)* (Frankfurt: Peter Lang 1999).
61 Walter Mogk, *Paul Rohrbach und das 'Größere Deutschland'. Ethischer Imperialismus im Wilhelminischen Zeitalter. Ein Beitrag zur Geschichte des Kulturprotestantismus* (Munich: Goldman 1972).
62 Furber, 'Near as far in the colonies'.
63 See Jan Esche, *Koloniales Anspruchdenken in Deutschland im Ersten Weltkrieg, während der Versailler Friedensverhandlungen und in der Weimarer Republik (1914 bis 1933)* (Hamburg: Jan Esche 1989); Klaus Hildebrand, *Vom Reich zum Weltreich—Hitler, NSDAP und koloniale Frage 1919–1945* (Munich: Fink 1969); and Karsten Linne, *Weiße 'Arbeitsführer' im 'Kolonialen Ergänzungsraum'. Afrika als Ziel sozial- und wirtschaftspolitischer Planungen in der NS-Zeit* (Münster: Monsenstein and Vannerdat 2002).
64 See Jürgen Zimmerer, 'Von der Bevormundung zur Selbstbestimmung. Die Pariser Friedenskonferenz und ihre Auswirkungen auf die britische Kolonialherrschaft im Südlichen Afrika', in Gerd Krumeich (ed.), *Versailles 1919: Ziele—Wirkung—Wahrnehmung* (Essen: Klartext 2001), 145–58.

pacifists due to their experiences in the colonial wars and the First World War. Berthold von Deimling, a military man from the colonies, served as a general during the First World War but later became one of the most hated pacifists.[65] Similarly, Hans Paasche offered his resignation after the Maji-Maji war in German East Africa in disgust over the conduct of the German campaign. During the First World War, he was admitted to a Berlin 'lunatic asylum'; later he participated in the Berlin soldiers' council and was subsequently murdered in May 1920.[66]

As the example set by the Freikorps demonstrates, the experience of colonial violence could be transferred to other contexts.[67] I am concerned here with indirect transmission, such as that conveyed through personal networks or teacher–student relationships. Another example would be the racial anthropologist Eugen Fischer, who was granted a professorship for his work 'Rehobother Bastards und das Bastardisierungsproblem beim Menschen', that is, on an ethnic group of German South-west Africa. He was later appointed director of the Kaiser-Wilhelm Institut für Anthropologie, menschliche Erblehre und Eugenik (institute of anthropology, the teaching of human heredity and eugenics), and served from 1933–5 as chancellor of Berlin University.[68] Such a biographical trajectory can often be found among doctors and scientists. Ernst Rodenwaldt, Otto Reche, Philalethes Kuhn and Theodor Mollison, too, combined vast experience in the colonies with keen enthusiasm for National Socialism and active participation in its racial and extermination policies.[69] Richard Walther Darré, a student in the German Colonial School in Witzenhausen, was appointed chief of the SS Rasse- und Siedlungshauptamtes (race and

65 Christoph Jahr, 'Berthold von Deimling. Vom General zum Pazifisten. Eine biographische Skizze', *Zeitschrift für die Geschichte des Oberrheins*, vol. 142, 1994, 359–87; Christoph Jahr, '"Die reaktionäre Presse heult auf wider den Mann". General Berthold von Deimling (1853–1944) und der Pazifismus', in Wolfram Wette (ed.), *Pazifistische Offiziere in Deutschland 1871 bis 1933* (Bremen: Donat 1999), 131–46.

66 Werner Lange, *Hans Paasches Forschungsreise ins innerste Deutschland. Eine Biographie* (Bremen: Donat 1995).

67 See, for example, Diner, *Das Jahrhundert verstehen*, 52f. Klaus Theweleit had already pointed to the connection between colonial military culture, the Freikorps, and the National Socialists; K. Theweleit, *Männerphantasien* (Frankfurt: Roter Stern 1977).

68 Kathrin Roller, 'Der Rassenbiologe Eugen Fischer', in Ulrich van der Heyden and Joachim Zeller (eds), *Kolonialmetropole Berlin. Eine Spurensuche* (Berlin: Berlin Edition 2002), 130–4, 302; Niels C. Lösch, *Rasse als Konstrukt. Leben und Werk Eugen Fischers* (Franfurt: Peter Lang 1997); Bernhard Gessler, *Eugen Fischer (1874–1967). Leben und Werk des Freiburger Anatomen, Anthropologen und Rassenhygienikers bis 1927* (Frankfurt: Peter Lang 2000).

69 Ehmann, 'Rassistische und antisemitische Traditionslinien'; Wolfgang Uwe Eckart, *Medizin und Kolonialimperialismus. Deutschland 1884–1945* (Paderborn: Schöningh 1996).

resettlement office) during the Third Reich and was responsible for racial reports on East European children who qualified for 're-Germanization'.[70]

Graduates from those special institutions established to train future colonial staff also belong in this category; their subsequent career paths have so far not been studied. In addition to the already mentioned Colonial School in Witzenhausen, there was the Koloniale Frauenschule (colonial school for women) in Rendsburg and the Hamburg Tropeninstitut (tropical institute).[71] These institutions aimed to convey the kind of practical knowledge that was also desirable in the East, a fact that justified the existence of the colonial schools, even well after the battle of Stalingrad when direct colonial engagement was no longer official Nazi policy. The Koloniale Frauenschule, for example, offered Russian as an elective subject, established a second campus in Potok Zloty and sent some of its students to the East.[72]

Such initiatives were welcomed by the German state and the Nazi Party. Not only were former German colonists in Africa the preferred settlers in the East, where their 'pioneer qualities' were thought to be useful,[73] but trained specialists were also in great demand. Franz Ritter von Epp, director of the Imperial Colonial Office, called for colonial experts to volunteer for the East:

> As the Director of the Colonial Office I urge all colonial farmers and experts from the German colonies or other tropical regions, who had volunteered for duty in our colonies, now to assist with their expertise in the southern part of the occupied East. . . . Those who prove themselves are assured preferential treatment in the colonies in the future.[74]

And it was not only governmental institutions that turned their attention eastward. German African companies also became more and more engaged there as relations with their traditional overseas trading partners dissolved.[75] Immediately after the invasion of Poland, German colonial companies were preferred as they had, among other things, experience in commerce with 'primitive' societies.

70 Gustavo Corni, 'Richard Walther Darré—Der "Blut-und-Boden" Ideologe', in Ronald Smelser, Enrico Syring and Rainer Zitelmann (eds), *Die braune Elite: 21 weitere biographische Skizzen*, 4th edn (Darmstadt: Wissenschaftliche Buchgesellschaft 1999), 15–27.
71 See Stefan Wulf, *Das Hamburger Tropeninstitut 1919 bis 1945. Auswärtige Kulturpolitik und Kolonialrevisionismus nach Versailles* (Berlin: Reimer 1994).
72 Linne, *Weiße 'Arbeitsführer'*, 180.
73 Furber, 'Near as far in the colonies'.
74 Letter from von Epp to Leiter der Deko Gruppe, Weigelt, 20 November 1941, quoted in Karsten Linne, 'Deutsche Afrikafirmen im "Osteinsatz"', *1999*, vol. 16, no. 1, 2001, 49–90 (88).
75 See Linne, 'Deutsche Afrikafirmen'.

Institutional connections also played an important role. In addition to military academies,[76] universities and individual academic disciplines acted as major transmission channels for colonial ideas. Universities have been subject to more recent attention, as their significance for the Third Reich's 'race' and 'space' politics has become a focus for historians. But, whereas the involvement of individual researchers in National Socialist politics has been examined in detail,[77] in-depth studies of the different disciplines have for the most part not been undertaken. Diachronic analyses of particular subjects over long periods remain—with the exception of euthanasia and eugenics—rare. But academic theories are not formed in a vacuum; they are imbedded in synchronic as well as diachronic discourses. It is important to reconstruct these institutional sites in order to understand how the sciences received concepts that were then passed on to the rulers. Colonial science, from the end of the nineteenth century, is an important point of reference as it was the 'showpiece' of population studies prior to 1933.[78] Already under the Kaiser, scientists volunteered for government service and the colonies with great enthusiasm and thus made their mark in their own disciplines.

76 We know nothing concerning their treatment and transmission of tactical knowledge gained during the colonial wars. For Great Britain, we know more: Colonel Callwell's book, which also deals with colonial wars (i.e. the Herero war), was mandatory reading in anti-guerrilla warfare training; it was first published in 1896, but subsequent editions followed; Charles E. Callwell, *Small Wars. Their Principles and Practice* (London: Stationery Office 1896).

77 Various academic disciplines were directly or indirectly involved in the restructuring of 'race' and 'space' in Eastern Europe as well as in Germany itself: eugenics, medicine, biology and social sciences, on the one hand, and geography, economics and engineering, on the other. Law and the humanities contributed to racial legislation and settlement history, and helped to legitimize both racial policy and expansion; academics developed plans and lent their expertise to various projects, serving as advisors in the administration of the occupied territories. A vigorous debate has arisen in recent years about the participation of scientists and experts generally in Nazi crimes; see Michael Fahlbusch, *Wissenschaft im Dienst der nationalsozialistischen Politik? Die 'Volksdeutschen Forschungsgemeinschaften' von 1931–1945* (Baden-Baden: Nomos 1999); Mechthild Rössler and Sabine Schleiermacher (eds), *Der 'Generalplan Ost'* (Berlin: Akademie 1993); Bruno Wasser, *Himmlers Raumplanung im Osten* (Basel: Birkhäuser 1993); and Franz-Rutker Hausmann, *'Deutsche Geisteswissenschaft' im Zweiten Weltkrieg. Die 'Aktion Ritterbusch' (1940–1945)* (Dresden: Dresden University Press 1998).

78 Research on this topic is still rather unsatisfactory. As an introduction, see the articles on various academic disciplines in van der Heyden and Zeller (eds), *Kolonialmetropole Berlin*; and Pascal Grosse, *Kolonialismus, Eugenik und bürgerliche Gesellschaft in Deutschland, 1850–1918* (Frankfurt: Campus 2000). The academic disciplines that explicitly dealt with the colonized peoples belong in this context; see Christoph Marx, *'Völker ohne Schrift und Geschichte'. Zur historischen Erfassung des vorkolonialen Schwarzafrika in der deutschen Forschung des 19. und frühen 20. Jahrhunderts* (Stuttgart: Steiner 1988); and Sara Pugach, 'Afrikanistik and Colonial Knowledge. Carl Meinhof, the Missionary Impulse and the Development of African Studies in Germany 1887–1919', Ph.D. thesis, University of Chicago, 2000.

Geography, for example, exploited the bourgeoisie's colonial enthusiasm to gain prestige in society and enhance its academic reputation.[79] Geographers such as the Berlin professor Ferdinand von Richthofen, doyen of his discipline, competed for research grants in the full knowledge that his work could be made available for the development of the colonies. Von Richthofen's successor in Berlin, Albrecht Penck, was the founder of *Kulturbodenforschung* (research on the relationship between territory and culture) and contributed greatly to the Third Reich's Eastern expansion. He was a supporter of both *Volkstum* politics and 'colonial revisionism' after 1933.[80] It is not too farfetched to ask whether both were informed by similar notions.

Geography is a discipline that is worth examining further because it overlapped with so many other disciplines. Political geography, for instance, comprised the sub-disciplines of colonial population science, colonial economics and production, colonial settlement and transport geography, colonial ethnology, colonial government, colonial empires and comparative government, all of which were interested in 'racial research', tropical medicine, the colonial exchange of commodities, colonial production, the economic exchange process between the metropole and the colonies, as well as in 'cultural mixing', colonial settlement and conditions in other colonies. All these subjects still need to be researched with regard to their influence on the development and exploitation of the colonies and their inhabitants. Even if the findings of colonial researchers were not as radical as that of their successors during the Third Reich, the earlier studies doubtless paved the way for later scientists to meet the needs of the Nazi regime.[81]

79 See Jürgen Osterhammel, 'Die Wiederkehr des Raumes: Geopolitik, Geohistorie und historische Geographie', *Neue Politische Literatur*, vol. 43, 1998, 374–96.

80 I have dealt with geography between colonialism and Nazism in Jürgen Zimmerer, 'Im Dienste des Imperiums. Die Geographen der Berliner Universität zwischen Kolonialwissenschaften und Ostforschung', in Andreas Eckert (ed.), *Universitäten und Kolonialismus*, a special issue of *Jahrbuch für Universitätsgeschichte*, vol. 7, 2004, 73–99; Jürgen Zimmerer, 'Wissenschaft und Kolonialismus. Das Geographische Institut der Friedrich-Wilhelms-Universität vom Kaiserreich zum Dritten Reich', in van der Heyden and Zeller (eds), *Kolonialmetropole Berlin*, 125–30.

81 Detailed analyses exist only for colonial medicine, engineering and geopolitics; see Eckart, *Medizin und Kolonialimperialismus*; Dirk van Laak, *Imperiale Infrastruktur. Deutsche Planungen für eine Erschließung Afrikas, 1880 bis 1960* (Paderborn: Schöningh 2004); and Jürgen Osterhammel, 'Raumerfassung und Universalgeschichte im 20. Jahrhundert', in Gangolf Hübinger, Jürgen Osterhammel and Erich Pelzer (eds), *Universalgeschichte und Nationalgeschichten* (Freiburg: Rombach 1994), 51–72. See also the articles in Irene Diekmann, Peter Krüger and Julius H. Schoeps (eds), *Geopolitik. Grenzgänge im Zeitgeist, 1890–1945*, 2 vols (Potsdam: Verlag für Berlin-Brandenburg 2000). On Haushofer, see Bruno Hipler, *Hitlers Lehrmeister. Karl Haushofer als Vater der NS-Ideologie* (St Ottilien: EOS-Verlag 1996); Hans-Adolf Jacobsen, *Karl Haushofer. Leben und Werk*, 2 vols (Boppard: Boldt 1979); and Frank Ebeling, *Geopolitik. Karl Haushofer und seine Raumwissenschaft 1919–1945* (Berlin: Akademie-Verlag 1994).

The transmission of colonial ideas was not only accomplished through the efforts of individuals who served in the colonies or the institutions that studied these ideas but, more importantly, through monuments, education, early films, lecture tours, exhibitions and literature. Journalists such as Paul von Lettow-Vorbeck and Paul Rohrbach transformed their colonial experiences for the mass media, and proved the importance of the media for the dissemination of colonial notions.[82] A wide-ranging genre of colonial literature developed,[83] including memoirs and fiction, such as (to name but three) von Lettow-Vorbeck's *Heia Safari*,[84] Margarethe von Eckenbrecher's *Was Afrika mir gab und nahm. Erlebnisse einer deutschen Frau in Südwestafrika*,[85] and Maximilian Bayer's *Mit dem Hauptquartier in Südwestafrika*.[86] The most famous of them all was Gustav Frenssen's *Peter Moors Fahrt nach Südwest*,[87] the bestselling book for German youth up until 1945. Hans Grimm's *Volk ohne Raum* enjoyed incredible success during the 1930s and 1940s.[88] It was regarded as a modern classic by the Nazis and compulsory reading in German schools, and the only book by a German author represented in the category 'German Literature' at the Chicago World Fair of 1933–4.[89]

This imaginary colonial history even embraced the western expansion of the United States through the fantasy of the Wild West: one has only to think

82 See the contributions in Kundrus (ed.), *Phantasiereiche*.

83 See Joachim Warmbold, '*Ein Stückchen neudeutsche Er . . .' Deutsche Kolonialliteratur. Aspekte ihrer Geschichte, Eigenart und Wirkung dargestellt am Beispiel Afrikas* (Frankfurt: Haag and Herchen 1982); Sibylle Benninghoff-Lühl, *Deutsche Kolonialromane 1884–1914 in ihrem Entstehungs- und Wirkungszusammenhang* (Bremen: Übersee Museum 1983); Amadou Booker Sadji, *Das Bild des Negro-Afrikaners in der Deutschen Kolonialliteratur (1884–1945). Ein Beitrag zur literarischen Imagologie Schwarzafrikas* (Berlin: Reimer 1985); and Rosa B. Schneider, '*Um Scholle und Leben*'. *Zur Konstruktion von 'Rasse' und Geschlecht in der deutschen kolonialen Afrikaliteratur um 1900* (Frankfurt: Brandes and Apsel 2003).

84 Paul von Lettow-Vorbeck, *Heia Safari! Deutschlands Kampf in Ostafrika* (Leipzig: Koehler 1920).

85 Margarethe von Eckenbrecher, *Was Afrika mir gab und nahm. Erlebnisse einer deutschen Frau in Südwestafrika* (Berlin: Mittler 1907). By 1940 an eighth edition had already been published.

86 Maximilian Bayer, *Mit dem Hauptquartier in Südwestafrika* (Berlin: Weicher 1909).

87 Gustav Frenssen, *Peter Moors Fahrt nach Südwest* (Berlin: Grote 1906). See also Rolf Meyn, 'Abstecher in die Kolonialliteratur. Gustav Frenssens Peter Moors fahrt nach Südwest', in Kay Dohnke and Dietrich Stein (eds), *Gustav Frenssen und seine Zeit. Von der Massenliteratur im Kaiserreich zur Massenideologie im NS-Staat* (Heide: Boyens 1997), 316–46; Medardus Brehl, '"Das Drama spielt sich auf der dunklen Bühne des Sandfeldes ab." Die Vernichtung der Herero und Nama in der deustchen (Populär-) Literatur', in Zimmerer and Zeller (eds), *Völkermord in Deutsch-Südwestafrika*, 86–96.

88 Hans Grimm, *Volk ohne Raum* (Munich: Langen 1926).

89 Jürgen Hillesheim and Elisabeth Michael, *Lexikon Nationalsozialistischer Dichter. Biographien—Analysen—Bibliographien* (Würzburg: Königshausen and Neumann 1993), 211–22 (211).

of Karl May.[90] Similar to the real world, this imaginary world created a framework that could hold the Nazis' colonial fantasies of Eastern European. It contributed to the conquerors' self-image as messengers of civilization, and the construction of Poles and Russians as 'savages' to be educated as servants, to be 'resettled' or 'removed' in order to make the country more efficient.

Throughout history, colonial adventurers felt motivated to live in the 'wild' in order to be able to pursue a lifestyle that was or had become unaffordable at home. Hence, an aristocratic lifestyle was exported to Africa. During National Socialism, the *Herrenmenschentum* (the 'master race' mind-set) returned to Europe. The binary encoding of white–black, natives–non-natives, rulers–servants, human–subhuman, worthy of life–unworthy of life, was profoundly colonial. The discursive formation of colonial ideas contributed to a broad and wide-ranging acceptance of such categories by the population.

Towards a global perspective on the Third Reich

Both at the time of the German empire and in subsequent decades, the German population's awareness of colonial history, including the conquest and rule of wide areas of the world by the English, French, Spanish, Portuguese, Belgians, Dutch and so on, was much stronger than is generally presumed. Sites for the dissemination of this knowledge included colonial clubs, geographical societies, political parties as well as popular novels and magazines, and university lectures. Consequently, ordinary citizens would have had some contact with notions such as the 'racial society', 'mixed marriage', 'expulsion and resettlement to special reserves', 'a declining and ailing race' or 'uneducated natives', even if they only came across them in reports by the various missionary societies. Attending to the colonial dimension in German history for an understanding of Nazi politics enables the recognition of various types of precursors and models. Some practices that, from a narrow Eurocentric perspective, seem unprecedented prove, on closer inspection, to be radicalized versions of forms found in earlier colonial times.

A truly global history of military or political occupation should disregard a Eurocentric distinction between occupation in Europe and colonial rule overseas. Nazi policies for the occupied areas of Poland and the Soviet Union must also be viewed as part of the global historical tradition of colonial rule. German as well as European history can only benefit from such a global perspective. The evidence of the long history of racial thinking can

90 See, for example, Rolf-Bernhard Essig and Gudrun Schury, 'Karl May', in Etienne François and Hagen Schulze (eds), *Deutsche Erinnerungsorte*, vol. 3, 2nd edn (Munich: Beck 2002), 107–21.

also help in understanding why so many Germans participated in the Nazi military campaign and the occupation without too many scruples. Indeed, it was the positive reading of European colonialism especially—which lasted well past the middle of the twentieth century—that contributed to concealing the criminal character of the German occupation from contemporary witnesses. For the perpetrators, the fact that brutal guerrilla warfare, resettlement and a slave economy had always accompanied colonialism helped to inspire and legitimize their own participation.

Jürgen Zimmerer is currently Visiting Assistant Professor at Essen University and a research fellow at the Centro de Estudos Interdisciplinares do Século XX at the University of Coimbra in Portugal. He is researching and writing on the relationship between colonialism and National Socialism, and on comparative genocide. He is the author of *Deutsche Herrschaft über Afrikaner. Staatlicher Machtanspruch und Wirklichkeit im kolonialen Namibia* (3rd edn 2004), and the editor of *Voelkermord in Deutsch-Südwestafrika. Der Kolonialkrieg (1904–1908) in Namiba und seine Folgen* (co-edited with Joachim Zeller) (2nd edn 2004) and *Schweigen—Erinnern—Bewältigen. Vergangenheitspolitik in globaler Perspektive* (2004). He is president of the European Network of Genocide Scholars and editor of the *Journal of Genocide Research*.

The concentration camp and development: the pasts and future of genocide[1]

VINAY LAL

A long prolegomenon to an allegedly short twentieth century

One of the more recent works of the esteemed British historian Eric Hobsbawm takes as its title *The Age of Extremes: The Short Twentieth Century,*

1 I am grateful to A. Dirk Moses, Dan Stone and two other readers for their careful reading of an earlier draft and incisive observations and queries.

1914–1991.[2] Though European powers were at war with each other over several centuries preceding the nineteenth century, their rapid acquisitions of overseas territories, their drive towards industrialization and nation-building, and the revolutions of 1848 all had the cumulative effect of shifting the terrain of war from Europe to the colonies. It was not only the scale of the war that engulfed Europe between 1914 and 1918, a war whose very characterization as the First World War suggests how far European conflicts are routinely assumed to have meaning for the rest of the world,[3] but rather the shattering of the dream that violence could, both casually and system-atically, be inflicted on colonized peoples while Europe itself remained inured to its effects, that perhaps justifies marking 1914 as the inauguration of a new century. It is also during the war years that the Bolsheviks gained power in Russia, and so brought into being an experiment that placed in strange but not atypical apposition the ideas of emancipation and orche-strated terror, and that crumbled only with the decimation of the Soviet Union in 1991.

As apparently reasonable as is Hobsbawm's framework for understanding the twentieth century, it remains resolutely Eurocentric, as well as driven by a rather conventional notion of history as the unfolding of events: events tethered, in particular, to violence and revolution. At this juncture of intellectual history, the charge of being Eurocentric is an all too familiar one, often levied to score polemical points rather than from serious intellectual intent; but its commonplace character or abuse makes it no less serious when the object of the critique is a scholar of extraordinary repute with pretensions to being progressive, ecumenical in his conception of history, and having the world at his fingertips. One wonders why, for example, the twentieth century should not be viewed as having been inaugurated in 1905 when Japan dealt Russia a crushing blow and so

2 London: Michael Joseph 1994.
3 It is true, of course, that many countries not involved in the conflict were, in one manner or another, dragged into the war. Over a million Indian men were dispatched overseas by the British government of India to fight a war which by no stretch of the imagination could be described as their war. Their needless sacrifice, not even of the some 50,000 men who laid down their lives in the battlefields of Mesopotamia and Flanders, has barely been noticed in Britain. The war's consequences for India were far-reaching: as prices of essential commodities shot up, standards of living declined precipitously. Defence expenditures increased by 300 per cent, and the usual shenanigans, once again so amply on display in George Bush's war on Iraq, about the imperative to preserve the world for freedom could be heard while people starved. See Sumit Sarkar, *Modern India 1885–1947* (Delhi: Macmillan India 1983), 168–72; Indian National Congress, Punjab Subcommittee, *Report of the Commissioners* [appointed to look into the Jallianawala Bagh massacre], vol. 1: *Report* (Bombay: Karnataka Press 1920). But my larger argument here is that Europe unthinkingly remains the template for the history we do, even if it is the history of some other place such as India, and that this hubris of knowledge creates its own forms of oppression.

became, to nationalists in India and Indonesia, a wondrous sign of resurgent Asia. 'Japanese victories stirred up my enthusiasm', wrote Nehru in his autobiography, 'and I waited eagerly for the papers for fresh news daily.... Nationalistic ideas filled my mind. I mused of Indian freedom and Asiatic freedom from the thralldom of Europe.'[4] One can say that subjugated natives no longer were obliged to believe in the inherent superiority of the white race, and that there has seldom been so momentous an awakening. From the point of view of colonized subjects, the most important phenomenon of the twentieth century was decolonization, however much its mention has receded if not disappeared from contemporary political commentary and academic tomes on modernity. Subhas Chandra Bose, the founder of the insurgent Indian National Army, writing about Japan's military prowess three decades after the destruction of the Russian naval forces, deplored Japan's occupation of China but nonetheless recalled the 'great things' Japan had done 'for herself and for Asia. Her re-awakening at the dawn of the present century sent a thrill throughout our Continent. Japan has shattered the white man's prestige in the Far East and has put all the Western imperialist powers on the defensive.'[5]

If Japan's victory over Russia in 1905 is proposed as one possible way, among many others, of imagining the beginnings of the twentieth century, one can similarly be tempted into marking its close with something other than the fall of the Soviet Union, most notably and ominously the Rwandan genocide of 1994. For years the western powers, chastened by the nightmarish experience of the Holocaust perpetrated upon the Jews, had been shouting themselves hoarse with the slogan 'Never Again'. And yet, despite mounting signs of the fratricidal conflict between Hutus and Tutsis, and with full knowledge of the atrocities that began to be perpetrated before their very eyes, France, the United States and the United Nations mutely partook, by their permissive indifference, of the ferocious killings that in a little over three months had left 800,000 Tutsis dead.[6] The former European colonial powers and the United States furnished a new meaning to the term 'free world', a world that frees one from moral responsibility and yet insists that borders that are not one's own should be free to trafficking by multinational corporations and arms dealers. (Nearly the entire world should be placed on the 'free' side of the ledger, considering that it is ringed by McDonald's franchises and American

---

4 J. Nehru, *Toward Freedom: The Autobiography of Jawaharlal Nehru* [1941] (Boston: Beacon Press 1958), 29–30.

5 S. C. Bose, 'Japan's role in the Far East', in *Through Congress Eyes* (Allahabad: Kitabistan 1938), 212.

6 Philip Gourevitch, *We Wish to Inform You That Tomorrow We Will Be Killed with Our Families: Stories from Rwanda* (New York: Farrar Straus and Giroux 1998).

military bases.) On the one hand, as has been indisputably documented, the United Nations Assistance Mission in Rwanda was ordered to wind up its operations in the midst of the killings; on the other hand, the French, who had inherited the colonial mantle from the Belgians, were supplying arms to the Hutu-led Rwandan army even as their ambassador to the United Nations was describing France's objective as 'naturally exclud[ing] any interference in the development of the balance of military forces between the parties involved in the conflict'.[7]

The numerous peculiarities of the Rwandan genocide apart, such as the extraordinary ethnic and cultural proximity of the perpetrators to the victims,[8] or the fact that amidst the late twentieth century's unparalleled arsenal for destruction the bulk of the killing was achieved with machetes, spears and clubs, one must also pause to ask whether at least some people who might have been in the position of restraining the killers or calling them to account were not emboldened in their indifference by the fact that these were black-on-black killings. The phrase 'primordial conflicts' is all too easily available to those who are predisposed to viewing certain conflicts, whether in the Balkans or in Africa, as not merely intractable but as opaque to the enlightened West. The West, one had every reason to believe from what was allowed to transpire in Rwanda, had given up on Africa. The Cambridge School of historians famously wrote about the 'scramble for Africa' among the colonial powers towards the end of the nineteenth century, but a century later western powers all seem to be ready to disown that troubled legacy. The scramble now is to get out. Africa had a way of inserting itself into the western consciousness then; it still does so today. Africa cannot be forgotten; nor can it be forgiven. The gruesome violence of the twentieth century seems, then, to have served no purpose other than to warn us, brutally and unceremoniously, that it had no purpose, however profuse the atonements, however widespread the epidemic of apologies that engulfed the last decade of the twentieth century. The precise terror of Rwanda is that our moral sensibilities appear to have been diminished rather than enhanced over the course of a century.

That Hobsbawm treats history as 'event' rather than 'category' is, as I have already hinted, a problem of a different order, one to which I shall turn in due course. Much more nuanced than the more commonly known pretenders to the enterprise of world cosmologies, Francis Fukuyama and Samuel Huntington, Hobsbawm never quite declared that history has come

---

7 Ibid., 149–57.
8 See David Newbury, 'Irredentist Rwanda: ethnic and territorial frontiers in Central Africa', *Africa Today*, vol. 44, no. 2, 1997, 211–22; Mahmood Mamdani, *When Victims Become Killers: Colonialism, Nativism, and the Genocide in Rwanda* (Princeton, NJ: Princeton University Press 2001), 41–75.

to an end, and that it only remains for people belonging to the under-developed or developing worlds to embrace the multiple and related virtues of globalization, electoral democracy and free enterprise. Nevertheless, he has come precipitously close to embracing this view, as the brackets he places on *his* twentieth century suggest. The inexorable and iron laws of history that Hobsbawm's Marxism trumpeted were surely not vindicated with the demise of the Soviet Union, but the moral support that many so-called progressives have offered to political and military interventions as necessary humanitarian gestures, from the bombing of Serbia to the invasion of Iraq, suggests that the free world's achievements are seen as the *telos* of *all* human history.[9] At the end of the Cold War, as we might recall, there was considerable rejoicing that the entire world could gain from what was termed the 'peace dividend'. One view that quickly gained wide currency was that since most of the wars fought between 1945 and 1991 were, to varying degrees, engagements that the United States and the Soviet Union waged through their proxies—partly by necessity, since a direct conflagra-tion between the two superpowers spelled annihilation, and partly by choice, since these proxy wars, besides feeding the armaments industries of both nations, were the most expedient way of disseminating their respective ideologies and passing on the casualties to purportedly inferior races—the fragmentation of the Soviet Union and the collapse of Communism throughout the Eastern bloc would necessarily diminish the resort to violence.

That we would have anything but 'peace' should have been clear from the fact that the demise of the Soviet Union and the decimation of Iraq went nearly hand-in-hand: indeed, the Gulf War was conducted partly with the justification that it was the most desirable and morally efficacious way of putting into effect what Bush Senior termed the 'new world order'. In each of the three principal military engagements of the United States since the Soviet bloc disintegrated and before the invasion of Iraq in 2003 by the American-led and comically named 'coalition of the willing'—the Gulf War, NATO's bombing of Yugoslavia and the war to hunt down Osama bin Laden and members of al-Qaeda and the Taliban—the word 'genocide' lurked in the air, occupying in the discursive space the same place as does an

---

9 Some readers might insist on consistency and ask why I should deplore the failure of the West to intervene in Rwanda while critiquing the interventions that did take place in Iraq and Serbia. This quest for consistency, whatever its assumed virtues, can become another mode of evading the politics of knowledge behind all such phenomena. It is more important to probe why the West does intervene on some occasions and not on others, the relationship of such interventions to geopolitical ambitions, the particular nature of the intervention and the location of political action within the matrix of ethical thinking. For some reflections on these questions, see Samantha Power, *'A Problem from Hell': America and the Age of Genocide* (New York: HarperCollins/Perennial 2003).

uninvited guest who is neither inside nor outside. In each instance, the chief villain of the piece—Saddam Hussein, Slobodan Milosevic and Osama bin Laden—could be viewed with some justification as evil incarnate, indeed as a person full of genocidal intent: Saddam had gassed the Kurds; bin Laden harboured genocidal fantasies against the Americans and, more broadly, certain enemies of Islam; Milosevic, transformed from the good Communist into the Serb nationalist, became one of the principal architects of the destruction of the culture of Bosnian Muslims and Kosovars.[10] Even the Taliban were, to all practical purposes, genocidal towards their women, if by genocide we mean that members of a specific group, here chosen on account of their gender, were targeted by a political regime and systematically stripped of their rights to education, health, livelihood and everything else that ordinarily makes possible a fulfilled life.[11] And, yet, in each case there seemed some reluctance to encompass the villains under the rubric of

10 With respect to Kosovo, it is now clear that stories of the mass disappearance of Albanian men, and of mass graves, were grossly exaggerated, perhaps planted by NATO and the American administration. Moreover, the Kosovar Liberation Army, hailed in the West as the supreme liberator of Albanians from the monstrous grip of Serbia, carried out as many killings as did the Serbian armed forces and their supporters.

11 There are important distinctions that come to mind that I cannot develop here, from the idea of war itself as a highly gendered activity and the cruel caricature of men who refuse to fight as 'effeminate' to the disproportionate impact that wars generally have on women and children, the sexual license that wars are seen to confer on men, the deployment of rape as a weapon of war, and 'genocidal rape' or 'rape warfare'. On the policy of what American feminist law professor Catherine MacKinnon has termed 'procreation by rape', see Vesna Kesic, 'Muslim women, Croatian women, Serbian women, Albanian women . . . ', in Dušan I. Bjelic and Obrad Savic (eds), Balkan as Metaphor: Between Globalization and Fragmentation (Cambridge, MA: MIT Press 2002), 313. The treatment of women under the Taliban illustrates some of the difficulties attendant on prevailing conceptions of genocide as well as femicide. Doubtless, there were women who were subjected to sexual abuse, but I am not aware that the Taliban, notwithstanding the disputes between Pathans, Tajiks and Hazara, subjected women of other ethnic and linguistic groups to rape and sexual abuse as a matter of policy. (Indeed, in the early months of the ascendancy of the Taliban, they were vigorously defended by many people as restoring order to a country that had descended into complete chaos, and women were described as feeling safe for the first time in years.) But the denial of medical facilities, education and social services to women was so prevalent as to go well beyond what is ordinarily captured by the phrase 'gender discrimination'. Are there circumstances under which the deliberate isolation of a specific group of people, who are allowed to regress to an earlier stage of development—and by development I denote not what is encompassed by the modern and statist ideology of development, but rather by the growth of human consciousness, moral sensibilities and civic institutions—can be construed as genocidal in intent? For valuable discussions, see Nancy Hatch Dupree, 'Afghan women under the Taliban', in William Maley (ed.), Afghanistan and the Taliban: The Rebirth of Fundamentalism?, rev. edn (New Delhi: Penguin 2001), 145–66; and Ahmed Rashid, Taliban: The Story of the Afghan Warlords, rev. edn (London: Pan Books 2001), 105–16.

'genocide'. Only a few thousand Kurds had been killed;[12] both Saddam and bin Laden had, at one time, been befriended by the Americans, and the Americans were not keen on being viewed as partners in crime. The Taliban had brutally sequestered their women, but no one could say that their numbers had been drastically reduced; if anything, it is Afghan men, whether belonging to the Taliban or otherwise, who have suffered huge losses since fighting first broke out with the Soviet invasion of Afghanistan in 1979.

Arguably, then, the fall of the Soviet Union was much less the definitive moment than the commonly accepted readings of it suggest, and the bookends that Hobsbawm places around the twentieth century, 1914 and 1991, derive from the received view of history: a view in which, as shall also be seen, history itself remains the supreme uncontested category. The twentieth century is now recognized as an exceptionally violent period, and estimates of those killed in wars, insurrections and genocides run to at least 200 million. In the 1980s, 60 per cent of scientists were described as being engaged, directly or indirectly, in defence research,[13] a fact that, however much scientists, defence officials, policy experts and counter-terrorism specialists may wish to resist its implications, has some bearing on the totalizing nature of violence in the twentieth century. If we take the twentieth century to be a category not so much of time as of mentality, a category signalling disposition towards a certain kind of violence that was eroding the restraints that societies had often times placed upon themselves, then it may be much more fitting to think of the twentieth century as interminably long, a century that began well before its allotted moment and that shows few signs of receding. The Kentucky-based farmer and writer Wendell Berry noted with his usual perspicacity following the attacks on the World Trade Center and the Pentagon that the modern doctrine of warfare 'was set forth and enacted by [Union] General William Tecumseh Sherman, who held that a civilian population could be declared guilty and rightly subjected to military punishment'.[14] Sherman was articulate in the expression of his passionately

12 I refer only to the chemical attack on Halabja under Ali Hassan al-Majid (also known as 'Ali Anfal' or 'Ali Chemical') on 16 March 1988, which caused between 4,000 and 7,000 fatalities. This received far more coverage than the entire Anfal campaign against Kurds in Northern Iraq over a seven-month period in 1988, which is estimated to have led to the loss of as many as 100,000 Kurdish lives. See Middle East Watch, *Genocide in Iraq: The Anfal Campaign against the Kurds* (New York: Human Rights Watch 1993), available online at www.hrw.org/reports/1993/iraqanfal (viewed 10 March 2005).

13 Ashis Nandy, 'The twentieth century: the ambivalent homecoming of homo psychologicus', *Hitotsubashi Journal of Social Studies*, vol. 33, no. 1, July 2001, 22.

14 Wendell Berry, 'Thoughts in the presence of fear', in *In the Presence of Fear: Three Essays for a Changed World* (Great Barrington, MA: The Orion Society 2001).

held belief that nothing was impermissible in the endeavour to break the spirit of the enemy. One of his more critical biographers credits him with the invention of the concept of 'total war';[15] and Berry himself concludes his thoughts on Sherman with the telling observation: 'We [in the United States] have never repudiated that doctrine.'[16]

Terror has a much longer history than terrorism, and the unknown soldier of the First World War, who has come to epitomize the anonymity of modern warfare, was already lurking in the unmarked graves of the Civil War. However, the Civil War had been fought between near equals, and victory, allowing for certain contingencies, could well have gone to the other side. What often gives a genocidal edge to total violence is immense disparities of power, and the late nineteenth century witnessed a number of developments that heralded the formal arrival of the genocidal twentieth century. Advances in military technology had in part facilitated the expansion of colonial rule: as a British officer fighting in Multan in western India at the end of 1848 confided to his diary, there was much cause to exult in the triumph of 'that true weapon the bayonet, which never yet failed to bring success to the British soldier'.[17] Yet the bayonet could only go so far, as the introduction of the machine gun so amply demonstrated. The disequilibrium in military strength, these days suggested by images of Israeli F-16s pounding Palestinian settlements from the air, was beginning to acquire a new meaning. The bullets fired from the Maxim gun in rapid succession tore into the flesh, splintering bone, puncturing large holes in the body. Mounted on a gunboat, the Maxim gun appeared to Winston Churchill, who took part in Kitchener's campaigns that led to the conquest of the Sudan in 1898, as a 'beautiful white devil' that floated 'gracefully on the waters', wreathed in smoke.[18] The loving lyricism with which Churchill describes the battle of Omdurman, at the end of which 20 Britons were dead and 11,000 Dervishes had sunk down in tangled heaps, should obscure neither the terrible tedium experienced by Kitchener's men nor the moral lessons drawn from this conflict by European observers. The 'mere physical act' of firing 'became tedious', noted Churchill, as one Dervish after another was cut into pieces: this was 'the most signal triumph ever gained by the arms of science over barbarians'.[19]

---

15 John Walters, *Merchant of Terror: General Sherman and Total War* (Indianapolis: Bobbs-Merrill 1973).

16 Berry, 'Thoughts in the presence of fear', 6.

17 Quoted in V. G. Kiernan, *Colonial Empires and Armies 1815–1960* (Stroud, Gloucestershire: Sutton Publishing 1998), 123.

18 Winston Churchill, quoted in Daniel R. Headrick, *The Tools of Empire: Technology and European Imperialism in the Nineteenth Century* (New York: Oxford University Press 1981), 118–19.

19 Quoted in Headrick, *Tools of Empire*, 118. See also John Ellis, *A Social History of the Machine Gun* (New York: Pantheon 1975).

A huge army, what Churchill described as 'the strongest and best-armed savage army yet arrayed against a modern European Power', had been almost effortlessly destroyed in the space of a few hours with minimal loss of life to the victors. But had Churchill been more prescient, he would perhaps have underscored the 'tedium' experienced by white men as they buried black bodies under mounds of bullets rather than the enormous chasm opened up by western arms between the 'civilized' and the 'savages'. Hannah Arendt had a different phrase to capture not only the bureaucratization of killing, but the moral distancing that takes place when the pulling of the trigger and the filing of papers become tasks akin to one another.[20] Evidently, 'the banality of evil' has many forms: once Kitchener had dealt with the Dervishes, and a number of other recalcitrant savage tribes, he eventually turned his attention to the troublesome Boers further south. Unlike the Dervishes, who had appeared in battle *en masse*, and died likewise, the Boers engaged in guerrilla tactics. Kitchener sought to decimate them with what one writer has described as a 'double sweeping operation': one measure consisted in flushing them out through systematic drives, 'organized like a sporting shoot, with success defined in a weekly "bag" of killed, captured and wounded'.[21] This was not wholly exceptional, considering that hunting for the scalps of Native Americans was a popular past-time for the white man. Scalps were exhibited to an admiring public, and the trophy hunters were local heroes. Kitchener was somewhat more innovative with his second measure, arguably showing himself in numerous ways to be the forerunner of the Nazis. To prevent civilians from offering material and moral support to the guerrillas, Kitchener conceived of a plan to sweep the country clean of them, and he herded Boer women and children into refugee camps as though they were cattle, sheep or horses.[22] Their rations were set absurdly low in the hope that the men would be encouraged to surrender, and disease was rampant in the camps. Recalling

20 See Hannah Arendt, *Eichmann in Jerusalem: A Report on the Banality of Evil* [1963] (New York: Penguin 1977).

21 Thomas Pakenham, *The Boer War* (New York: Random House 1979), 522.

22 There is, in principle, an important distinction to be drawn between camps intended to hold or sequester civilians, such as the internment camps for Japanese-Americans created by Franklin Roosevelt's Executive Order, and the extermination camps established by the Nazis. One effect of such distinctions has been to reinforce arguments that plead for the uniqueness of the Holocaust, just as this form of reasoning unduly focuses on intent. The hardening of boundaries does not allow for the easy accommodation of numerous cases in which the lines between internment or segregation and extermination were blurred. Kitchener's contemporary (and forerunner, one might say), General Valeriano Weyler (1838–1930), the governor of Cuba, initiated the policy of reconcentration (*reconcentrado*) in 1897 in his attempt to inflict defeat on Cuban insurgents. Weyler, who admitted to great admiration for Sherman, hit upon a plan to separate peasant men, women and children from guerrillas by placing them in camps. Those who were not in camps were dubbed rebels and seditionists, and were liable to be shot on the spot; but those inside the camps did not fare much better, and as many as 400,000 succumbed to disease,

Churchill's description of the tedium involved in cutting down Dervishes with a machine gun, one is not surprised that, as Thomas Pakenham puts it, 'administrative problems' involving civilians 'always bored' Kitchener. Pakenham is remarkably forthright in his assessment of the contribution of Kitchener, once lionized as one of the greatest proconsuls of empire, to civilization: 'Today, Kitchener is not remembered in South Africa for his military victories. His monument is the camp— "concentration camp", as it came to be called. The camps have left a gigantic scar across the minds of Afrikaners: a symbol of deliberate genocide.'[23]

A short prolegomenon to an interminably long past

The twentieth century, then, might have been much more than the 'short' century that has been described by Hobsbawm, and that it is assumed to be by all those who jointly mark the disappearance of the Soviet Union, and the emergence of the space of the Internet as a radical possibility for the fulfilment of the ideas of democracy and liberty, as the twin signs of the inauguration of a new period in human history. Hannah Arendt was among the first scholars to recognize that concentration camps were not an invention of totalitarian governments, having been used not only in South Africa but in India for the retention of 'undesirable elements'.[24] But she was

medical negligence, malnutrition and mistreatment. See G. J. A. O'Toole, *The Spanish War: An American Epic 1898* (New York: Norton 1986), 56–8. The tactic of herding rural populations into camps in an effort to deprive insurgents of food and shelter was used during the Malay insurgency, and resurfaced in the form of the Strategic Hamlet programme initiated by the Americans in Vietnam in 1962. See Stanley Karnow, *Vietnam: A History* (New York: Penguin 1984), 255–8. The term 'concentration camps', as used by Hannah Arendt (see below) and myself, encompasses a broad semiotic register.

23 Pakenham, *The Boer War*, 522–4.
24 Hannah Arendt, *The Origins of Totalitarianism*, rev. edn (New York: Harcourt Brace Jovanovich 1973), 440. Arendt's mention of India is unaccompanied by any reference, but she is almost certainly referring to the practice, adopted by the British in the late nineteenth century, of keeping people who were considered to belong to 'criminal castes' and 'criminal tribes' under 'protective custody'. British officials construed members of these allegedly criminal castes and tribes, running into the millions rather than the tens of thousands, as 'criminals by birth', as firm a recipe for genocide as one can imagine. The severe disabilities imposed upon these criminal castes and tribes for well over a century point to deliberate and systematic attempts to reduce their numbers. Members of criminal castes and tribes are among those unfortunate victims of genocide who have not been recognized as such; invisibility takes on new meanings with reference to them. Most histories of India do not even spare a word for them, but the work of Sanjay Nigam has been exemplary in drawing attention to them; see his 'Disciplining and policing the "criminals by birth"', *Indian Economic and Social History Review*, vol. 27, no. 2, April–June 1990, and no. 3, July–September 1990. The Criminal

even more perspicacious in her identification of concentrations camps as sites of total domination of an unusual kind. She described them as 'the laboratories in which the fundamental belief of totalitarianism that everything is possible is being verified': here the intention was not only to 'exterminate people and degrade human beings', but to eliminate, 'under scientifically controlled conditions, spontaneity itself as an expression of human behavior and of transforming the human personality into a mere thing, into something that even animals are not'.[25] The vast scale on which the Nazis committed their crimes made them improbable to others; equally improbable, the Nazis might have thought, would be the accounts of survivors. Those who dared to speak the unspeakable would be viewed with suspicion: having returned to the world of the living, Arendt writes, the survivor who bears witness 'himself is often assailed by doubts with regard to his own truthfulness, as though he had mistaken a nightmare for reality'.[26]

If Arendt could reach back to the Boer War and to British colonialism in India to describe the origins of that totalitarian form of terror known as the concentration camp, it is just as reasonable to ask what the concentration camp of the future might look like. Is the concentration camp only a thing of the past, or has it metamorphosed into different forms? When Theodor Adorno declared that to write poetry after Auschwitz is barbaric, could he also have meant to say that we did not, after all, survive the concentration camp? Dazed women, men and children walked out of the camps, but did civilization outlive the onslaught? 'The idea that after this war', reflected Adorno,

> life will continue 'normally' or even that culture might be 'rebuilt'—as if the rebuilding of culture were not already its negation—is idiotic. Millions of Jews have been murdered, and this is to be seen as an interlude and not the catastrophe itself. What more is this culture waiting for?[27]

Has the concentration camp, unmoored from its precise location, shorn of its physicality, freed from its chains, bounded no longer by barbed wires, come to occupy a different space? If the concentration camp never really

---

Tribes Act was first passed in 1871, amended in 1882, and extended by turn to various parts of India, including the Madras presidency in 1911. The government of India has made half-hearted attempts to 'denotify' these castes and tribes, but their living conditions remain wretched and stigma continues to be attached to them.

25 Arendt, *Origins of Totalitarianism*, 437–8.
26 Ibid., 439.
27 Theodor Adorno, *Minima Moralia: Reflections from Damaged Life*, trans. from the German by E. F. N. Jephcott (London: Verso 1978), 55.

disappeared, even as the only form in which we 'knew' it vanished, might that point to an ominous future for genocide and the categories through which we have hitherto understood it? Will it suffice to speak of genocide as the wilful elimination, in part or in whole, of groups of people, whether conceived through the categories of nationality, religion, ethnicity, gender, sexual preference or linguistic identity, and point to continuing violence in the Sudan, Chechnya, the Chittagong Hill Tracts and elsewhere as instances of genocide in our time, or do our times call for some radical rethinking of genocide? Does our present understanding of genocide permit us to recognize the numerous forms, institutions and socio-cultural practices, many cast as benevolent interventions, through which it might be practised?

I am by no means merely adverting to the argument, considerable as its merits indubitably are in some instances, that many recent military engagements have been tethered on the slimmest ideas, generally a strange conjoining of infantilism with a moral rhetoric as offensive and hypocritical as it is an invitation to perpetuate terror in the name of eliminating terrorism. The 'new world order' of 1991 gave way to the notion of 'humanitarian intervention' in 1999, and this in turn was succeeded, in the war against terror, by the terrifying notion that 'if you are not with us, you are against us'.[28] It is the Gulf War (1991), as well, that serves as the template for what has now become firmly enshrined as the philosophy of American military engagement, namely, the notion that the loss of lives on the other side is acceptable if not desirable 'collateral damage' so long as no lives are lost on one's own side. The triumph in the Balkans was trumpeted with the observation that not a single American life had been lost to enemy gunfire. That is one principal reason why bombing from altitudes of 10,000 feet or more, where it becomes extremely difficult to distinguish military targets from the civilian infrastructure, is now considered normative, even a form of moral bravery. These forms of 'humanitarian intervention' are, let us recognize, just as asymmetrical as those colonial wars of expansion, conquest and self-aggrandizement that decimated entire tribes or communities in the Americas, Australia and Africa. One might argue that each age has its own form of benevolent violence, and that 'humanitarian interventions' have only supplanted the discourse of 'civilizing mission' that was rampant in the nineteenth century. Civilizing missions entailed punitive expeditions to bring 'unruly' tribes to their senses and the 'pacification' of warlike people and entire villages, and humanitarian interventions now appear to operate in somewhat similar idioms. What, then, should strike us as distinct in the idea of 'humanitarian intervention', and why should we think of it as

28 For a more extended discussion, see Vinay Lal, 'Terrorism, Inc.: the family of fundamentalisms', *The Little Magazine* (New Delhi), vol. 2, no. 5, September–October 2001, 33–43.

anything other than a very contemporary form of state politics that has been us with for a long time?

To gain some sense of just how far we have traveled along the road to more evolved forms of oppression that will, at least in part, have the effect of making genocide invisible, it is necessary to begin with the observation that we live amidst times when the categories deployed in the service of cognitive frameworks have become overwhelmingly oppressive. A case in point is furnished by the categories—the bedrock of political science and modern nation-state systems and nearly always prevalent in discourses surrounding genocide—of 'majority' and 'minority'. Every nation-state has its minorities, and the keenest political observers are, it is reasonable to aver, in agreement that any political system that safeguards the rights of minorities is least likely to gravitate towards violence and oppression. No lesser a person than Mohandas Gandhi, whose political acumen was not less remarkable than the moral sensibility that he brought to politics, took the view that the litmus test of a democracy is its treatment of its minorities. Minorities have often had good reasons to fear majorities. Nonetheless, even a modicum of reflection suggests that genocides or systematic acts of repression are not always perpetrated by majorities upon minorities, and the Sunni stranglehold over power (and thus the appropriation of state-sanctioned violence) in Shia-majority Iraq under the regime of Saddam Hussein is only the most contemporary and well-known illustration of the phenomenon of a minority wielding immense power over a majority. Over 500 years of colonialism, European minorities, whether in settler colonies or otherwise, and sometimes dwarfed by native majorities as in India under the British, rendered extinct large indigenous populations, exercised naked and hegemonic power over their subjects, and transformed the colonies that fell under their jurisdiction.

What, then, if a minority acted with the confidence of a majority and, contrariwise, a majority thought of itself as a minority? And what if, to bring a sharply political edge to our reflections, the minority was not so transparently emboldened by its monopoly over the use of force, but was rather a minority that had almost seamlessly assimilated itself into the social fabric of the country? While they have doubtless occupied a disproportionately important place in the socio-economic life of India, the Parsis or Zoroastrians, whose share of India's population has always been minuscule, never exercised military influence and seldom displayed any interest in wielding political power, and there is little to suggest that they have ever been resented by the comparatively gargantuan Muslim, not to mention Hindu, majorities. Hindus, on the contrary, constitute the overwhelming majority of India's population, and even in undivided India would have accounted for 70 per cent of its people, but nonetheless have for nearly a century imagined themselves as a besieged people. They today frequently rehearse the complaint that they are treated akin to a discriminated minority and view Hindu-dominant India as an anomaly in world politics, a nation whose outright majority is cowed into submission by one or more minorities. The modern movement of Hindu nationalism that goes under the name of Hindutva has been fuelled, in part, by the perception that Hindus are the largest majority in the world that allows itself to be oppressed by a minority, namely the Muslims. Hindutva's websites, magazines, official pronouncements and various other instruments of propaganda are awash with the claim that the largest ever genocide perpetrated in history took place with the Muslim occupation and brutalization of India.[29]

The excessive tolerance of a majority can, on this account, make it vulnerable to the depredations of a depraved minority; moreover, from the standpoint of militant Hindus, Muslims are never anywhere in a minority, since Islam does not, in principle, recognize the idea of the nation-state, and Muslims imagine themselves as part of a worldwide community, the *ummah*, as Hindus never can. Thus the Muslim 'minority' in India is really a majority, and not merely the advance column of a world-conquering faith. Leaving aside the particularly egregious distortions that inhere in this view, such as the propensity to view Islam as a monolith, or the occlusion of the fact that Muslims are conspicuous among those who belong to the lower strata of society, the more general point about how categories of 'majority' and 'minority' have been naturalized needs reinforcement. Once the ideas of proportional political representation and the census had become firmly etched in the modern political imaginary, it became impossible to dislodge the notions of 'minority' and 'majority', and political science has done everything to consolidate this modality of thinking. The notions of 'majority' and 'minority' are the bread and butter of modern constitutional politics, as discussions over the recently concluded elections in the 'liberated' countries of Iraq and Afghanistan so amply demonstrate.

I have elsewhere advanced the argument that, as we move along in the twenty-first century, oppression will increasingly be exercised through the categories of knowledge, and that naked force, military might and the brutal class oppression of industrial society will be less visible instruments of violence.[30] This may seem a particularly inopportune moment to put forth such an argument, considering the instances of contemporary violence, whether genocidal or otherwise, that I have already enumerated in this paper. Besides the wars in Iraq and Afghanistan, and the conflicts in Rwanda, Uganda, Congo, Sudan and the Ivory Coast, there are more complicated cases of violence targeted at specific groups that appear to fall

29 For an elaboration of this point, see Vinay Lal, 'North American Hindus, the sense of history, and the politics of Internet diasporism', in Rachel C. Lee and Sau-ling Cynthia Wong (eds), *AsianAmerica.Net: Ethnicity, Nationalism, and Cyberspace* (London: Routledge 2003), 98–138. The anxiety that informs Hindutva is analysed in Vinay Lal, 'India in the world: Hinduism, the diaspora and the anxiety of influence', *Australian Religion Studies Review*, vol. 16, no. 2, Spring 2003, 19–37.
30 Vinay Lal, *Empire of Knowledge: Culture and Plurality in the Global Economy* (London: Pluto 2002).

short of 'genocide' as the term is commonly used by scholars. Many human rights activists in India have not been reticent in describing the pogrom that was directed at Muslims in Gujarat in early 2002, which took the lives of at least 2,000 people and left another 150,000 homeless, as genocide. The evidence is indisputably clear that the violence, though perhaps not instigated by the state in the first few hours, was then carried out with the full force of state power and with the active participation of functionaries of the state charged with checking the violence.[31] The genocides of the future will likely be directed not at entire populations, but rather at what one might term sufficiently symbolic sectors—and not necessarily, as one might be tempted to infer from previous genocides, intellectuals, political elites or the wealthy—of the targeted group. Human rights activists who have investigated the killings in Gujarat found that the murderers and arsonists directed their wrath not only at Muslim-owned shops and buildings but at a disproportionately large number of mosques and, even more ominously, at *dargahs*.[32] In Gujarat, as in many other parts of India, the burial sites of Sufi saints attract Muslim and Hindu worshippers. That the perpetrators of violence viewed *dargahs* and other sites associated with Sufis as particularly deserving of destruction is illustrative of the argument, to which I shall return in closing, that the fear of oneself is often greater than the fear of the other. Hindus who worship at *dargahs* are not only, from the perspective of militant Hindus, apostates, traitors and friends of Pakistan: they are palpable reminders of the syncretism that has historically characterized what later assumed the corporate identity of Hinduism, uncomfortable reminders indeed of everything that advocates of a masculinist (and often genocidal) faith masquerading as Hinduism have disowned in their own past. The genocide perpetrated against Muslims masks Hindutva's genocidal impulses towards Hinduism.

While it is transparently obvious that sheer military might subjugated the Taliban, the stubborn resistance of the Palestinians in the face of the overwhelming military superiority of Israel, which has not denied itself such obscene advantages as the deployment of F-16s in Palestinian neighbourhoods, should alone give some pause to reconsider the supposedly inevitable success accompanying the application of military force. Consequently, in suggesting that oppression and genocide should increasingly be understood as an aspect of the imperialism of categories, it becomes necessary to enquire into the origins of these categories and how they

31 Siddharth Varadarajan (ed.), *Gujarat: The Making of a Tragedy* (New Delhi: Penguin 2002) is a good compendium, and the role of the state is also heavily documented in Human Rights Watch, *'We Have No Orders to Save You': State Participation and Complicity in Communal Violence in Gujarat*, Human Rights Watch Report, vol. 14, no. 3 (New York: Human Rights Watch 2002).

32 See, for example, *Genocide: Gujarat 2002*, a special issue of *Communalism Combat* (Mumbai), vol. 8, nos 77–8, March–April 2002, 94–7.

operate. These categories are the handiwork of social scientists and other academic workers, and it is my submission that, in the era of globalism, when the same icons of popular culture proliferate everywhere, trade disputes universally come under the jurisdiction of the World Trade Organization or some other economic regime such as NAFTA, and financial markets are inextricably linked, nothing is more global than modern knowledge and its categories. The modern academic disciplines, especially the social sciences, are now replicated in universities around the world, though the prodigious discussion around globalization scarcely gives a hint of this development. The formal frameworks of knowledge have bequeathed to every corner of the globe a universal and supposedly tested and verifiable recipe for development, technological progress, successful management and democracy—the last enshrined in the idea of 'free elections' and further guided by the magical incantation of 'one person, one vote'. Gestures against globalization of a certain kind—the stone-throwing that accompanied the opening of a Kentucky Fried Chicken restaurant in Bangalore, the burning of the warehouses of the Indian subsidiaries of Monsanto upon the introduction of a terminator seed or the destruction of a McDonald's by a French farmer—are captured in popular memory, but it is useful to recall that American-style business schools are being embraced around the world, that for well over one generation the economics textbooks of Paul Samuelson have reigned supreme around the globe, and that no one protested when social science in the American, British or French idiom began to prevail in the 'developing' and 'underdeveloped' worlds. Indeed, the very ideas of 'development', 'growth', 'scarcity' and 'poverty' with which economists, social planners, sociologists and politicians in the non-Euro-American world work are sanctified by several generations of western experts. Even more so than Coca-Cola, Disney or manifestations of American-style youth culture, formal modeling and other mathematized forms of social science have reached into every corner of the world. Economists in dictatorships, democracies and dukedoms are, in so far as their work as social scientists is in question, fundamentally alike, however acute the degree of variance in the constraints placed on their ability to contribute to scholarly literature. The well-meaning protestors in Seattle and Genoa may have been echoing popular sentiments about globalization, but when we speak of the growing polarities, the extension of the ranks of the very poor as well as those of the very rich, it becomes incumbent on us to reflect upon how the categories of 'poverty' and 'scarcity' themselves operate to produce oppression.

Not all categories are alike; they have greater or lesser epistemic force, by which I partly mean that some—'poverty' and 'scarcity', to name two—have become so naturalized that the discursive fields generally concerned with enquiring into such phenomena, among them economics, geography and sociology, no longer feel they have to perform much explanatory work. Economists might dispute how poverty is to be alleviated, and the concept of purchasing power parity (PPP) allows them to understand that a dollar buys half a dozen eggs in American cities but a full meal at a roadside restaurant in India. The World Bank and United Nations bodies use some such figure as $1 or $2 per capita spending money per day to compute how many people the world over can be described as living in poverty, but seldom allow any other conceptions of poverty to enter into their calculations. Since economists seldom if ever think dialectically, none would think of writing about poverty by writing about the super-rich. Similarly, the economist is unable to distinguish between the poverty that one is born into, the poverty into which one is forced, the poverty that the supposed victim imagines as a form of wealth, the poverty that draws a line between needs and wants, the poverty that stands forth in repudiation of consumption, the poverty that becomes (as in the traditions of both Indian renunciates and warrior saints) one's armour and so on. Indeed, in many post-industrial societies, most particularly the United States, the poor are despised only because they cannot partake of the consumer society and are, thus, traitors to the notion of the ultimately good life.

Some categories are provisional, others are more enduring; some, such as 'development', have an extraordinary tenacity. Some categories are of recent vintage, the 'international community' being a notable case in point. If today the United States acts to subjugate, chastise or warn another people, it attempts to do so in the name of the international community. That was never much of a consideration when the United States fought in Vietnam, initiated the bombing of Cambodia or mined the harbours of Nicaragua. Other categories have been invested with newer meanings and have received different and revived forms of circulation. The idea of being literate, to take one example, has been in circulation since at least the late mediaeval period, and it set up a hierarchy between literates and illiterates; however, the category of literacy, as a perusal of the *Oxford English Dictionary* suggests, is much more modern than we might suppose. Literacy is a form of measurement, one used to browbeat nations into shame, contrition or submission. Where previously ethnologists drew on anthropometry and craniometry to draw distinctions between superior and inferior civilizations, or to delineate 'criminal types', today the ranking of civilizations draws on other criteria. Naked forms of racism are no longer tolerated, and there would be universal outrage at the suggestion that women and men with shapely or pointed noses are more elevated beings than those who are snub-nosed.[33] Instead, those people among whom literacy rates are low now substitute for

33 'They grabbed what they could get for the sake of what was to be got', comments Marlow in the first chapter of Joseph Conrad's *Heart of Darkness*. He is describing European adventurers. 'It was just robbery with violence, aggravated murder on a great scale, and men going at it blind—as is very proper for those who tackle a darkness. The conquest of the earth, which mostly means the taking it away from those who have a different complexion or slightly flatter noses than ourselves, is not a pretty thing when you look into it too much'; Joseph Conrad, *Tales of Land and Sea* (New York: Hanover House 1953), 37.

those with unshapely noses: they are the pathetic ones, ripe for interven-tion.[34] The United Nations, for one, is unequivocal in its various pronounce-ments that literacy rates are one of the three principal measures for determining where a nation-state shall stand on the scale of civilization.

Modern, largely invisible, holocausts are being perpetrated on significant sections of the world's population. I have so far desisted from establishing a catalogue of genocides, partly because the twentieth century has been particularly fecund in this respect and we are in any case far from completing the catalogue. Hitler infamously precipitated the elimination of the Jewish population with the observation that no one remembered the extermination of the Armenians, and there is every possibility that the twenty-first century might be richer still in other, hitherto still invisible, holocausts. Nothing furnishes more vivid illustrations of this argument than the idea of 'development', which remains indubitably the clearest example of the genocidal violence perpetrated by modern knowledge systems on the integrity of human communities. The saga of Soviet terror originated in the brutal collectivization of Russian agriculture and in the impulse to industrialize rapidly, and consequently increase productivity, by the use of forced labour. Millions of deaths were achieved, not by superior forms of armament, but by coolly and rationally conceiving of these deaths as the necessary price to pay for development. In a similar vein is the Chinese Communist Party's heartless embrace of ruinous economic policies, the attempt by political functionaries to make the subjects of the state partake in the Great Leap Forward, and the consequence of this extreme folly: 25–30 million people dead from starvation.

Yet these starvation deaths are not routinely thought of as constituting a genocide or a holocaust, and they have not impacted our memory and sensibility with anything even remotely resembling the force and effect with which the Holocaust has nearly everywhere become part of the awareness of diverse political communities. On the one hand, denying the veracity of the Holocaust is a criminal offence under the law in Germany, and Holocaust-deniers face considerable opprobrium in various other countries as well; on the other hand, demographers and specialists in Chinese history and politics aside, the world has never been very much bothered by the history of famine mortality in modern China. Nor were these starvation deaths the only ones that took place in the name of development, or in the interest of proving right the pet theory of some economist. The famine mortality in India from 1876–1902 alone has been estimated, quite conservatively, at anywhere between 12 and 29 million, and at least one progressive British commentator who had the misfortune of witnessing the 1876 Madras famine prophesized

34 Michael Ward, in his otherwise novel study, *Quantifying the World: UN Ideas and Statistics* (Bloomington: Indiana University Press 2004), misses the entire politics of literacy measurements, such as those encountered in the United Nations Development Programme's *Human Development Report*.

that when 'the part played by the British Empire in the nineteenth century is regarded by the historian fifty years hence, the unnecessary deaths of millions of Indians would be its principal and most notorious monument'.[35] This pronouncement has gone the way of many other moral denunciations, deep into oblivion, and there are still British historians ready to pronounce British rule in India as well intentioned and, on the balance, good for India; but none of that should obscure the critical word in William Digby's assessment, namely his observation that the deaths were 'unnecessary'. Had Digby said 'wilful', he would still not have been doing injustice to his material. Farmers, villagers and communities were sacrificed not merely to poor policy, or to keep the Indian army and railways in good shape, but because colonial officials were of the firm view that purportedly tested theories of economic advancement and human development could not be surrendered to compassion, moral sentiment or emotional responses to which inferior beings, such as natives and women, were susceptible. In 1877 Richard Temple, charged with enforcing the famine code in the severely affected areas of the Deccan during the Viceroyalty of Lytton, was insistent that principles of free market economics should be brought to bear on the management of the famine. Half a million affected people were removed from public works. Temple refused permission to colonial officials to remit land taxes even in famine districts, and engineered, during the height of the famine, the passage of the Anti-Charitable Contributions Act of 1877, which (in Mike Davis's words) 'prohibited at the pain of imprisonment private relief donations that potentially interfered with the market-fixing of grain prices'.[36] Cutting rations for male coolies assigned to heavy labour, Temple set the daily caloric intake for them at 1,627, which compares with the approved diet (in 1981) of 2,050 calories for a seven-year-old child engaged in normal activity and the diet of 1,627 calories assigned to inmates of Buchenwald engaged in hard labour.[37] Davis rightly minces no words in describing Temple as the 'personification of free market economics as a mask for colonial genocide'.[38]

We are likely to see starvation deaths and the killings in concentration camps as discrete forms of violence, when in fact they are equally derived from the categories—development, bureaucracy, progress, instrumental rationality—of modernity. The victims of social engineering will surely not care to choose between different forms of death, but some victims are assured at least of monuments in their name. There are no monuments or

---

35 William Digby, quoted in Mike Davis, *Late Victorian Holocausts: El Niño Famines and the Making of the Third World* (London: Verso 2002), 8.

36 Davis, *Late Victorian Holocausts*, 39–40; this paragraph draws more generally on chs 1, 4, 5 and 10.

37 Ibid., 39. The exact diet at Buchenwald from 1939 until the liberation of the camp in 1945 is specified in *The Buchenwald Report*, trans. and ed. David A. Hackett (Boulder, CO: Westview Press 1945), 146–9.

38 Davis, *Late Victorian Holocausts*, 39.

memorials to the victims of development; ironically, they remain singularly 'underdeveloped' even in this respect. Many people would insist on knowing how one can speak of development's victims at all, and there a re even scholars who, while claiming to speak as progressive spokespersons on behalf of the 'genuinely' oppressed, can barely disguise their scorn at groups on behalf of whom victimhood status is sometimes claimed.[39] The very word 'development' perpetually unsings its own grave, so to speak: every parent is rightfully persuaded, for instance, that nothing should obstruct the development, or growth and well-being, of her or his child. A battery of experts exists in most modern cultures to provide the optimum conditions under which the development of children can transpire,[40] and no reasonable person considers the objective as less than laudable, though we all are also aware that many of the 'experts' are entirely dispensable.

What passes as 'common sense' impedes the placement of development alongside the Holocaust, genocide, wanton killing, destruction and dispossession. That is one obstacle to the construction of a political archaeology of the idea of development. Moreover, by the second half of the nineteenth century, if not earlier, social thinkers in the West had largely come to accept the idea that civilizations were to be placed alongside a scale, and a form of evaluative scale still survives, indeed thrives, in the idea of development. For this idea to be at all meaningful, it must presuppose that there are nations that are developed, others that are developing and yet others that doggedly persist in remaining underdeveloped, a testament to Oriental laziness or the savagery of a dark continent. Frequently, these terms are substituted by others, though each set has its own particular resonance. The term 'third world' had extraordinarily wide currency until very recently; among other terms that abound, one hears of 'post-industrial societies', of nations in the throes of 'advanced' or 'flexible' capitalism and of countries, which when not outright 'backward' are merely 'industrializing'. The countries of sub-Saharan Africa, as I have previously suggested, are sometimes called 'failed' states, and we know what remedies—structural adjustment, subjection to a regime of sanctions, even recolonization—lie in wait for those who fail; at the other extreme, the proponents of the 'development' lexicon are reluctant to use the word 'over-developed' to describe some of the developed states, though that description seems apt for

39 A particularly good example of such extreme insensitivity to, and mockery of, victims of development is Meera Nanda, *Prophets Facing Backward: Postmodern Critiques of Science and Hindu Nationalism in India* (New Brunswick, NJ: Rutgers University Press 2003).
40 For example, Betty Farber, *Guiding Young Children's Behavior: Helpful Ideas for Parents and Teachers from 28 Early Childhood Experts* (Garden City, NY: Preschool Publications 1998). The discussion in Colin Heywood, *A History of Childhood* (Cambridge: Polity Press 2001), is useful.

at least some countries whose appetite for consumption and self-aggrand-izement is also reflected in their obesity rates.[41]

In the near aftermath of the Second World War, the 'underdeveloped' areas of the world were invited to open themselves to intervention by the more 'developed' countries, as though genocide were so imbricated in the human sensibility at that juncture that another avenue had to be found for it, albeit couched in the language of benevolence. No one had quite reflected on Gandhi's observation that if a small island had to occupy a good deal of the world to satisfy its wants and vanity, one shuddered to think what the consequences would be for the world if a large country such as India resolved to imitate Britain. Had Gandhi been alive to witness the burgeoning economic 'development' of China and (to a somewhat lesser extent) India, one can be certain that he would have, far from wanting to recant his assessment, been firmly convinced that the ideology of development always hungers for sacrificial victims. Amidst widespread disease, hunger and malnutrition, numerous world organizations, such as the Department of Social and Economic Affairs at the UN, boldly inferred that rigorous demands, from the forfeiture of traditional livelihoods and the rejection of religious values to the painful adjustments required by the erosion of the moral economy and the conception of the commons,[42] could be placed upon those who wished to answer the irresistible calls to development.

By the mid-1950s, the idea of development had achieved the status of unimpeachable certainty, global in its reach and totalizing in its capacity to order and evaluate human relations. This was unequivocally the way to the future, and all who dared to reject development as an ill-thought panacea were condemned to become pariahs, the burnt carcasses and rejects of history. Yet the violence perpetrated in the name of development was never recognized as violence, and not merely because it makes for poor media coverage or less than sensational journalism. In what was more than a fleeting moment of fancy, Nehru conveyed the idealism that allowed his generation to view dams as the future 'temples' of humanity. Little thought would be given, over the next few decades, to the 40–80 million people conservatively estimated by the World Commission of Dams to have been displaced from their traditional homelands by dams, a displacement that, for

41 Some of these terms have other insidious histories: to take one example, 'flexible' capitalism is a short-hand for the corporate strategies that have led to 'downsizing', increase in part-time labour, the reduction of the permanent work force and the emasculation of labour unions. The discussion of development in this paragraph and the following draws largely on Lal, *Empire of Knowledge*, 111–13.

42 By 'commons' I mean not only the idea of shared public spaces, communal property and the common inheritance of communities (from the wisdom of the elders to shared knowledge about medicinal plants), but also everything that is implied in the phrase 'moral economy' as it is encountered in the writings of E. P. Thompson, the reflections of E. F. Schumacher and the intellectual and political practices of Mohandas Gandhi.

people whose attachment to their land cannot be measured by monetary worth, was often tantamount to loss of soul and life. Developmental violence on this scale has every characteristic of ethnic cleansing—the open targeting of a particular group, in this case the 'poor' and the 'underdeveloped', drawn largely from the ranks of ethnic minorities or indigenous peoples, and their subsequent eviction—but it is not recognized as such. Unlike practitioners of open genocide, who may have to face the gallows or the humiliation of trial before an international tribunal, the stalwarts of this form of ethnic cleansing are often fêted for their humanitarian contributions to human welfare. As Ivan Illich has suggested, what is particularly insidious in the idea of development is that, following the Nazi practice of employing Jews in unpaid labour as their own contribution to their death, it 'enlist[s] people in their own extinction'.[43] The future of concentration camps may be more grim than we commonly recognize.

Coda

The study of genocide has, as I have attempted to argue, been constrained: in part by the emphasis on groups or communities who have borne the brunt of oppression on account of their ethnicity, nationality or religious outlook; and in part by the tendency to dwell on violence in its most palpably naked forms, such as the extermination camps in which Jews were herded and then dispatched to their death or the brutally open incitements to violence of the sort witnessed in Rwanda where radio announcements spurred the Hutus to massacre the 'cockroaches'. Various other forms of genocide have gone wholly or largely unnoticed, and there is little prospect that we will even recognize the holocausts unfolding before our eyes until we understand the oppression of categories that have come to exercise a tyrannical sway over our lives. At least a few commentators have begun to recognize the truly genocidal potential of categories that are seen as innocent, as can be witnessed in the skepticism with which they receive invocations by the United States to the 'international community'. However much 'the international community' is presented as something of a natural, self-generated phenomenon, embodying the collective and moral will of humanity, there are also good reasons for viewing it as a newer, apparently more 'democratic', form of imposing the depraved morality of the powerful upon the powerless. Let us not forget that the decade-long sanctions regime put in place against Iraq, during which mortality rates in Iraq (and not only of children, though their deaths expectedly evoked more sympathy) skyrocketed, would not be terminated by the United States on the grounds

43 Ivan Illich, quoted in Claude Alvares, *Science, Development and Violence: The Revolt against Modernity* (Delhi: Oxford University Press 1994), 137.

that the 'international community' could not condone Iraq's flagrant violation of UN resolutions.[44]

There is, on sustained investigation, a transparency about 'international community' as a category of oppression that eludes many other categories. I commenced this paper with Eric Hobsbawm, and have previously remarked that Hobsbawm treats history as the unfolding of events, but never really pauses to understand history as a relatively recent category of now universal import. Let me, in closing, return to history and to its attempted monopoly over our conceptions of the past. Most societies lived without history textbooks—or, indeed, other textbooks, though here again history textbooks, over which controversies are often bitter and deep, have a salience in modern societies that is quite distinct—until they emerged as nation-states, although now a society without textbooks is all but inconceivable. Textbook publishing is a phenomenally huge and profitable business, and there is at least as much reason to be alarmed by textbook cartels as there is to fear oil cartels. Textbooks have homogenized forms of knowledge throughout the world, and societies that had numerous ways to engage with the past—myth, vernacular forms of knowing, the wisdom of elders, folktales, among others—have increasingly turned to history textbooks and to the narratives produced by professional historians to access the past and resolve disputes arising from its interpretation. As numerous historians, myself included, have documented in substantial detail, the controversy in India over the Babri Masjid, a sixteenth-century mosque in the north Indian city of Ayodhya, alleged by Hindu extremists to have been the site of a particularly significant Hindu temple before the temple was razed to make way for the mosque, was turned over to historians. On 6 December 1992, the Babri Masjid was destroyed by a crowd numbering in the thousands.[45] In the wake of this act of desecration, violence erupted in many parts of India.

Whatever the precise history of the now-extinct Babri Masjid, the mosque survived for well over 450 years, mostly during the time when Hindus did not care much for their history, and were certainly content to settle for what might be described as a very muddled history of the Babri Masjid. What makes modern forms of knowledge particularly oppressive for much of humankind is our diminishing capacity to live with ambiguity, an argument to which both George W. Bush and Osama bin Laden stand forth as sinister witnesses. Nothing can make nineteenth-century colonialism look benign, except of course to those who are still predisposed towards looking at colonialism as an endless variant of the narrative of 'Custer Died with His Boots On', but nonetheless the forms of colonization being attempted today suggest that the goriest chapters in genocide have yet to be written, most

---

44 Anthony Arnove, *Iraq under Siege: The Deadly Impact of Sanctions and War*, rev. edn (Cambridge, MA: South End Press 2002).

45 Vinay Lal, *The History of History: Politics and Scholarship in Modern India* (New Delhi: Oxford University Press 2003).

particularly if we keep in mind the most expansive conception of genocide as the extinction of distinct lifeforms and cultures. The present of the developing world, in the worldview of those who have set out to bring development to the unenlightened, is none other than the past, sometimes the very remote and mist-shrouded past, of the developed world; and, indeed, in this lies one of the greatest uses of the developing world, which preserves in its institutions and social practices the memory of a European past that is lost or of which there are only very dim traces. The 'barbarism' of the developing world is always a reminder to the 'developed' world of the past it left so long ago, and of the profound blessings of Christianity, reason and western science. The future of the developing world: well, there is no future, since its future is already known to Europe and America. Indeed, the developed world already lives the distant future of the developing world. As the future of the developing world as a whole is none other than the present of the developed world, so the future of the tribal or the peasant is only to live the limited conception of life of the planner, economist, policy analyst and management guru. The other word for such a future is 'genocide'.

Vinay Lal is Associate Professor of history at the University of California, Los Angeles (UCLA). His recent books include *Empire of Knowledge: Culture and Plurality in the Global Economy* (2002), *The History of History: Politics and Scholarship in Modern India* (2003), *Of Cricket, Guinness, and Gandhi: Essays on Indian History and Culture* (2003), *Introducing Hinduism* (2005), and (co-edited with Ashis Nandy) *The Future of Knowledge and Culture: A Dictionary for the Twenty-first Century* (2005).

Conceptual blockages and definitional dilemmas in the 'racial century': genocides of indigenous peoples and the Holocaust

A. DIRK MOSES

The author is grateful to Adrian Carton, Robert Cribb, Ned Curthoys, John Docker, Nick Doumanis, Geoff Eley, Andrew Fitzmaurice, Max Friedman, Simone Gigliotti, Martin Jay, Mark Levene, Ben Kiernan, Amelia Klein, Konrad Kwiet, Geoffrey Brahm Levey, Ken Macnab, Lawrence McNamara, Sam Moyn, Glenda Sluga, Ulrich Speck, Dan Stone, Eric Weitz and Jürgen Zimmerer for encouragement, references and constructive criticisms of earlier drafts. They are neither responsible for the views expressed here nor, of course, for any errors. I also thank Delwyn Elizabeth for her able research assistance, which was funded by the University of Sydney.

But even regarding History as the slaughter-bench at which the happiness of peoples, the wisdom of States, and the virtue of individuals have been victimized—the question involuntarily arises—to what principle, to what aim, these enormous sacrifices have been offered? [1]

Hegel was well aware of the terrible cost exacted by the march of civilization. Yet, precisely because the 'History of the World is not the theatre of human happiness', as he put it rather coyly, Hegel felt compelled to develop a philosophy of history that invested cosmic meaning in what otherwise would be an intolerable spectacle of pointless carnage. [2] He was thereby proposing a secular 'theodicy', a term coined by the German philosopher G. W. Leibniz in 1710 to mean 'justification of God'. [3]

In 1940, at the beginning of a European catastrophe that would urgently re-pose the question of evil, the German-Jewish critic Walter Benjamin poured scorn on theodicies because they necessarily view the past through the eyes of its victors and retrospectively justify their actions and morality. Could the European civilization that produced colonial violence and the First World War be the greater good that redeemed the immeasurable suffering it caused? 'There is no document of civilization which is not at the same time a document of barbarism', Benjamin wrote famously in his 'Theses on the philosophy of history'. [4] Rather than continue the destruction wrought by such barbarism, he urged 'anamnestic solidarity' with its victims as a way of interrupting the supposedly ineluctable and necessary 'progress' of civilization. [5]

Benjamin's plea for the primacy of the victims' point of view has certainly been absorbed by the scholarly community that studies genocides. But Hegel, or at least theodicy, still commands a following, for the enquiry into

1 G. W. F. Hegel, *The Philosophy of History* (New York: Dover 1956), 14.

2 Hegel, 26.

3 Zachary Braiterman incorrectly asserts that Leibniz coined the term 'after an earthquake devastated Lisbon in 1755', but Leiniz died in 1716!: Z. Braiterman, *(God) after Auschwitz* (Princeton, NJ: Princeton University Press 1998), 19.

4 Walter Benjamin, 'Theses on the philosophy of history', in W. Benjamin, *Illuminations*, ed. Hannah Arendt (New York: Schocken Books 1969), 256. Michael Löwy, 'Revolution against "progress": Walter Benjamin's romantic anarchism', *New Left Review*, no. 152, July–August 1985.

5 For an analysis of the concept of 'anamnestic solidarity' and its appropriation, see Max Pensky, 'On the use and abuse of memory: Habermas, "anamnestic solidarity", and the *Historikerstreit*', *Philosophy and Social Criticism*, vol. 15, no. 4, 1989, 351–81.

the extermination of so-called native or indigenous peoples continues to be overshadowed by the nationalistic and totalitarian 'cleansing' programmes of the twentieth century, particularly the Holocaust. Mark Mazower suggests two reasons for this low priority:

> I think there may have ... been a widely-held unspoken assumption that the mass killing of African or American peoples was distant and in some senses an 'inevitable' part of progress while what was genuinely shocking was the attempt to exterminate an entire people in Europe. This assumption may rest upon an implicit racism, or simply upon a failure of historical imagination.[6]

Another reason is the fact that the nation-states of 'the West', which are responsible for upholding human rights and the moral universalism on which they are based, profitted enormously from imperialism, and often owe their very existence to their projects of settlement. The genocides of indigenous peoples by colonial powers and settlers necessarily pose thorny questions today regarding the dark past or provenance of these societies.[7] Then there is the prosaic problem that very few scholars dispose over sufficient knowledge to make plausible comparisons and linkages between different genocidal episodes. The upshot is that the genocide of European peoples in the twentieth century strikes many American, Anglo-European and Israeli scholars as a more urgent research question than the genocide of non-Europeans by Europeans in the preceding centuries or by postcolonial states of their indigenous populations today.[8]

Underlying this asymmetry is the claim that the Holocaust is 'unique', 'unprecedented' or 'singular'. Its implications for the study of indigenous genocide are as significant as they are dire: that such 'lesser' or 'incomplete' genocides—if indeed they are considered genocides at all—are marginal or even 'primitive', thereby reinforcing hegemonic Eurocentrism;[9] and that the moral caché of the indigenous survivors of colonialism is less than that of Jews. Predictably, they are rejected by some scholars who counter that

6 Mark Mazower, 'After Lemkin: genocide, the Holocaust and history', *Jewish Quarterly*, vol. 5, winter 1994, 5–8.

7 For useful surveys of issues surrounding genocide and indigenous peoples today, see Robert T. Hitchcock and Tara M. Twedt, 'Physical and cultural genocide of various indigenous peoples', in Samuel Totten, William S. Parsons and Israel W. Charny (eds), *Genocide in the Twentieth Century* (New York and London: Garland Press 1995), 483–514; Katherine Bischoping and Natalie Fingerhut, 'Border lines: indigenous peoples in genocide studies', *Canadian Review of Sociology and Anthropology*, vol. 33, no. 4, 1996, 481–506; John H. Bodley, *Victims of Progress* (Menlo Park, CA: Cummings 1975).

8 Ziauddin Sardar, Ashis Nandy and Merryl Wyn Davies, *Barbaric Others: A Manifesto on Western Racism* (London and Boulder, CO: Pluto Press 1993); Donald Bloxham and Tony Kushner, 'Exhibiting racism: cultural imperialism, genocide and representation', *Rethinking History*, vol. 2, no. 3, 1998, 349–58.

9 Scott L. Montgomery, 'What kind of memory? Reflections on images of the Holocaust', *Con tention*, vol. 5, no. 1, autumn 1995, 101.

genocide lies at the core of western civilization,[10] and by others who extend its meaning to a wide variety of phenomena, for example, to a European interest in indigenous spirituality, birth control for African Americans, disease in Hawaii and the murder of street children in South American city slums.[11] 'The coinage has been debased', observes Michael Ignatieff with exasperation: 'What remains is not a moral universal which binds us all together, but a loose slogan which drives us apart.'[12] Identity politics and academic enquiry are often conflated in polemical expressions of group trauma, and rancour sets the tone. The question almost raises itself: should the victim's point of view be authoritative in this field when different victim groups make incommensurable, indeed competing, claims?[13]

If we are to move beyond this unproductive intellectual and moral stalemate, rehearsing the now familiar arguments is insufficient.[14] A critical perspective that transcends that of victims (articulated by Benjamin) and perpetrators and their descendants (advanced by Hegel) is clearly necessary. Whether it can be done with sensitivity is a question I am not in a position to answer. One method has been undertaken by the anthropologist Michael Taussig. Turning to Benjamin for inspiration, he invokes the presentational strategy of montage to disrupt the normative status of the given order, placing stress not on 'facts and information in winning arguments ... [but] ... the less conscious image realm and in the dreamworld of the popular imagination'.[15] But what if the popular imagination is

10 Native American scholar and activist Ward Churchill goes so far as to claim that the unique ness argument is tantamount to the denial of indigenous genocides; indeed, that it is worse, because it dovetails with the exculpatory imperatives of colonial-national governments at the expense of their impotent indigenous minorities, and is purveyed by those with institutional power: *A Little Matter of Genocide* (San Francisco: City Lights Books 1997), 31–6, 50.

11 Bron Taylor, 'Earthen spirituality or cultural genocide? Radical environmentalism's appro priation of native spirituality', *Religion*, vol. 27, 1997, 183–215; Simone M. Caron, 'Birth control and the black community in the 1960s: genocide or power politics?', *Journal of Social History*, vol. 31, no. 3, 1998, 545–69; O. A. Bushnell, *The Gifts of Civilisation: Germs and Genocide in Hawai'i* (Honolulu: University of Hawaii Press 1993); Nancy Scheper-Hughes, 'Small wars and invisible genocides', *Social Science and Medicine*, vol. 43, no. 5, 1996, 889–900.

12 Michael Ignatieff, preface, in Simon Norfolk, *For Most of It I Have No Words* (London: Dewi Lewis 1998).

13 Arlene Stein, 'Whose memories? Whose victimhood? Contests for the Holocaust frame in recent social movement discourse', *Sociological Perspective*, vol. 4, no. 3, autumn 1998, 519–41.

14 The relevant arguments have been analysed thoroughly in two recent publications: Gavriel D. Rosenfeld, 'The politics of uniqueness: reflections on the recent polemical turn in Holo caust and genocide scholarship', *Holocaust and Genocide Studies*, vol. 13, no. 1, 1999, 28–61; Alan S. Rosenbaum (ed.), *Is the Holocaust Unique?*, 2nd edn (Boulder, CO: Westview Press 2001).

15 Michael Taussig, *Shamanism, Colonialism, and the Wild Man* (Chicago and London: Univer sity of Chicago Press 1987), 368f.

hopelessly divided about the identity of the 'real' victims of history or the hierarchy of their suffering?[16] In that case, an approach that lays bare the group traumas blocking conceptual development and mutual recognition can aid in their working through, as well as in stimulating the critical reflection needed to rethink the relationship between the Holocaust and the indigenous genocides that preceded it.[17]

Trauma, the sacred and the profane

What is at stake in the 'uniqueness' question? In order to grasp its existential importance, it is necessary to appreciate that the events of the Holocaust were experienced by members of the victim group as a trauma of virtually metaphysical proportions, a defining rupture in personal and collective identity with world-historical significance. Many Jews, especially the direct survivors, accordingly treat this genocide as sacred,[18] and it has become an important marker of collective Jewish identity,[19] notwithstanding considerable discomfort in that community with such a heteronomous determination.[20]

Emile Durkheim's theory of the sacred provides a useful tool for understanding this phenomenon. Group identity, he wrote, is constituted by a shared sense of the basic division of the world into two domains, the sacred and the profane. The former comprises objects and events that are loved, venerated or dreaded, and that are superior in dignity to the ordinary world of the profane. This division implies an obvious hierarchy: the sacred is special, and the profane is not. Without a shared sense of the sacred, group identity would dissolve. But preserving the sacred status of certain objects

16 Katherine Bischoping and Andrea Kalmin, 'Public opinion about comparisons to the Holo caust', *Public Opinion Quarterly*, vol. 63, no. 4, winter 1999, 485.

17 Dominick LaCapra, *Writing History, Writing Trauma* (Baltimore and London: Johns Hopkins University Press 2001).

18 Adi Ophir, 'On sanctifying the Holocaust: an anti-theological treatise', *Tikkun*, vol. 2, no. 1, 1987, 61–7. Ophir calls it 'a new religion' with its own commandments: 'Thou shalt have no other holocaust'; 'Thou shalt not make unto thee any graven image or likeness'; 'Thou shalt not take the name in vain'; and 'Remember the day of the Holocaust to keep it holy, in memory of the destruction of the Jews of Europe'. Cf. Mark Levene, 'Is the Holocaust simply another example of genocide?', *Patterns of Prejudice*, vol. 28, no. 2, 1994, 6.

19 Peter Novick, *The Holocaust in American Life* (New York: Houghton Mifflin 1999). For critical discussion, see Harold Kaplan, 'Americanizing the Holocaust', in John K. Roth and Elisabeth Maxwell (eds), *Remembering for the Future*, vol. 1 (London: Palgrave 2001), 309–21; and Berel Lang, 'On Peter Novick s *The Holocaust in American Life*', *Jewish Social Stud ies*, vol. 7, no. 3, 2001, 149–58.

20 For a plea that the Holocaust not become 'the crucible of [Jewish] culture', see David G. Roskies, *Against the Apocalypse: Responses to Catastrophe in Modern Jewish Culture* (Cam bridge, MA: Harvard University Press 1984), 9. See also Michael André Bernstein, *Foregone Conclusions: Against Apocalyptic History* (Berkeley: University of California Press 1994), 10, 13.

and events is not only a matter of communal survival; it is a response to suffering. For the cosmic order provided by the sacred-profane division endows the survivor of trauma with 'more force either to endure the trials of existence or to conquer them'.[21]

Durkheim's analysis also helps expose other aspects of the Holocaust's sacredness. He calls the group's most holy thing or object its 'totem', the sacred aura of which extends to two further domains: the sign or representation of the totem, and the members of the clan (Durkheim had in mind indigenous Australians) who comprise the core of the community.[22] On this account, the survivors themselves assume a sacred status, and it is no surprise that they also vigilantly guard representations of the Holocaust lest it be defiled or contaminated.[23] This endeavour is necessarily sectarian. Finally, the Holocaust is read as a negative cult, a *piaculum*, as Durkheim would have it: the commemoration of a calamity, that is, a trauma.[24] Utilizing the literature on trauma, the historian Dominick LaCapra has come to similar conclusions:

> Those traumatized by extreme events, as well as those empathizing with them, may resist working through because of what might almost be termed a fidelity to trauma, a feeling that one must somehow keep faith with it ... Moreover ... there has been an important tendency in modern culture and thought to convert trauma into the occasion for sublimity, to transvalue it into a test for the self or the group and an entry into the extraordinary ... Even extremely destructive or disorienting events, such as the Holocaust or the dropping of the bombs on Hiroshima and Nagasaki may become occasions of negative sublimity or displaced sacralization. They may also give rise to what may be termed founding traumas—traumas that paradoxically become the valorized or intensely cathected basis of identity for an individual or a group rather than events that pose the problematic question of identity.[25]

Of course, contemporary Jewish individual and religious identity precedes the Holocaust and continues apart from it. Jewish identity is not automatically Holocaust-centric.[26] Yet, for some influential contributors to the field, the Holocaust does in fact possess this status, due perhaps to their catholic interest in the fate of all Jews, since all Jews, irrespective of religious

21 Emile Durkheim, *The Elementary Forms of Religious Life* (New York: Free Press 1915), 52–4, 142, 240, 464.
22 Ibid., 140, 150ff.
23 Witness the bitter protest of survivors against the New York exhibition, 'Mirroring evil: Nazi imagery/recent art', which opened on 17 March 2002. See Walter Reich, 'Appropriating the Holocaust', New *York Times*, 15 March 2002, A23.
24 Durkheim, 434ff.
25 LaCapra, 22–3.
26 Space does not permit considering the differences between Jewish identity in different countries.

or political hue, whether religious or secular, were potential victims of National Socialist designs. 'I admit that my personal starting point, my bias if you will', confesses the historian Yehuda Bauer, 'is formed by my overriding interest in the fate of the Jews'.[27] The Holocaust is the trauma that all Jews share and it functions thereby, George Steiner observes, as the cement binding post-Holocaust Jewry. The *Shoah* (a term he prefers to 'Holocaust' because of its connotation of sacrifice), he writes,

> is the one and only bond which unites the Orthodox Jew and the atheist, the practising Jew and the total secularist, the people of Israel and the Diaspora, the Zionist and the anti-Zionist, the extreme conservative Jew ... and the Jewish Trotskyite or Communist. Above all else, to be a Jew in the second half of this century is to be a survivor, and one who knows that his survival can again be put into question ... We are, in certain respects, a traumatised, a crazed people. How could we not be? Especially where it is that trauma which keeps us from final dispersal.[28]

Elie Wiesel has made the logical connection between trauma, group identity and the insistence of uniqueness:

> I always forbade myself to compare the Holocaust of European Judaism to events which are foreign to it. Auschwitz was something else. The Universe of concentration camps, by its dimensions and its design, lies outside, if not beyond, history. Its vocabulary belongs to it alone.[29]

Accordingly, he has expressed alarm that other victim groups are 'stealing the Holocaust from us ... we need to regain our sense of sacredness'.[30] Renowned scholars such as Lucy Dawidowicz, Steven T. Katz and Bauer do not differ from Wiesel and survivors in this regard, even if they locate the Holocaust in history. Bauer himself has pointed out the traumatizing effect of the Holocaust on Israeli society, demonstrated, above all, by its instrumentalization by all

27 Yehuda Bauer, 'A past that will not go away', in Michael Berenbaum and Abraham J. Peck (eds), *The Holocaust and History* (Bloomington: Indiana University Press 1998), 20. To be sure, Bauer maintains, against theologians, that the Holocaust is 'meaningless', but it none theless remains for him a sacred event in the Durkheimian sense.
28 George Steiner, 'The long life of metaphor: an approach to "the Shoah"', *Encounter*, February 1987, 57.
29 Elie Wiesel, 'Now we know', in Richard Arens (ed.), *Genocide in Paraguay* (Philadelphia, PA: Temple University Press 1976), 165. To be sure, in the Paraguayan genocide of the Aches, Wiesel recognizes the analogy: 'it is indeed a matter of a Final Solution: It simply aims at exterminating this tribe' (166).
30 Quoted in Robert G. L. Waite, 'The Holocaust and historical explanation', in Isidor Wallimann and Michael N. Dobkowski (eds), *Genocide and the Modern Age* (Westport, CT: Greenwood Press 1987), 169. Cf. Zev Garber and Bruce Zuckerman, 'Why do we call the Holocaust "the Holocaust"?', *Modern Judaism*, vol. 9, no. 2, 1989, 197–211.

sides in public debate for partisan political purposes.[31] And with characteristic forthrightness Katz insists on its centrality for Jewish identity:

> To understand ourselves [as Jews] requires ineluctably that we come to some
> grasp of these events [the Holocaust] and our relation to them ... Those who
> would enquire what it means to be a Jew today must ask not, or even pose
> primarily, vague and unformed questions about Jewish identity and the relation
> of Judaism and modernity and Judaism and secularity, but must rather articulate
> the much more precise and focused question through which all other dimensions
> of our post-Holocaust identity are refracted and defined: 'What does it mean to be
> a Jew after Auschwitz?' Auschwitz has become an inescapable *datum* for all
> Jewish accounts of the meaning and nature of covenantal relation and God's
> relation to man. Likewise, all substantial answers also need to be open and
> responsive to the subtleties of the dialectical alternation of the contemporary
> Jewish situation: that is, they must also give due weight to the 'miracle' which is
> the state of Israel. They must thoughtfully and sensitively enquire whether God is
> speaking to the 'survivors' through it, and if so how.[32]

Because Katz and Bauer locate the Holocaust at the centre of Jewish life, they
are forced to insist on its uniqueness, for to do otherwise would undermine
their personal identity and concept of collective Jewish existence.[33] The
significance Katz and Bauer attach to the Holocaust cannot be sustained if it
is 'merely' another case of the mass killing that punctuates human history,
for the problem of evil—the mystery of undeserved suffering—cannot be
faced without the sense of a cosmic meaning subtended by the division of
the world into sacred and profane domains.[34]

Consequently, both men have devoted considerable energy to establishing the logical corollary of their implicit faith in the sacredness of the
Holocaust, namely, the division of all genocide victims into the same two
categories, sacred and profane.[35] Although they profess not to posit a

---

31 Yehuda Bauer, 'We are condemned to remember', *Jerusalem Post*, 19 April 2001. Bauer
  assumes the posture of the analyst.
32 Steven T. Katz, *Post-Holocaust Dialogues* (New York and London: New York University
  Press 1983), 142f. and the chapter 'The "unique" intentionality of the Holocaust',
  287–318. Cf. Yehuda Bauer, who makes the same point in 'The place of the Holocaust
  in contemporary history', *Studies in Contemporary Jewry*, vol. 1, 1984, 224. Emil
  Fackenheim, 'Why the Holo caust is unique', *Judaism*, vol. 5, no. 4, autumn 2001,
  438–47.
33 Durkheim, 427–33, 462–79. Conversely, Jews that do not put the Holocaust at the
  centre of Jewish identity presumably do not have to insist on its uniqueness.
34 This point is elaborated in A. Dirk Moses, 'Structure and agency in the Holocaust:
  Daniel J. Goldhagen and his critics', *History and Theory*, vol. 37, no. 2, 1998, 194–219.
  See also Braiterman.
35 This observation is John M. Cuddihy's in 'The Holocaust: the latent issue in the
  uniqueness debate', in Philip F. Gallagher (ed.), *Christians, Jews and Other Worlds*
  (London and New York: University Press of America 1988), 62–79.

hierarchy of victims or to claim that individual Jewish victims suffered more than non-Jewish ones, the burden of their argument nonetheless is that the Jewish victims of the Holocaust are sacred, and that those of other genocides are not, because only the Jews as a group were singled out for total extermination.[36] For this reason, Bauer dismisses David E. Stannard's claim of an 'American Holocaust' (that is, of the Native Americans) with the telling statement that it 'cannot be seen on a *par* with the Holocaust'.[37]

Indeed, Bauer decries such equivalences as antisemitic. The temptation to 'submerge the specific Jewish tragedy in the general sea of suffering caused by the many atrocities committed by the Nazi regime', he fears, is in fact a 'worldwide phenomenon connected with dangers of anti-Semitism'.[38] Herewith, he acts out the two collective traumas of European Jewry: the suffering caused by more than a millennium of Christian anti-Judaism (including the Holocaust), and the 'second victimization' through the 'unspeakability' of the Holocaust in the immediate post-war years.[39] Now only the memory of the Jewish Holocaust can prevent the flourishing of the antisemitism that led to the catastrophe in the first place: 'A reversion back to "normalcy" regarding Jews requires the destruction of the Holocaust-caused attitude of sympathy'.[40] Understandable as this position is, it leaves Bauer open to the charge of Norman Finkelstein and denialists that he instrumentalizes the Holocaust to gain a moral advantage for Jews.[41]

Certainly, Bauer has made a career not only of policing the compound around the Holocaust, but also of regulating its meaning for Jewish self-understanding:

> all these universalizing attempts [regarding the Holocaust] seem to me to be, on the Jewish side, efforts by their authors to escape their Jewishness. They are

36 Steven T. Katz, *The Holocaust in Historical Context*, vol. 1 (New York: Oxford University Press 1994). See also Steven T. Katz, 'The Holocaust: a very particular racism', in Berenbaum and Peck (eds), 56–63, in which Katz takes pains to distinguish between the eugenic world-view that underlay Nazi policies towards all supposed racially inferior people from anti-Jewish racism.

37 Yehuda Bauer, 'Comparison of genocides', in Levon Chorbajian and George Shirinian (eds), *Studies in Contemporary Genocide* (New York: St Martin's Press 1999), 33, emphasis added.

38 Yehuda Bauer, 'Whose Holocaust?', in Jack Nusan Porter (ed.), *Genocide and Human Rights: A Global Anthology* (Lanham, MD: University Press of America 1982), 35, 38, reprinted from *Midstream*, vol. 26, no. 9, November 1980.

39 Jean-Michel Chaumont, *Die Konkurrenz der Opfer: Genozid, Identiät und Aerkennung*, trans. Thomas Laugstein (Lüneburg: Dietrich zu Klampen Verlag 2001). See also Gerd Korman, 'The Holocaust in American historical writing', *Societas*, vol. 2, no. 3, 1972, 251–70.

40 Bauer, 'Whose Holocaust?', 44.

41 Norman Finkelstein, *The Holocaust Industry* (London and New York: Verso 1999).

expressions of a deep-seated insecurity; these people feel more secure when they can say 'we are just like all the others'. The Holocaust should have proved to them that the Jews were, unfortunately, not like the others. Obviously it did not.[42]

The link between the ongoing maintenance of group identity and the sacredness of the Holocaust could hardly be made more explicitly than in this extraordinary statement.

Even Bauer's elucidation of the universal meaning of the Holocaust denies other victims of Nazi racial policies a place around its holy penumbra. The 'unique situation of Jewry in Western culture', he insists, meant that it alone was the object of fantasies of complete destruction; consequently, the specifically Jewish experience must be raised above all others in order to serve as a general warning for all minority groups, since they too could one day suffer a holocaust.[43] But this reasoning is muddled, because if the Jewish position in Europe was unique then the likelihood of another ethnic minority becoming the object of the same rhetoric of total extermination is more than highly improbable.[44] In fact, the logical conclusion of the argument that the less-than-total, non-Jewish, profane genocides are much more common is that they should be the focus of scholarly attention and public memory.

To be sure, Bauer has developed his position over the years, now characterizing the Holocaust as 'unprecedented' rather than 'unique', and pleading for a 'spectrum' of genocides, with the Holocaust at one end as the most extreme example of extermination. His sincere and generous advocacy on behalf of other victim groups is well known.[45] Yet, this concession to comparison does not alter significantly his consistently held belief since the 1970s that the differences between the Holocaust and other genocides outweigh any similarities, and that the Holocaust is thereby special (or sacred). He appears to confuse two, distinct tasks: on the one hand, reflecting specifically on the burden of history and identity for post-Holocaust Jewry; on the other, explaining generally how and why genocides occur. By collapsing the latter into the former, he ends up at times proffering identity politics in the name of disinterested scholarship.

Both in his and Katz's particular and universal rendering of the Holocaust, then, the centrality of Jewish victims must be foregrounded lest its meaning be traduced. In order to maintain the border between sacred

42 Bauer, 'A past that will not go away', 17.
43 Ibid., 43; Yehuda Bauer, *A History of the Holocaust* (New York: Franklin Watts 1982), 332.
44 See Dan Stone, *Constructing the Holocaust: Genocide and History* (London: Vallentine Mitchell, forthcoming). Bauer, *Rethinking the Holoca ust* (New Haven: Yale University Press, 2001), ch. 3: 'Comparisons with other genocides'; and Yehuda Bauer, 'Plenary address', in Roth and Maxwell (eds), 21–4.
45 Bauer is an active member of the Elmau Initiative: An International Taskforce to Prevent Genocide.

and profane victims of genocide, they have to downplay the similarities between all victims of genocide by referring, somewhat ironically, to Hitler's own faith in the 'redemptive' act of killing all Jews, an unfortunate authority to which to appeal.[46] The point of drawing attention to their strategies, however, is not to dispute the fact that the Holocaust can be distinguished from other genocides in important respects. It is to note in this field of enquiry that group trauma is acted out in truculently held intellectual positions whose articulators are prepared to climb out on very thin limbs to make their cases.

As might be expected, the uniqueness argument is a particular anathema to members of the victim groups it consigns to profane status.[47] Historians from these groups have responded in three ways. First, they question whether there was in fact a Nazi will for total extermination of Jews, thereby desanctifying Jewish victims.[48] Second, they claim that the Holocaust was a copy of the mass exterminations that had already taken place in the European colonies, thus claiming priority for such genocides. 'In fact, the holocaust of North American tribes was, in a way, even more destructive than that of the Jews', claims Russell Thornton provocatively, 'since many American Indian peoples became extinct'.[49] A third argument substitutes total regularity for absolute uniqueness: 'Queen Elizabeth, King Ferdinand, Queen Victoria, King Louis and so on were the "Adolf Hitler's" [sic] of their day', a collective of Canadian authors suppose. '"Auschwitz " was an everyday reality for many people across the world during the years of colonialism and the years that followed.'[50] The indignation stems from the fact that Native American deaths are considered 'unworthy' because they died at the hands of 'our very own [white] forebears', as Stannard notes: that

---

46 Cuddihy, 72.

47 It is also the object of attack by Jewish scholars. Ismar Schorsch warns that the insistence of uniqueness 'impedes genuine dialogue, because it introduces an extraneous, contentious issue that alienates political allies from among other victims of organized human depravity': 'The Holocaust and Jewish survival', *Midstream*, vol. 17, no. 1, January 1981, 39. Steven T. Katz attempts a refutation in his *The Holocaust in Historical Context*, 39–42; David Biale critically reviews Katz and attacks the uniqueness thesis in *Tikkun*, vol. 10, no. 1, January-February 1995, 79–82. See also the differentiated discussion by Irving L. Horowitz, 'Genocide and the reconstruction of social theory', in Wallimann and Dobkowski (eds), 61–80.

48 Ian Hancock, 'Uniqueness as denial: the politics of genocide scholarship', in Rosenbaum (ed.), 163–208. Hancock is greatly irritated by Bauer's contention that Gypsies represented only a 'minor irritant' for the Nazis.

49 Russell Thornton, *American Indian Holocaust and Survival* (Norman and London: Univer sity of Oklahoma Press 1987), xvi; M. Annette Jaimes, 'Sand Creek: the morning after', in M. Annette Jaimes (ed.), *The State of Native America* (Boston: South End Press 1992), 1–12; Churchill, *A Little Matter of Genocide*; David E. Stannard, *American Holocaust* (New York and Oxford: Oxford University Press 1992), 255.

50 Antoon A. Leenaars *et al.*, 'Genocide and suicide among indigenous people: the North meets the South', *Canadian Journal of Native Studies*, vol. 19, no. 2, 1999, 338.

is why there is no Holocaust Memorial for Native Americans or other victims.[51] This is a telling point, for most American public leaders and intellectuals are happy to pontificate about genocide in every country but their own.[52] Because of this taboo, Stannard has to resort to making creative analogies with the Holocaust: if Jews who died as slave labourers or of disease in the camps rather than in the gas chambers were equally victims of the Holocaust, then Native Americans who died in analogous circumstances, that is, from 'natural causes', were similarly victims of the 'American Holocaust'.[53]

Such reasoning is not the innocent product of the ivory tower as the prolific Native American scholar and activist Ward Churchill makes clear with endearing candour when he proclaims the purpose of his scholarship to be 'unequivocally political'. His explicit aim is to invest American Indians with 'every ounce of moral authority we can get. My first purpose is, and always has been, to meet my responsibilities of helping deliver that to which my people is due.'[54] Here are echoes of Bauer's position, and not surprisingly Churchill goes on also to claim uniqueness for the suffering of his group: 'The American holocaust was and remains unparalleled, both in terms of its magnitude and the degree to which its goals were met, and in terms of the extent to which its ferocity was sustained over time by not one but several participating groups.'[55]

That such a claim cannot be dismissed out of hand, as writers like Katz are inclined, has been shown recently by David Moshman in a searching article entitled 'Conceptual constraints on thinking about genocide'. The problem with definitions of genocide so far, he argues, is that they have been based on prototypes: a paradigmatic genocide underlies the normative definition against which all others are measured. Hitherto, the prototype has been the Holocaust, especially in relation to the centrality of state intention. But such a choice is conceptually capricious, he thinks, and there is no reason why another genocide could not be prototypical.

51 David E. Stannard, 'Preface', in Churchill, A Little Matter of Genocide, xviii. Here Stannard is influenced by the thesis of Edward Herman and Noam Chomsky that the West divides victims of genocide and government oppression into two categories, worthy and unworthy, depending on its foreign policy agenda. See their Manufacturing Consent: The Political Economy of the Mass Media (New York: Pantheon Books 1988), 37.

52 Symptomatic of this taboo is Samantha Power, A Problem from Hell: America and the Age of Genocide (New York: Basic Books 2002). She is scathing of the United States as an impotent bystander to genocides abroad, but does not consider the possibility that her country might be a co-perpetrator or that it was founded on genocide.

53 Stannard, American Holocaust, 255. By contrast, Gavriel Rosenfeld thinks that the unique ness thesis is a defensive response to attempts by writers like Stannard to equate all genocides (Rosenfeld). There is insufficient space here to address this issue.

54 Churchill, A Little Matter of Genocide, 11.

55 Ibid., 4.

Suppose, for example, that we construed the European conquest of the Americas as a singular and ultimate set of interrelated genocides. This mega-genocide ... has been deliberately aimed at, and has succeeded in eliminating, hundreds of discrete cultures throughout the Americas. Moreover, it has for the most part been a consensus policy, pursued generation after generation by the governments of multiple colonial and emerging nations ... The Holocaust, from this perspective, might be dismissed as relatively minor, having targeted only a handful of cultures and having ended after just a few years when the Nazi regime was defeated.[56]

Such a minimization of the Holocaust, Moshman adds, would be 'indefensible', but no less so than the 'routine genocide denials that result from taking the Holocaust as unique and/or prototypical'. The point, then, is to avoid one kind of mass death as prototypical.[57]

Indeed, there are good reasons to regard the indigenous critiques, at least in certain modes, with caution, for they too seek to be prototypical and proffer a metaphysics of their own. Consider Lilian Friedberg's 'Dare to compare' and John C. Mohawk's *Utopian Legacies*. Both authors attribute the colonial and twentieth-century genocides to the essence of the western intellectual tradition, namely, the epistemological hubris according to which all things are knowable and possible, and in the name of whose 'master race' other cultures and peoples can be destroyed.[58] For Friedberg, the universal meaning of the Native American Holocaust is elucidated when it is placed next to the Jewish Holocaust, for only in this way can the incubus of western civilization be laid bare. 'If we are to divert the disaster [of human self-destruction], Mount Rushmore must be placed on a par with burning synagogues, whose fires can never be extinguished.'[59]

Clearly, the problem with Holocaust-indigenous genocide discourse is that it is structured as a zero-sum game. Where Bauer and Katz see equations with the Jewish Holocaust as antisemitic and as the occlusion of its world-historical meaning, Friedberg regards the resistance to precisely such analogies as anti-Native American and the enabling condition for the continuing rape of the world by the western spirit. The discourse is also remarkably static because each side dogmatically asserts the similarities or differences between cases for its own advantage without exploring the conceptual and historical relations between them. What is more, whether the similarities are more significant than the differences is ultimately a political

56 David Moshman, 'Conceptual constraints on thinking about genocide', *Journal of Genocide Research*, vol. 3, no. 3, 2001, 436.
57 Ibid.
58 Lilian Friedberg, 'Dare to compare: Americanizing the Holocaust', *American Indian Quar terly*, vol. 24, no. 3, 2000, 353–80; John C. Mohawk, *Utopian Legacies: A History of Conquest and Oppression in the Western World* (Santa Fe, NM: Clear Lights Publishers 2000).
59 Friedberg, 373.

and philosophical, rather than a historical, question and, as we have seen, the answers are driven by passionate, extra-historical considerations. Consequently, creative research questions about the processes that link the genocides of modernity are hindered by the mechanism that prompts each side to stress the specialness (or sacredness) of its respective genocide in the face of contrary assertions.

This game has no winner, unless the dreary spectacle of assertion and counter-assertion can pass for innovative scholarship. It is time for historians in the field to play by other rules, namely, those of the community of scholars dedicated to presenting arguments directed to and for the world at large, rather than primarily to and for an ethnic or political group. It is necessary also for them to dispense with the vocabulary of uniqueness they have all appropriated and abused. Uniqueness is not a useful category for historical research; it is a religious or metaphysical category, and should be left to theologians and philosophers to ponder for their respective reading communities.[60] Where historians employ it, they stand in danger of relinquishing their critical role and assuming that of the prophet or sage who offers perspectives for group solidarity and self-assertion.

Indigenous scholars and their supporters may object that this entreaty sounds like yet another technology of western domination from which they can derive little benefit, because they need to cultivate group solidarity in the face of colonialist dissipation.[61] Yet, abandoning the communicative rationality inherent in the appeal to the putative universal reader risks relinquishing the very weapon with which to unmask exploitation and extermination. Moreover, an overarching moral consensus on the value of alterity is necessary to secure its existence, and this perforce entails appealing to standards of verification to which everyone can assent. To valorize difference implies the universalization of this particular good.[62] But what if most readers view colonial genocide through the lenses of the Holocaust and thereby discount it, as Churchill and others complain? Counter-claiming uniqueness or primacy of indigenous genocides may have raised the profile of the latter, but it can no longer advance the scholarly or political

60 Philosophical reflections include: Raimond Gaita, *A Common Humanity: Thinking about Love, Truth and Justice* (London: Routledge 2000); Avishai Margalit and Gabriel Motzkin, 'The uniqueness of the Holocaust', *Philosophy and Public Affairs*, vol. 25, no. 1, 1996, 65–83. There is insufficient space here to consider Steven T. Katz's claims to have access to a 'phenomenological' reality in which the Holocaust is unique: *The Holocaust in Historical Context*, 51–64. Surprising is the little space he devotes to justify posing the question in the first place.

61 In the place of numerous references: Hayden White, *The Content of the Form* (Baltimore and London: Johns Hopkins University Press 1987), 80f.; and Jan Kociumbas, 'Introduction', in Jan Kociumbas (ed.), *Maps, Dreams, History: Race and Representation in Australian History* (Sydney: Department of History, University of Sydney 1998).

62 Thomas McCarthy, 'Doing the right thing in cross-cultural representation', *Ethics*, no. 3, 1992, 644. McCarthy calls the resulting ethic 'multicultural universalism'.

discussion. The categories and critical tools with which historians approach the subject need to be rethought.

Rival theories of colonial genocide

How might we replace the current static relationship between Holocaust and preceding genocides with one that allows the reconstruction of the dynamic historical relations between them?[63] The place to start is with an examination of the contending theories of colonial/indigenous genocide. Broadly speaking, they fall into two camps. The first I call 'liberal' because it stresses the agency of the state as the intending genocidal subject. The second I call 'post-liberal' because it emphasizes the structural determinants of policy development as well as the social forces in civil society that precipitate mass death and disperse centralized exterminatory intention and agency. The former corresponds to the Holocaust paradigm, the latter to the alternative proposed by its indigenous and other critics. Somewhat confusingly, both approaches revolve around the Holocaust and both lay claim to the authority of Raphael Lemkin, the first theorist of genocide. Yet, the underlying issue is the definition of 'genocide' itself, because whether or not colonialism has an inner affinity with genocide depends on how one defines the term, conceptualizes exterminatory intention and locates the agent that can possess it.

A liberal theory of colonial genocide

Consistent with the uniqueness paradigm, liberal theorists insist that genocide, both as a concept and as formulated in the United Nations Convention of 1948, entails the eventual physical extermination or extinction of a people or ethnic group, and not cultural genocide, that is, the effacement of group identity without killing.[64] Or they distinguish between genocide (partial destruction of a group, physical or otherwise) and holocaust (intended complete physical destruction).[65] Although Bauer, for example, regards Lemkin's 1944 definition of genocide as muddled because it supposedly does not distinguish clearly between the two, he exemplifies the liberal position with its emphasis on premeditation as the key element of

---

63 An admirable study that avoids playing the uniqueness game without diminishing the obvi ous importance of the Holocaust to modern European history is Omer Bartov, *Mirrors of Destruction* (Oxford: Oxford University Press 2000).

64 Pieter N. Drost, *Genocide* (Leiden: A. W. Sijthoff 1959); Pieter N. Drost, *The Crime of State: Penal Protection for Fundamental Freedoms of Persons and Peoples* (Leiden: A. W. Sijthoff 1959). Drost recommended that political groups should also be included in the definition.

65 Gaita; Andrew Markus, 'Genocide in Australia', *Aboriginal History*, vol. 25, 2001, 50–70.

the crime.[66] Did not Lemkin himself deliver the formulation when he wrote that genocide is 'a synchronized attack' and 'a co-ordinated plan of different actions aiming at the destruction of the essential foundations of life of national groups, with the aim of annihilating the groups themselves'?[67] On this reading, the agency of the perpetrator and its exterminatory *mens rea* is clearly identifiable. Genocide is established when an agent, in particular the modern state, can be determined to possess the requisite genocidal intention. This focus has a number of important consequences.

The first concerns the origin of intention, which is held to lie in the motives of the perpetrator. Liberals, who are mostly North American political scientists, are inclined to typologize genocides according to motive, distinguishing for example between 'developmental' or 'utilitarian' genocides of indigenous peoples and 'ideological' genocides of scapegoated or hostage groups.[68] According to one prominent liberal, Roger W. Smith, the motive in colonial situations is easy to identify, namely, 'greed': 'The basic proposition of utilitarian genocide is that some persons must die so that others can live well.'[69]

The second consequence is that liberals insist on the primary role of the state as the genocidal perpetrator.[70] As Frank Chalk argues, the United Nations Convention was aimed at states because only they have the power at once to commit and prevent genocide. So even when the actual killing of indigenous groups is carried out by ranchers or land speculators, the state is turning a blind eye and is therefore ultimately responsible. Because the state is conceived of in Rankean terms as an individual personality, genocide is held to issue from ideologies about it (like fascism) rather than a prior cause in civil society.[71] The phenomena scholars should study are therefore clear when Chalk reminds his readers: 'we must never forget that the great genocides of the past have been committed by [state] perpetrators who acted

66 Bauer, 'Whose Holocaust', 43f.
67 Raphael Lemkin, *Axis Rule in Occupied Europe* (Washington, DC: Carnegie Foundation 1944), xi, 79; Yehuda Bauer, *The Holocaust in Historical Perspective* (Seattle: University of Washing ton Press 1978), 35.
68 See the discussion of the various positions in Barbara Harff and Ted Robert Gurr, 'Toward empirical theory of genocides and politicides', *International Studies Quarterly*, vol. 32, 1988, 359–71; Helen Fein, 'Scenarios of genocide and critical responses', in Israel Charny (ed.), *Towards the Understanding and Prevention of Genocide* (Boulder, CO: Westview Press 1984), 3–31.
69 Roger W. Smith, 'Human destructiveness and politics: the twentieth century as an age of genocide', in Wallimann and Dobkowski (eds), 25.
70 Helen Fein, 'Genozid als Staatsverbrechen. Beispiele aus Rwanda und Bosnien', *Zeitschrift für Genozidforschungen*, vol. 1, 1999, 36–45; Frank Chalk and Kurt Jonassohn, *The History and Sociology of Genocide* (New Haven and London: Yale University Press 1990), 23.
71 The legacy of German historicism in the liberal mindset awaits its analyst. An excellent study of Rankeanism is Georg G. Iggers, *The German Conception of History*, rev. edn (Middletown, CT: Wesleyan University Press 1983).

in the name of absolutist or utopian ideologies aimed at cleansing and purifying their worlds.'[72] Liberal theories of genocide are really theories of totalitarianism.

There are a number of problems with the liberal position. To begin with, its account of genocidal intentions is radically voluntarist and can only 'explain' why they develop with circular logic by referring to the intentions of the perpetrator. The liberal categorization of genocides simply names the different contexts in which genocides occur and comes to the solipsistic conclusion that perpetrators commit them because they want to. Such a perspective conceptually insulates the state from powerful social forces that push for the expulsion or extermination of native peoples on coveted land. The individualistic motive of 'greed' in indigenous genocides, for example, is left dangling in the air, a consequence of imagining the world in terms of atomistic agents somehow free from the tangled skein of relations that mediate state agency and make it the articulator, however oblique, of deeper social conflicts. The economic system and inter-state rivalry are ignored as salient factors.

Then there is the prioritization of the 'great genocides' of the twentieth century, based as they were on totalitarian ideologies. Who would gainsay their enormity, but the argument is hardly conclusive when seen in light of the fact that, as Katz himself admits, 'sheerly as a matter of quantity the Indian catastrophe [between the sixteenth and nineteenth centuries] is unparalleled'.[73] Scholars from non-western backgrounds can point out that 'more people have been killed in the name of "development" this century [the twentieth] than have been killed by all the genocides put together, but we are still overwhelmingly reluctant to recognize "development" as another form of "genocide"'.[74]

Clearly, the emphasis on state intention and totalitarian ideology directs attention away from the social forces extant in all modernizing and colonizing societies that seek to sequester indigenous land and kill its owners if they are resisted. Implicitly, the liberal position deems the massive deaths on which European and North American societies are based as non-genocidal and therefore less worthy of scholarly attention.[75] They were but the unintended consequences of colonization. Where conscious extermination did occur, it issued from individual vice ('greed') rather than the structural imperatives or logics of the colonization process. The real enemy is

---

72 Frank Chalk, 'Redefining genocide', in George J. Andreopolous (ed.), *Genocide: Conceptual and Historical Dimensions* (Philadelphia: University of Pennsylvania Press 1994), 58ff.

73 Katz, *Holocaust in Historical Context*, 91. Cf. Tzvetan Todorov, *The Conquest of the Ameri cas* (New York: HarperCollins 1985), 5.

74 Vinay Lal, 'Genocide, barbaric others, and the violence of categories', *American Historical Review*, vol. 103, October 1998, 1190.

75 Symptomatic is Kurt Glaser and Stefan T. Possony, *Victims of Politics: The State of Human Rights* (New York: Columbia University Press 1979).

the totalitarian drive to perfection, a deviant form of modernity resisted heroically by the West, itself largely innocent of the intended physical destruction of a people. The liberal position reveals itself thereby as a theodicy, justifying the suffering of indigenous peoples in the name of the western civilization that has been constructed on their land and graves. Here indeed are faithful disciples of Hegel.

The attendant conceptual blockage is evident in the liberal reaction to the foregrounding of non-state genocidal pressures that post-liberals stress. One of their number dismisses such thinking because it 'suggests the normal-ization of the genocidal process and the concomitant impossibility of devising preventive measures', an observation that both understands and misunderstands the post-liberal critique in equal measure.[76] Another is happy to concede that 'it was the hand-in-glove pressure of American settlers and the military might deployed by the government of the United States that destroyed large numbers of the American Indians', yet concludes astonishingly that this fact reveals nothing about 'the nature of American society'.[77] In the end, liberals offer no coherent account of why genocides take place in colonial situations. Either they deny the mass death that attends colonization is genocidal, or they ascribe extermination to contingencies like 'greed', a human vice hardly confined to colonial situations. Here we have a spectacular failure of what C. Wright Mills called 'the sociological imagina-tion', that is, the complex interplay of structure and agency necessary to understand individuals, their inner life and action.[78] Does the post-liberal conception of genocide offer any more?

Post-liberal theories

Where liberals legitimize western societies, post-liberals delegitimize them by essentially equating genocide and colonialism, thereby sullying their liberal foundation myths.[79] And they do so by appealing also to the Holocaust and Lemkin's definition of genocide. For, while some statements in his book *Axis Rule in Occupied Europe* do indeed emphasize planning and premeditation, others cast the German policies in Eastern Europe as emphatically colonial. As Robert Davis and Mark Zannis, Ward Churchill and, most recently, Ann Curthoys and John Docker have stressed, Lemkin regarded the German project in these terms because it was the Nazis' sure

76 George J. Andreopolous, 'Introduction: the calculus of genocide', in Andreopolous (ed.), 9.
77 Chalk, 'Redefining genocide', 56ff.
78 C. Wright Mills, *The Sociological Imagination* (New York: Oxford University Press 1959), ch. 1.
79 On the importance of foundation myths, see A. Dirk Moses, 'Coming to terms with the past in comparative perspective: Germany and Australia', *Aboriginal History*, vol. 25, 2001, 91–115.

intention to secure permanent biological superiority over the indigenous peoples (Slavic and Jewish) by settling ethnic Germans in their stead.[80]

> Genocide has two phases [Lemkin wrote]: one, destruction of the national pattern of the oppressed group; the other, the imposition of the national pattern of the oppressor. This imposition, in turn, may be made upon the oppressed population which is allowed to remain, or upon the territory alone, after removal of the populations and the *colonization* of the area by the oppressors' own nationals.[81]

In elaborating his definition, Lemkin adumbrated the means by which such a destruction could take place, and mass murder was only one among them. Because genocide attacked 'nationhood', he included language restrictions on subject peoples, the abolition of their law courts and other such measures.[82] For this reason, post-liberals contend that the first formulation of the concept included cultural genocide in its core; that is to say, genocide did not necessitate mass murder or even eventual biological extirpation.[83] What is more, there is no qualitative difference between mass murder and cultural genocide, because the latter destroys the indigenous systems of meaning and ultimately the survivors' will to live, resulting ultimately in widespread death.[84]

All the more dismaying, post-liberals lament, was the incremental restriction of Lemkin's promising start in the immediate post-war years as Cold War politics conspired to produce the restrictive and anodyne UN Convention in 1948 with its requirement of explicit exterminatory intention, and the exclusion of cultural genocide as a crime and political groups as possible targets. In other words, the original post-liberal understanding of genocide was replaced by a liberal one for the benefit of nation-states, a limitation they instituted because they regularly utilize technologies of governance that post-liberals would define as genocidal. As Ward Churchill complains:

> Arguably ... the physical/cultural eradication of entire human groups, or their systematic reduction to whatever extents are deemed desirable by perpetrator

80 Robert Davis and Mark Zannis, *The Genocide Machine in Canada* (Montreal: Black Rose Books 1973), 12; Ann Curthoys and John Docker, 'Introduction—Genocide: definitions, questions, settler-colonies', *Aboriginal History*, vol. 25, 2001, 1–15.

81 Lemkin, 79, emphasis added.

82 Ibid., 82–90.

83 Ward Churchill, 'Forbidding the "G-word": Holocaust denial as judicial doctrine in Canada', *Other Voices: The (e)Journal of Cultural Criticism*, vol. 2, no. 1, February 2000: www.othervoices.org/2.1/churchill/denial.html (as of 25 July 2002).

84 In terms of group survival, Davis and Zannis (180) argue that cultural genocide is more dam aging than physical annihilation, because the survivors of the latter can garner more support than the deracinated remnants of assimilated indigenous groups.

societies, has increasingly become not only a mode by which racial, ethnic and religious conflicts are 'resolved', but a fundamental method employed by governments and attendant elites to attainment of political homogeneity, from adjustments at the micro level of their national economies to the tuning at the macro level of the international economy as a whole.[85]

Here he draws on the work of Davis and Zannis who argue that after 1945 traditional colonial terror was transformed into a 'genocide machine' as the nature of capitalist domination became less overtly racist, more attuned to American corporate imperatives, but above all driven by technological automation that issues in total wars, as in the Vietnam War. Accordingly, they can equate the Holocaust and the bombing of Hiroshima and Nagasaki as the culmination of the previous phase of colonial violence, characterized as it was by the imposition of genocidal terror on subject peoples to prevent their feared retaliation. The current post-war phase goes further in perpetrating an 'autogenocide' on the entire human race by creating a homogeneous western-world culture and thereby obliterating discrete ethnic and national groups.[86]

Here we are again with Mohawk's and Friedberg's attribution of exterminatory effects to western liberalism. But the originator of this link was Jean-Paul Sartre whose intervention in 1968 in the context of the Vietnam War is regarded by post-liberals as the breakthrough to the recovery of the original Lemkinian intention.[87] Sartre also distinguished between modes of colonial domination: until 1945, it always entailed cultural genocide because it 'cannot take place without the systematic elimination of the distinctive features of the native society', but physical annihilation was checked by the need for indigenous labour.[88] With the post-war anti-colonial struggles for national liberation, however, the mobilization of the entire subject populations made impossible the distinction between combatants and civilians, so the only way for colonial powers to respond to the inevitable guerrilla resistance was to annihilate part of the population in order to terrorize the rest, a policy he denounced as genocidal.[89]

Sartre concluded with the elliptical statement that highly industrialized and under-developed countries must perforce exist in 'a relationship of genocide expressed through racism', but it is unclear what he meant.[90] The tantalizing suggestion of an objective dimension to genocide that supersedes

85 Churchill, A Little Matter of Genocide, 400.
86 Davis and Zannis, 30ff., 175ff.
87 Churchill, A Little Matter of Genocide, 416.
88 Jean-Paul Sartre, 'On genocide', *New Left Review*, no. 48, 1968, 16. Cf. Davis and Zannis, 30.
89 Sartre, 17.
90 Ibid., 24.

the subjective exterminatory intention was made explicit by Tony Barta in a much-discussed book chapter, 'Relations of genocide: land and lives in the colonization of Australia'.[91] Unlike Sartre, Barta is interested in explaining the 'genocidal outcomes' in colonial societies before the Second World War, and he finds in the concept of 'relations of genocide' a way of obviating the centrality of state policy and premeditation in the hegemonic liberal definition of the term. Indigenous deaths more often were the result of the unintended consequences of colonization (diseases, starvation, declining birthrate), but should they therefore be excused as accidental? Barta refutes the inference thus:

> Genocide, strictly, cannot be a crime of unintended consequences; we expect it to be acknowledged in consciousness. In real historical relationships, however, unintended consequences are legion, and it is from the consequences, as well as the often muddled consciousness, that we have to deduce the real nature of the relationship.[92]

He concludes that all Australians live in objective 'relations of genocide' with Aborigines, and that Australia was a 'genocidal society' because its original inhabitants were fated to die in enormous numbers by the pressure of settlement despite the eventual protective efforts of the state and philanthropists. A similar argument has been made recently by Alison Palmer, who shows how colonial genocides are often 'society-led' rather than 'state-led'.[93]

The Australian historians Raymond Evans and Bill Thorpe have continued this line of thinking, proposing a new term altogether, 'indigenocide', which they distinguish from the Holocaust with its concerted, state-driven, bureaucratic and industrial killing. Although Lemkin does not appear in their footnotes, the concept has clear affinities with his definition:

> 'Indigenocide' is a means of analysing those circumstances where one, or more peoples, usually immigrants, deliberately set out to supplant a group or groups of other people whom as far as we know, represent the Indigenous, or Aboriginal peoples of the country that the immigrants usurp.[94]

It has five elements: the intentional invasion/colonization of land; the conquest of the indigenous peoples; the killing of them to the extent that

---

91 Tony Barta, 'Relations of genocide: land and lives in the colonization of Australia', in Wallimann and Dobkowski (eds), 237–52.
92 Ibid., 239.
93 Alison Palmer, *Colonial Genocide* (Adelaide: Crawford House 2000), 209. For Palmer, this distinction is more important than terms like 'colonial genocide'.
94 Raymond Evans and Bill Thorpe, 'The massacre of Aboriginal history', *Overland*, no. 163, September 2001, 36.

they can barely reproduce themselves and come close to extinction; their classification as vermin by the invaders; and the attempted destruction of their religious systems. Indigenocide is consistent with the continued existence of indigenous peoples where they are classified as a separate caste.[95] Accordingly, not all imperialisms are genocidal. The British occupation of India, for example, was not a project of settlement, and the colonizers relied on the labour of the locals, which, as Sartre had noted earlier, was an impediment to physical genocide.[96]

What are we to make of these post-liberal theories? Their obvious virtue is to correct the liberal blindness regarding the non-state determinants of genocidal behaviour and policy development. They show that indigenous genocides were not merely the contingent outcome of aberrant settler violence, but inhered in the structure and logic of the colonial project.[97] The implications of Barta's case are especially striking, in particular his point that, while colonial Australia was a genocidal society rather than a genocidal state, Nazi Germany was a genocidal state but not a genocidal society. Here is food for thought that liberals have been reluctant to digest.[98] Yet, the post-liberal insights come at the cost of a certain blindness, namely, blurring an important distinction and proposing a static model that bypasses rather than confronts the problem of the exterminatory consciousness.

To begin with, is it really satisfactory to equate cultural genocide and physical extermination? Few deny that the former is 'horrible', as Zannis, Davis and Churchill insist, but this equation defies deeply held intuitions that probably precede the Holocaust, and I wonder whether it would command a majority. And is Lemkin really an authority for the inclusion of cultural genocide in the core definition of genocide? He explicitly rejected denationalization as a synonym for genocide because it did not connote biological destruction of a people.[99] His listing of cultural measures that destroyed a people are subtended by the intention to eradicate them biologically, not merely to deculturate them. What befell the Jews, he thought, ultimately awaited many Slavic peoples even if less totally; and

95 Ibid., 37. Some of these items, particularly the question of intention to destroy a group 'in part', are discussed and approved by the International Criminal Tribunal for Former Yugo slavia: see Prosecutor v. Radislav Krstic at www.un.org/icty/krstic/TrialC1/judgement/ index.htm (as of 25 July 2002).
96 Whether land or labour is the object of the colonial economy is obviously a key variable. For discussions, see Palmer; Patrick Wolfe, 'Land, labor, and difference: elementary structures of race', American Historical Review, vol. 106, no. 3, June 2001; Michael Freeman, 'Genocide, civilization and modernity', British Journal of Sociology, vol. 46, no. 2, 1996, 207–23.
97 Cf. Patrick Wolfe, 'Nation and MiscegeNation: discursive continuity in the post-Mabo era', Social Analysis, vol. 36, 1994, 93–152.
98 Frank Chalk, Definitions of Genocide and Their Implications for Prediction and Prevention (Montreal: Montreal Institute of Genocide Studies 1988), 10–12.
99 Lemkin, 80.

sure enough the Germans did intend to starve tens of millions of Slavs to reduce the number of 'useless eaters' to make room for the colonization of ethnic Germans.[100] Bauer and Churchill both misread him on this point.[101] Of course, by insisting on cultural genocide as the core of genocide *per se*, the link to colonialism is much easier to establish, especially in relation to policies of assimilation after the conquest of indigenous resistance. It is open to question, also, whether by insisting on its equal status, post-liberals ignore the dynamic relations between cultural and physical genocide, namely, the potential for escalation from the one to the other when the former is successfully resisted, or the de-escalation to the former when indigenes have been 'pacified'.

Which leads to the static nature of most post-liberal theories. They either posit a checklist of features akin to the liberal love of typologies or, in their radical mode, make a straight equation between settler colonialism and the Holocaust based on the formal criteria of the common striving for living space based on the European sense of racial superiority.[102] Does the concurrence of such formal criteria prove the substantial similarity between the nineteenth-century colonization projects of western, liberal states and Nazi imperialism in Eastern Europe? One could object that the differences are also significant. The one was totalitarian, the other liberal enough that a Native American like Ward Churchill could eventually occupy an academic position at a state university of the perpetrator society (University of Colorado, Boulder). Here, too, the question of theodicy is apparent. The reluctance to advocate western civilization as the good that redeems indigenous suffering is understandable. In light of the knowledge about the fatal impact of colonization on indigenous peoples, who can now preach that gratitude is the appropriate response to the blessings of this civilization? But it is not necessary to commend this theodicy to insist that distinctions be made: Nazi universities did not hire the people it conquered and exterminated.

Ultimately, the post-liberals' account of *why* genocides occur to indigenous peoples is as unsatisfactory as the liberal one. It tends only to deal with the vexed question of intention by defining it away in terms of objective relationships in which no one may be responsible for the mass death.[103] Processes of colonization are denuded of conscious actors, which indicates as impoverished a sociological imagination as the one-sided liberal stress on

100 Ulrich Herbert (ed.), *National Socialist Extermination Policies* (New York: Berghahn Books 2000).
101 Cf. Alan Rosenberg, 'Was the Holocaust unique?', in Wallimann and Dobkowski (eds), 154ff.
102 Churchill, *A Little Matter of Genocide;* Jaimes, 4ff.; Lal, 1188.
103 Helen Fein, *Genocide: A Sociological Perspective* (London: Sage 1990), 80. Fein's own pro posal for the better specification of 'criminal acts and ... standards for social policy to differ entiate policies and strategies which protect and which destroy indigenous peoples' is vague and does not address the salient issues.

agency. The fact is that genocide was not an inevitable consequence of European penetration, exploitation, occupation and settlement of the New World. Certainly always racist, colonial regimes could be discriminatory, slaveholding or apartheid-like in character without resorting to extermination.[104] And yet, sometimes it became a policy option. Post-liberals do not examine how occupation policies that are not initially murderous can radicalize or escalate in an exterminatory direction when they are resisted. If the logic of settler colonialism is to occupy and exploit the land (rather than indigenous labour), then it displays *genocidal moments* when the process is put under pressure and is in crisis.[105] In other words, colonialism needs to be viewed as a dynamic process. And, as Mark Levene has stressed, it must also be set in international context. The struggle to construct viable nation-states is an imperative that plays itself out on the violent frontier far away from the metropolitan capitals of Europe.[106] Sartre saw this potential in post-war genocides, but it is in the pre-war context that they are in fact most apparent. And this is when the so-called 'unintended consequences' of civilization were indulged by colonial and metropolitan elites.

Towards a new theory of indigenous genocide and the Holocaust

It is too simple, then, to argue that colonialism is basically non-genocidal (the liberal view) or that it essentially is (the post-liberal view). But what of the philosophical argument that genocide is an 'essentially contested concept'? Like 'art', 'social justice' or 'the Christian life', it is necessarily open, persistently vague, and definable in various ways because no criteria exist by which to adjudge one definition as 'true', and no amount of discussion can settle the issue conclusively.[107] The conceptual blockages and definitional dilemmas we have canvassed so far suggest that the concept is fated to exist without an ultimate determination of its meaning. Too much trauma has been caused, and too many individual and group emotions and political claims are invested in the term for it to be regarded as a purely heuristic

104 George M. Fredrickson, *The Comparative Imagination: On the History of Racism, Nation alism, and Social Movements* (Berkeley: University of California Press 1997).

105 I attempt to apply this approach to Australian colonialism in A. Dirk Moses, 'An antipodean genocide? The origin of the genocidal moment in the colonization of Australia', *Journal of Genocide Research*, vol. 2, no. 1, 2000, 89–106.

106 Mark Levene, 'A dissenting voice: Or how current assumptions of deterring and prevent ing genocide may be looking at the problem through the wrong end of the telescope', *Journal of Genocide Research*, vol. 5, 2003, forthcoming; Mark Levene, *Genocide in the Modern Age*, vol. 1, *The Coming of Genocide* (Oxford: Oxford University Press 2003, forthcoming).

107 William E. Connolly, *The Terms of Political Discourse*, 3rd edn (Princeton, NJ: Princeton University Press 1993), 10–41. W. B. Gallie, 'Essentially contested concepts', in Max Black (ed.), *The Importance of Language* (Englewood Cliffs, NJ: Prentice-Hall 1962), 121–46.

device. And, after all, more than a strong whiff of criminality attends any policy or process associated with the term. But this does not entail intellectual defeat. If the positivism implicit in the vain search for a neutral definition is no longer sustainable on epistemological grounds, the challenge for historians and social scientists is to work through their often traumatic emotional investment in their own position and engage in two tasks: acknowledge the broad areas of consensus in the discussion; and try to imagine the genocides of modernity as part of a single process rather than merely in comparative (and competitive) terms. Let us address each in turn.

Despite the polemics, an implicit consensus exists regarding the relationship between structure and agency because the two can never be separated entirely. Structures cannot exist without their embodiment in human beings, a relationship recognized by Marx when he wrote: 'Men make their own history, but they do not make it just as they please.'[108] If agency is indispensable, then the question of intention cannot be defined away, especially if one wants to retain the radically transgressive nature of genocide, a heinous crime in international law. Criminality cannot inhere in processes or structures, only in conscious agents. A 'criminal' or 'genocidal' process is a misnomer that draws attention away from the fact that usually some agent of mass killing or death can be identified and held responsible, even if posthumously.[109] Consequently, Leo Kuper's suggestion of an 'affinity' between colonialism and genocide is to be welcomed, but his coining of the term 'genocidal processes' to cover the non-deliberate causes of indigenous death—'massacres [!], appropriation of land, introduction of diseases, and arduous conditions of labor'—is misleading.[110]

For this reason, even post-liberals prize identifiable exterminatory intention as 'smoking gun' evidence of genocide. Churchill, for example, proposes a differentiated schema of genocides based on the extent of self-conscious exterminatory consciousness. Using the analogy of the United States murder law, he distinguishes between genocide 'in the first degree' (subjective murderous *mens rea*), 'in the second degree' (genocide not directly intended, but attendant to other criminal behaviour) and 'in the third degree' (in which the death results from reckless conduct).[111] This approach is not

---

108 Karl Marx, *The Eighteenth Brumaire of Louis Bonaparte* (New York: International Publishers 1963), 15.

109 Jürgen Zimmerer, 'Colonialism and the Holocaust: towards an archaeology of genocide', in A. Dirk Moses (ed.), *Genocide and Settler Society* (New York: Berghahn Books 2003, forthcoming).

110 Leo Kuper, *Genocide: Its Political Use in the Twentieth Century* (Harmondsworth: Penguin 1981), 45; Leo Kuper, 'Other selected cases of genocide and genocidal massacres: types of genocide', in Israel W. Charny (ed.), *Genocide: A Critical Bibliographical Review* (London, Mansell 1988), 156.

111 Ward Churchill, 'Genocide: toward a functional definition', *Alternatives*, vol. 11, 1986, 413. See also his discussion in *A Little Matter of Genocide*, 4 31 ff. Chalk and Jonassohn, 118–20.

without precedent.[112] In nineteenth-century English law, persons were inferred to have intended the 'natural consequences' of their actions: if the results proscribed were reasonably foreseeable as a likely consequence of their actions, the presumption was that those accused had intended the result.[113] On this reading, the definition of intention is not limited to the subjectively intended result, and this is important for colonialism, in which the conscious agent is exceedingly difficult to pin down. Because colonial states did not exercise unlimited authority in their lands, ruled through 'mediating powers' and were supervised by distant, metropolitan governments in Europe, identifying the genocidal perpetrator is not straightforward.

Consider the case of the British in nineteenth-century Australia. The Colonial Office in London constantly warned the settlers—both the colonial governors and the pastoralists—not to exterminate the Aborigines. Yet, thousands of Aborigines were killed. The Aboriginal population declined drastically for a number of reasons, primarily disease, in all areas soon after contact with Europeans, but massacres were also prevalent. Was the catastrophic population decline genocidal? If we use a differentiated concept of intention, authorities in London cannot any more escape responsibility than the Australian-based governors and the direct perpetrators of the many massacres. For while they wrung their hands about frontier violence, they were unwilling to cease the colonization project despite the manifest consequences of tribal extermination through violence and extinction by disease. In the 1830s the humanitarian liberals in the Colonial Office were acutely conscious of the struggle transpiring on the other side of the world, on which a Select Committee report in 1837 urged the British government to assume moral responsibility for the indigenous peoples of South Africa, the Australian colonies and North America, lest they 'ceased to exist'.[114] But the report made virtually no impact, and despite admonishing missives from London and occasional colonial compromises, the fatal pattern of events continued to unfold unchanged such that Colonial Office officials ultimately resigned themselves to the inevitable:

> The causes and the consequences of this state of things are clear and irremediable [wrote one official], nor do I suppose that it is possible to discover any method by which the impending catastrophe, namely, the elimination of the Black Race, can be averted.[115]

112 Alexander K. A. Greenawalt, 'Rethinking genocidal intent: the case for a knowledge-based interpretation', *Columbia Law Review*, December 1999, 2259–94.
113 Lord Diplock in the House of Lords: R v. Lemon, AC [1979] 617 at 636.
114 See the discussion of R. H. W. Reece, *Aborigines and Colonists* (Sydney: Sydney University Press 1974), 132ff.
115 Ibid., 139; A. G. L. Shaw, 'British policy toward the Australian Aborigines, 1830–1850', *Australian Historical Studies*, vol. 25, 1992, 265–85; Henry Reynolds, *An Indelible Stain? The Question of Genocide in Australia's History* (Ringwood, Victoria: Viking Press 2001), ch. 6. See also Smith, 'Human destructiveness and politics', in Wallimann and Dobkowski (eds), 23.

The discourse of inevitability may be evidence for the proposition that colonialism was a process that no central agency controlled, and therefore that no one can be held responsible for its unfortunate consequences. After all, they regarded indigenous extinction as the regrettable aspect of the otherwise redeeming story of human progress, as biologists, anthropologists and naturalists were happy to assure them.[116] Certainly, colonialism in Australia, as elsewhere, could not be halted in the manner of flicking a light switch. The Colonial Office, for example, was only a small part of a massive state apparatus. But only a miserably attenuated concept of intention would absolve it in these circumstance. The rhetoric of inevitability also served to mask choices open to policymakers, choices they were not prepared to entertain because they fundamentally approved of the civilizing process in which they were engaged. The fact is that they did not take their own humanitarian convictions seriously enough to implement the radical measures necessary to prevent indigenous deaths, whether caused by massacre or disease, for it would entail relinquishing control of the land and jeopardizing the colonizing mission. Talk of inexorable extinction reflected a racist theodicy as much as governmental impotence. The disappearance of indigenous peoples from the face of the earth was a natural consequence of the (in)action of European elites, and they knew it on the frontier, in the colonial capital and back home at the imperial seat of power. Where genocide was not explicitly intended, then it was implicitly, in the sense of the silent condoning, sometimes agonized acceptance, of events held to be somehow 'inevitable'.[117]

The racial century, c. 1850–1950

Racial extinction, then, was a common notion in Europe long before the Holocaust.[118] But if claims of Australian or American holocausts are hyperbolic, is it possible nonetheless to relate colonial genocides to the mass exterminations of the twentieth century, in particular, to that of European Jewry?[119] It is, if they are linked as constituents of a *unified process*.

116 Russell McGregor, *Imagined Destinies: Aboriginal Australians and the Doomed Race Theory, 1880–1939* (Melbourne: Melbourne University Press 1997); Patrick Brantlinger, '"Dying races": rationalizing genocide in the nineteenth century', in Jan Nederveen Pieterse and Bhikhu Parekh (eds), *The Decolonization of Imagination* (London and Atlantic Highlands, NJ: Zed Books 1995), 43–56.
117 On the concept of implied intention, see Palmer, 194, and Hugo Adam Bedau, 'Genocide in Vietnam', in Virginia Held, Sidney Morgenbesser and Thomas Nagel (eds), *Philosophy, Morality and International Affairs* (New York and Oxford: Oxford University Press 1974), 5–46.
118 Sven Lindqvist, *'Exterminate all the Brutes'* (London: Granta Books 1996); Brantlinger.
119 Mark Levene, 'Why is the twentieth century the century of genocide', *Journal of World History*, no. 11, 2000, 305–36.

The earliest attempt to conceptualize them as a totality is Hannah Arendt's *The Origins of Totalitarianism* (1951).[120] It is customary at conferences now to refer to her linkage of imperialism (to which she devotes a third of her book) and the Holocaust, but so far only promissory notes have been issued, although historians like Jürgen Zimmerer are on the case.[121] What is striking about Arendt's explanatory strategy is her mediation of structural and cultural methods. Eschewing the intuitive and popular approach of seeking the roots of fascism in German history alone, she thematized European history as a whole to lay bare the various crises caused by modernization. Central to her analysis is what she calls 'the political emancipation of the bourgeoisie', a concept fundamental both to imperialism and totalitarianism. 'Imperialism must be considered the first state in political rule of the bourgeoisie rather than the last stage of capitalism.'[122] Contrary to modernization theorists who regarded incomplete bourgeois revolutions as the misdevelopment that led to fascism, Arendt saw the gradual increase in political power of the rising middle class after the mid-nineteenth century as the key issue.[123] For this class sought to use politics to expedite its economic aims, namely, to transcend the limits of the nation-state for the world-wide investment of its capital, and to cast the world in its own image.[124] She held this development to be disastrous for, as is well known, Arendt regarded the bourgeoisie as the agent of 'the social', the realm of material necessity, counterpoised to 'the political', which she prized as the space of collective decision-making that guaranteed human autonomy and freedom.[125] The odium of imperialism, then, inhered in the occlusion of the political realm by the social, with the consequence that the bourgeois political universe, exemplified and first articulated by Thomas Hobbes,

120 For fine appraisals of Arendt's work, see Ned Curthoys, 'The politics of Holocaust repre sentation: the worldly typologies of Hannah Arendt', *Arena Journal*, vol. 16, 2001, 49–74; Steven E. Aschheim, *In Times of Crisis: Essays on European Culture, Germans, and Jews* (Madison: University of Wisconsin Press 2001); and Margaret Canovan, *Hannah Arendt: A Reinterpretation of Her Political Thought* (Cambridge: Cambridge University Press 1992).
121 Zimmerer, 'Colonialism and Nazi genocide'. See also his *Deutsche Herrschaft überAfrikaner: Staatlicher Machtanspruch und Wirklichkeit im kolonialen Namibia*, 2nd edn (Münster and Hamburg: Lit Verlag 2002).
122 Hannah Arendt, *The Origins of Totalitarianism*, 2nd edn (London: George Allen and Unwin 1958), 138.
123 Barrington Moore, Jr., *Social Origins of Dictatorship and Democracy* (Boston: Beacon Press 1966); Ralf Dahrendorf, *Society and Democracy in Germany* (London: Weidenfeld and Nicolson 1968). See the fundamental critique of David Blackbourn and Geoff Eley, *The Peculiarities of German History* (Oxford: Oxford University Press 1984).
124 Arendt, 125.
125 See Hanna Fenichel Pitkin, *The Attack of the Blob: Hannah Arendt's Concept of the Social* (Chicago: University of Chicago Press 1998).

began to infect politics: the world became Hobbesian as brutal competition and racist domination replaced citizenship.

But that is not all. Arendt implied that totalitarianism is a radicalized form of the 'moderate imperialism' whose unrelenting and limitless striving for world domination was always fettered by the nation-state before 1914.

> National institutions resisted throughout the brutality and megalomania of imperialist aspirations, and bourgeois attempts to use the state and its instruments of violence for its own economic purposes were always only half successful. This changed when the German bourgeoisie staked everything on the Hitler movement and aspired to rule with the help of the mob.[126]

What Arendt is arguing bears closely on the previous discussion of theories of colonial genocide, for her vision of the modern pathology is that society (that is, the bourgeoisie) gradually takes over the state and uses it for social rather than political ends; indeed, that totalitarianism is the apogee of that process.[127] Clearly, liberal theorists of genocide and totalitarianism misunderstand Arendt if they invoke her as the authority for their propositions, as she is arguing that the totalitarian energy that produces the concentration camps emanates from the imperatives of the economic system. And yet, although there is an obvious post-liberal dimension to her account, she is interested in showing how this energy became embodied in ideology and state policies. What she achieves, then, is a sublation of liberal and post-liberal positions that incorporates the insights of both into a new perspective, the ideal methodological advance in the philosophy of the social sciences.[128] Similarly, the universal and particular are carefully negotiated. Rather than taking a 'special path' to modernity or standing apart *sui generis* from the other European powers, Germany is the exemplar of an experience they all underwent in varying degrees of intensity. It is the country where the process occurred most radically.[129]

There are good reasons today to revise central features of Arendt's account. Her talk of 'the mob' is anachronistic, her views on the Jewish question quixotic, the concept of totalitarianism is suspect, the section on

---

126 Arendt, 124.
127 Ibid., 123.
128 Geoffrey Brahm Levey, 'Theory choice and the comparison of rival theoretical perspectives in political sociology', *Philosophy of the Social Sciences*, vol. 26, no. 1, March 1996, 26–60; John Gerring, *Social Science Methodology* (Cambridge: Cambridge University Press 2001), 14–17.
129 Some commentators have accused Arendt—unfairly in my view—of thereby quarantining German intellectual traditions, to which she was in thrall, from fascism: Ernest Gellner, *Culture, Identity and Politics* (Cambridge: Cambridge University Press 1987), 89ff.

imperialism is based on the superseded views of Hobson and Lenin, and the contention false that empires weakened nation-states.[130] But such super-annuation is normal for a book written over fifty years ago. What is significant is Arendt's dazzling deployment of the full ensemble of modern sociological categories to track the emergence of modern extermination. What she produced was not a contribution to the stale debate between structure and agency, based as it is on an atomistic world-view in which causation and independent/dependent variables are supposed to explain this or that outcome. Nor did she write a conventional synthesis in which the narrative shows how 'one thing led to another'. *The Origins of Totalitarianism* is a *phenomenology* of modernity in that same way that Ernst Nolte's *Three Faces of Fascism* traces the evolution of fascism in the context of endogenous dynamics in Europe since the Enlightenment.[131] Their point is not to identify a single causal variable, nor to expose static structures,[132] but to lay bare the radical-ization of a system. By this method, the nation-state is not the 'sovereign ontological subject' of explanation,[133] yet neither is it discarded as an agent in the historical process in the manner of world systems theory.[134] Vertically distinctive national histories are only explicable in relation to the broader processes that a horizontally integrative history can better pro-vide.[135] Scholars in genocide studies need to look carefully at methodolo-gical developments in world history.

What is required, then, is an account of European modernity that links nation-building, imperial competition and international and intra-national racial struggle to the ideologically driven catastrophes of the twentieth century. The proposition I should like to advance is that the hundred years roughly following 1850 can be conceptualized as the 'racial century' whose most basic feature was competition between rival projects of nation-building and 'people making' (that is, the fashioning of ethnically homogeneous populations domestically) that culminated in the Holocaust of European Jewry and other racial minorities in the 1940s.[136] Such an approach links the

130 Ronald Hyam and Ged Martin, *Reappraisals in British Imperial History* (London: Macmillan 1975), 1–21; David Armitage, *The Ideological Origins of the British Empire* (Cambridge and New York: Cambridge University Press 2000), 14ff.
131 E. Nolte, *Three Faces of Fascism*, trans. Leila Vennewitz (London: Weidenfeld and Nicolson 1965).
132 See the critique of structuralism by Michael Adas, 'Bringing ideas and agency back in', in Philip Pomper, Richard H. Elphick and Richard T. Vann (eds), *World History: Ideologies, Structures, and Identities* (Oxford: Blackwell 1998), 81–104.
133 Antoinette Burton, 'Who needs the nation: interrogating "British" history', *Journal of His torical Sociology*, vol. 10, no. 3, September 1997, 232.
134 Stuart Ward, 'Transcending the nation: a global imperial history', in Antoinette Burton (ed.), *After the Imperial Turn* (Durham, NC: Duke University Press, forthcoming).
135 Richard Fletcher, cited in ibid. For a recent, splendid example of such an approach, see Mike Davis, *Late Victorian Holocausts* (London and New York: Verso 2001).
136 'The racial century' is the title of my current research project.

genocides that occurred in the European colonies with the intra-European population politics of the inter-war and war years. The nation-states of Europe, including the Ottoman empire and subsequent Turkish nation-state, engaged in increasingly extreme measures of self-assertion abroad and ethnic 'purification' at home, as they were forced to compete for survival as viable powers, which were universally articulated in terms of a race whose fate it was the role of the state to secure. Moreover, it was the hundred years in which explicitly racial categories were the prime source of policy legitimation.

European history in this period was a *dynamic process* rather than a succession of events. Consequently, it is necessary to situate the racial violence on the imperial periphery, essential for the retention of European dominance in the nineteenth century, as part of the same flow of events that led to the eruption of violence in Europe in 1914 and again a quarter of a century later. In this way, the genocidal episodes of the 'racial century' are linked in a complex causal nexus of upwardly spiralling violence against real and imagined threats to the viability of marginal nation-states. With the adoption of the UN conventions on human rights and genocide in the late 1940s and the subsequent sea-change in public opinion regarding racial issues, the 'racial century' came to an end.

To be sure, genocides of indigenous peoples by Europeans began centuries earlier, and the exterminatory dimension of nation-building was evident in the Vendée conflagration during the French Revolution.[137] Obviously, such processes so central to European modernity have long histories, and ethnic politics are hardly new. Remarkable about the racial century, however, is the coincidence of Great Power projection into and penetration of the world and the degree of self-consciousness and self-justification about what they are doing. In other words, the mid-nineteenth century marks the beginning of the especially intense phase of competition between rival projects of nation-building and people-construction at home and abroad ('competitive self-mobilization') that initiated a dynamic of 'cumulative radicalisation', culminating in the 'European civil war' (Arno Mayer) of the first half of the twentieth century.[138]

This approach thereby avoids the twin danger of absolute difference and absolute similarity. The former treats genocides episodically and in isolation

---

137 John Docker, *1492: Poetics of Diaspora* (London: Continuum 2001); Reynald Secher, *Le Genocide franco-français: La Vendée-Venge* (Paris: Presses Universitaires de France 1986). Cf. Arno Mayer, *The Furies: Violence and Terror in the French and Russian Revolutions* (Princeton. NJ: Princeton University Press 2000).

138 Cf. Michael Geyer and Charles Bright, 'World history in a global age', *American Historical Review*, vol. 100, no. 4, October 1995, 1034–60; Michael Geyer and Charles Bright, 'Global violence and nationalizing wars in Eurasia and America: the geopolitics of war in the mid- nineteenth century', *Comparative Studies of Society and History*, vol. 38, no. 4, 1996, 619–57.

from one another, the latter places the blame for the catastrophes of the twentieth century at the feet of a monolithically conceived 'modernity' or 'civilization', which tends to collapse the distinctions between the Holocaust and the preceding genocides.[139] The task is to relate each genocide to others in a way that allows them to retain their distinctive features. The concept of a cumulative radicalization and metaphor of upward spiral permit such a linkage. What is striking about the Holocaust is that it was a project of racial cleansing and self-assertion that sought *consciously* to achieve for Germans what the imperial endeavours of rival European powers had achieved in a largely haphazard manner before the First World War: permanent security and well-being for the domestic population conceived as the citadel and bearer of a superior European culture.[140] The dispersion of agency and consciousness in the period of 'classical' colonialism is gathered up and located centrally in a totalitarian state, notwithstanding recent research about the importance of peripheral initiatives in the first phase of killing in 1941. Here was the most radical genocidal moment of the racial century, the culmination of the violence directed towards inner and outer enemies.

Why, then, did Germany produce the Holocaust? Tentatively, one can speculate that, as a latecomer to the nation-building and imperialism game, its elites were forced to imitate and improve the models of the established powers. In the struggle to be a viable Great Power, it was not surprising that the usual colonial ruthlessness was intensified. But it is unsatisfactory to revert solely to national modes of explanation. Expansionist and racist lobby groups existed in all European powers.[141] The analytical task is to explain why they gained more or less influence in different countries during the racial century, and here too the context of international competition and population politics is central. The radical right in Germany was only able to achieve a breakthrough—and then only electorally in 1930—in the wake of the national and demographic catastrophe of the First World War.[142] There

---

139 Norman M. Naimark, *Fires of Hatred: Ethnic Cleansing in Twentieth-century Europe* (Cam bridge, MA: Harvard University Press 2001); Zygmunt Bauman, *Modernity and the Holocaust* (Ithaca, NY: Cornell University Press 1989); Zygmunt Bauman, *Modernity and Ambivalence* (Cambridge: Polity Press 1991). See the critical discussion in A. Dirk Moses, 'Modernity and the Holocaust', *Australian Journal of Politics and History*, vol. 43, 1997, 441–5.

140 Richard Rubinstein, 'Afterword: genocide and civilization', in Wallimann and Dobkowski (eds), 288; Annegret Ehmann, 'From colonial racism to Nazi population policy: the role of the so-called Mischlinge', in Berenbaum and Peck (eds), 115–33; Tony Barta, 'Discourses of genocide in Germany and Australia: a linked history', *Aboriginal History*, vol. 25, 2001, 37–56; Zimmerer, 'Colonialism and Nazi genocide'; Eric Weitz, *A Century of Genocide: Utopias of Race and Nation* (Princeton, NJ: Princeton University Press 2003, forthcoming).

141 Paul Kennedy, *The Rise and Fall of the Great Powers* (New York: Random House 1987).

142 Geoff Eley, 'Conservatives and the radical nationalists in Germany', in Martin Blinkhorn (ed.), *Fascists and Conservatives* (London: Unwin Hyman 1990), 50–70.

were peacemakers on both sides in 1917, but they were thwarted by those on both sides who insisted on holding out for total victory.[143]

By linking colonial genocides and the Holocaust in this way, I hope to achieve two things: to convince the believers in theodicy that they are not on the side of the angels; and to allow members of victim groups to situate their suffering, and that of others, in the sorry tale of European world domination. It would be idle to regard such contextualization as a consolation, but it may be the only way to work through trauma and thereby release the utopian potential that modernity promised, for the mutual recognition of common suffering is a powerful moral source for the solidarity needed to prevent future victims of progress.

A. DIRK MOSES teaches modern European history and comparative genocide studies at the University of Sydney. He has published articles on these subjects, and his edited volume, *Genocide and Settler Society: Frontier Violence and Child Removal in Australia*, will be published by Berghahn Books in 2003.

---

143 Douglas Newton, *British Policy and the Weimar Republic, 1918–1919* (Oxford: Clarendon Press 1997).

White men with low moral standards? German anthropology and the Herero genocide[1]

Dan Stone

I am convinced that in the next century people will slaughter each other by the million because of a difference of a degree or two in the cephalic index. It is by this sign, which has replaced the Biblical shibboleth and linguistic affinities, that men will be identified. ... And the last sentimentalists will be able to witness the most massive exterminations of peoples.

—Georges Vacher de Lapouge (1896)

... the historian of the future will have to register that Europeans in the past sometimes exterminated whole island peoples; that they expropriated most of the patrimony of savage races; that they introduced slavery in a specially cruel and pernicious form; and that even if they abolished it later, they treated the expatriated Negroes as outcasts and pariahs ...

—Bronislaw Malinowski (1945)

In the fifty years separating Vacher de Lapouge and Malinowski there were indeed several 'exterminations of peoples'. One of the most horrific, and still comparatively unknown, was the genocide of the Hereros in German South West Africa (now Namibia), who, after years of oppressive treatment, rose up against their colonial 'masters' in 1904. Following General von Trotha's famous 'annihilation order' (*Vernichtungsbefehl*) of 2 October 1904,

1 My thanks to Scott Ashley and Mark Hewitson for their comments on the first draft of this essay.

the Hereros were murdered or driven out into the desert to die of thirst and hunger. This murder was considered by the perpetrators to be the Hereros' 'terrible, but deserved fate'.[2] Of a population of approximately 80,000, by 1906 only some 15,000 remained alive, enticed out of the desert by missionaries, and held until 1908 in concentration camps,[3] after being tattooed 'GH', *Gefangene Herero* (imprisoned Herero). As one contemporary commentator boldly put it: 'the Herero people as such was annihilated.'[4]

I do not want to tell the history of the genocide, which has already been skilfully related by several historians.[5] What they have made clear is that the Germans prosecuted their campaign with savagery. Despite its ironic, propagandistic tone, the comments of one British author in 1939 are basically correct:

> The Hereros went into rebellion, under the Paramount Chief Samuel Maharero. They fought according to a certain savage code, according to which German soldier prisoners were in for a rough time, British and Dutch were treated as old friends, and white women and children of all races were not touched. The Germans fought them according to a more civilised code, according to which prisoners were not taken and women and children often raped and bayoneted.[6]

Rather, I want to investigate some of the strands of thought that accompanied the German colonial enterprise, and in particular the role of German anthropology. Anthropologists, especially before 1900, tended to be

2 K. Schwabe, *Der Krieg in Deutsch-Südwestafrika 1904–1906* (Berlin: Verlag von C. A. Weller 1907), 305. All translations, unless otherwise stated, are by the author.

3 Ibid. Schwabe uses the term *Konzentrationslager* (306).

4 Wilhelm Külz, *Deutsch-Südafrika im 25. Jahre deutscher Schutzherrschaft: Skizzen und Beiträge zur Geschichte Deutsch-Südafrikas* (Berlin: Wilhelm Süsserott 1909), 159.

5 The main studies are Jürgen Zimmerer, *Deutsche Herrschaft über Afrikaner: staatlicher Machtanspruch und Wirklichkeit im Kolonialien Namibia* (Münster: LIT Verlag, 2004). Helmut Bley, *South-west Africa under German Rule 1894–1914*, trans. Hugh Ridley (London: Heinemann 1971); Horst Drechsler, *Let Us Die Fighting: The Struggle of the Herero and Nama against German Imperialism*, trans. Bernd Zöllner (London: Zed Press 1980); and Jon M. Bridgman, *The Revolt of the Hereros* (Berkeley: University of California Press 1981). See also Woodruff G. Smith, *The German Colonial Empire* (Chapel Hill: University of North Carolina Press 1978), 51–65; Helmut Stoecker (ed.), *German Imperialism in Africa: From Its Beginnings until the Second World War*, trans. Bernd Zöllner (London: C. Hurst and Co. 1986), 39–62, 136–48; Mark Cocker, *Rivers of Blood, Rivers of Gold: Europe's Conflict with Tribal Peoples* (London: Jonathan Cape 1998), 269–357; Tilman Dedering, '"A certain rigorous treatment of all parts of the nation": the annihilation of the Herero in German South West Africa, 1904', in Mark Levene and Penny Roberts (eds), *The Massacre in History* (Oxford: Berghahn Books 1999), 205–22. An important study that recognizes the Hereros' agency is Jan Bart Gewald, *Towards Redemption: A Socio-Political History of the Herero of Namibia between 1890 and 1923* (Leiden: Research School CNWS 1996), now published as *Herero Heroes: A Socio-Political History of the Herero of Namibia between 1890 and 1923* (Oxford: James Currey 1999).

6 G. L. Steer, *Judgement on German Africa* (London: Hodder & Stoughton 1939), 62.

progressive thinkers by the standards of the time, and were therefore in no way directly responsible for the genocide. Nevertheless, the logic of their very enterprise, depending as it did on colonialism, encouraged a way of thinking that was hierarchical and racist on the one hand, romantic and primitivist on the other. Even if they defended a monogenist rather than a more explicitly racist polygenist thesis of human evolution, anthropologists held certain assumptions about racial and cultural divisions. When German human and biological sciences turned to a more fundamentalist Darwinism after 1900, these assumptions fed neatly into social Darwinist and eugenic theories of racial selection and the 'disappearance' of backward peoples. Such assumptions—conferring the authority of 'objective science'—were used by those involved in the murder of the Hereros to justify their actions.

Anthropology and race

From the 1860s on, German medical students—it was medical men who were predominant in the then professionally inchoate German anthropological circles—learned about racial concepts and, as Paul Weindling says, these concepts and the ethnological studies they engendered 'gave a sense of the great rift between "primitive" cultures and European civilizations'.[7] Although German anthropologists were initially opposed to colonial imperialism, because they believed this would threaten the existence of diverse human groups, by the 1890s positions were hardening, and anthropologists, like the rest of the population, became more vociferous in their support for colonialism and their disregard for notions of biological homogeneity.[8]

There remained, nevertheless, quite a gulf between the scientific undertakings of the anthropologists and the popular understanding of racial difference. Anthropologists tried, largely in vain, to modify the more extreme claims of colonial 'experts'. In a book devoted to bush warfare, one British military man noted the result of exercising too strong a show of force over the natives: 'Things are apparently all right for a time, and then suddenly the savages rise, cut up, and probably eat, the white man and his troops, and a

---

7 Paul Weindling, *Health, Race and German Politics between National Unification and Nazism 1870–1945* (Cambridge: Cambridge University Press 1989), 50.
8 Ibid., 57. On the change in anthropological ideas, see also Benoit Massin, 'From Virchow to Fischer: physical anthropology and "modern race theories" in Wilhelmine Germany', in George W. Stocking Jr. (ed.), *History of Anthropology. Vol. 8: Volksgeist as Method and Ethic: Essays on Boasian Ethnography and the German Anthropological Tradition* (Madison: University of Wisconsin Press 1996), 79–154, and Sheila Faith Weiss, 'The race hygiene movement in Germany', *Osiris*, vol. 3, 1987, 193–236. See also Robert Ross (ed.), *Racism and Colonialism* (The Hague: Martinus Nijhoff Publishers 1982); Gérard Leclerc, *Anthropologie et colonialisme* (Paris: Fayard 1972); and T. O. Ranger, 'From humanism to the science of man: colonialism in Africa and the understanding of alien societies', *Transactions of the Royal Historical Society,* vol. 26, 1976, 115–41.

punitive expedition results.'[9] Or, to take a German example, one member of the colonial troops involved in the genocide asked rhetorically: 'can one hope that a Negro people [*Negervolk*] can have developed so far in fifty years that beasts have become civilized people?'[10] At least in their scientific publications, anthropologists were not to be found making such claims, at any rate not until the final triumph of Nazism and the *Gleichschaltung* (co-ordination) of anthropological institutes under scientists such as Eugen Fischer, Otmar Freiherr von Verschuer and Josef Mengele.[11]

Anthropologists were, nonetheless, ambivalent towards colonized peoples. They may have scorned *völkisch* ideologies such as Aryanism or antisemitism, but they did not question the presuppositions of racial hygiene: that racial differences could be identified, racial-cultural hierarchies established and positive racial qualities encouraged. Rudolf Virchow (1821–1902), for example, along with T. H. Huxley a consultant in the exhumation of the human remains found at Neanderthal in 1856, and co-founder of the German Anthropological Society in 1869, considered Darwinism only one possible explanation for the origins of the human race, preferring to place more emphasis on cellular pathology. His survey of German schoolchildren, collating statistics on hair and eye-colour, skin and skull shape, led him to conclude that there was no such thing as a pure German race, 'only a mixture of morphological types'.[12] Nevertheless, although Virchow condemned antisemitism, he still spoke of the Jews as a distinctive racial type. Furthermore, as the Lamarckianism of Virchow and other early anthropologists increasingly came under attack, so too did their relatively liberal political positions.

Another example of this ambivalence is the case of Felix von Luschan (1854–1924), who became professor of anthropology in Berlin in 1900. Von Luschan had extensive links with colonial societies, and lauded the colonial enterprise whilst simultaneously attacking the increasingly racist notions that were creeping into German physical anthropology. In a paper delivered to the German Colonial Congress in Berlin in 1902, he made remarks that illustrate what one scholar aptly calls a 'combination of generous humanitarian feelings and callous scientific utilitarianism'.[13] On the one hand, he

9 Lieut.-Colonel W. C. G. Heneker, DSO, *Bush Warfare* (London: Hugh Rees 1907), 164.
10 Schwabe, 67.
11 For these, see Weindling, *Health, Race and German Politics*; Max Weinreich, *Hitler's Professors: The Part of Scholarship in Germany's Crimes against the Jewish People*, 2nd edn (New Haven and London: Yale University Press 1999); Robert N. Proctor, *Racial Hygiene: Medicine under the Nazis* (Cambridge, MA and London: Harvard University Press 1988); Ute Deichmann, *Biologists under Hitler*, trans. Thomas Dunlap (Cambridge, MA and London: Harvard University Press 1996). See also Hans-Walter Schmuhl, Grenzüberschreitungen: Das Kaiser-Wilhelm-Institut für Anthropologie, Menschliche Erblehre und Eugenik 1927–1945 (Gottingen: Wallstein Verlag, 2005).
12 Ivan Hannaford, *Race: The History of an Idea in the West* (Washington DC: Woodrow Wilson Center Press/ Baltimore: Johns Hopkins University Press 1996), 262.
13 Massin, 95, is referring to Virchow, but the description applies just as well to von Luschan.

voiced a typical concern of anthropologists, that primitive peoples needed to be protected:

> Modern communication [*Verkehr*] is a terrible and relentless enemy of all primitive conditions; what in the coming years we are unable to secure and to save for posterity is heading for complete disaster, and can never be recreated. Conditions and institutions that have developed in their own way over the course of thousands of years change under the influence of the white man almost from one day to the next. That is to say, act quickly, before, moreover, it becomes forever too late.[14]

Von Luschan went on to note that all attempts to establish criteria of differentiation between *Kulturvölkern* (civilized people) and *Wilden* (savages) were destined to failure.[15] He nevertheless defended the utility of anthropology, appealing to the 'loyal co-operation of most missionaries' and claiming that 'the warm goodwill that our colonial government and colonial societies evince for our ethnographic endeavours certainly first emerged out of respect for the practical value of ethnology [*Völkerkunde*]' .[16] In the light of the German massacres of the Hehe in East Africa in 1897 such statements take on a less innocent aspect than at first appears.

Indeed, they became even more noteworthy since, after the Herero genocide of 1904–6, von Luschan was one of several western anthropologists to give keynote papers at the first Universal Races Congress in London in 1911. The congress was designed to bring together anti-racist intellectuals from around the world to combat the claims of racial science and promote international peace.[17] Yet in his paper von Luschan's cultural-hierarchical claims outweighed his assertions of racial equality. He attacked as scientifically absurd the polygenist view of human evolution—the notion that there was more than one human race—yet held that racial differences were important and merited investigating.[18] Indeed, when he suggested that the 'brotherhood of man is a good thing, but the struggle for life is a far better one',[19] he gave vent to a crude social Darwinism. And von Luschan was in no doubt that the civilizations of white Europe represented the

14 Felix von Luschan, 'Ziele und Wege der Völkerkunde in den deutschen Schutzgebieten', in *Verhandlungen des Deutschen Kolonialkongresses 1902, zu Berlin am 10. und 11. Oktober 1902* (Berlin: Verlag von Dietrich Reimer (Ernst Vohsen) 1903), 163–74 (165).
15 Ibid., 169.
16 Ibid., 171.
17 See Paul Rich, ' "The baptism of a new era": the 1911 Universal Races Congress and the liberal ideology of race', *Ethnic and Racial Studies,* vol. 7, no. 4, 1984, 534–50.
18 Felix von Luschan, 'Anthropological view of race', in G. Spiller (ed.), *Papers on Inter-Racial Problems Communicated to the First Universal Races Congress Held at the University of London, July 26–29, 1911* (London: P. S. King 1911), 13–24 (16).
19 Ibid., 23.

pinnacle of human achievement; the only danger came from the rare examples of white men with low moral standards:

> I am still seriously convinced that certain white men may be on a lower
> intellectual and moral level than certain coloured Africans. But this is a mere
> theoretical statement and of little practical value, except for the Colonial Service.
> In the Colonies, naturally, a white man with a low moral standard will always be a
> serious danger, not only for the natives, but also for his own nation.[20]

Coming so soon after the murder of the Hereros—of which von Luschan, with his colonial contacts, must have been especially conscious—this is quite an understatement, and hardly constitutes an attack on racism. Ascribing genocide to the 'low moral standards' of 'certain white men' does not constitute one of the great insights of anthropological thought. Besides, von Luschan seems more concerned with the effects of such low moral standards on Germans than on their victims. It is important to remember that at this point in Germany, liberal anthropology was almost a thing of the past, and these comments of von Luschan's represent the death knell of progressive notions of racial equality and the rise of a cold Darwinian explanation of racial selection.

No one articulated this change more powerfully in Germany than Otto Ammon, perhaps the most influential of the German social Darwinists. Ammon (1842–1916) was a member of the Alldeutsche Verband, an influential German pro-colonial society, and a self-designated social anthropologist who combined the notion of race with the idea of natural selection to arrive at one of the clearest statements of the social Darwinist philosophy.[21] He set out his application of the idea of natural selection with the explicit aim of rubbishing the campaign for social equity of social democrats and to argue for the protection of the 'long-headed' Germans from 'round-headed' Catholics, socialists and Jews. 'The consequences of Darwin's theory', he wrote in 1891, 'are not democratic, still less social democratic, but thoroughly preservative [*erhaltend*], anti-levelling [*anti-nivellistisch*], aristocratic and monarchical.'[22] Thus, even though he began by acknowledging that anthropology had revealed there to be no such thing as a pure race, Ammon's study of military recruits in the region of Baden praised the work of Virchow, agreed with August Weismann that 'there exists continuity of the germ-plasm, the hereditary substance, from one generation to the next', noted that purity of type was favourable, and

20 Ibid., 22.
21 On the question of what was novel in social Darwinism, see Gregory Claeys, 'The "survival of the fittest" and the origins of social Darwinism', *Journal of the History of Ideas*, vol. 61, no. 2, 2000, 223–40.
22 Otto Ammon, *Der Darwinismus gegen die Sozialdemokratie: Anthropologische Plaudereien* (Hamburg: Verlagsanstalt und Druckerei A. G. 1891), 112.

claimed that the progeny of race-mixing should be 'abandoned to annihila-tion [*Vernichtung*] in the struggle for existence [*Kampf ums Dasein*]'.[23]

In his next book, a biological justification of a hierarchical social order, Ammon was in even more of a triumphalist mode. He noted in the foreword that 'the future unarguably belongs to the world-view that is based on the theory of evolution', and then went on to predict the glittering career that anthropology would inevitably soon enjoy as 'the foundation of various other sciences'. In his analysis of social democracy in Germany, Ammon immediately made clear what that new role for anthropology would be. Social democracy, Ammon argued, ran counter to everything that Darwin's theory taught. Social democrats, so Ammon said, accepted that everything was 'adapted to social need [*dem Bedürfnis angepaßt*]' with the exception of the social order, which they saw as unnatural. In other words, through sheer pigheadedness they refused to recognize the 'aristocratic character of Darwinism' that guaranteed, for 'peoples and races' no less than for individuals, that the weak would go under and the strong would prosper. Ammon found proof of these claims in the Prussian victory over France in 1870, which demonstrated the validity of belief in 'the German type [*Art*], German cold-bloodedness, breeding [*Mannszucht*] and tenacity'. And the general lesson that Ammon drew from these discoveries: 'Should a people [*Volk*] get left behind, it will be overthrown by a better organized neigh-bouring people, and will have to accept that neighbour's more purposeful organization.' The importance of this work in the 1890s—which witnessed the rise of the Social Democratic Party as a powerful revolutionary force in domestic German politics, and as a significant opponent of German colonialism—should not be underestimated.[24]

Depicting the Herero

The switch in anthropology from von Luschan's ambivalence to Ammon's 'cold-bloodedness' is reflected in depictions of Hereros in contemporary German scholarly works and the colonial literature on South West Africa. Such depictions reflected the tension between romantic, primitivist notions of 'noble savages' on the one hand, and racist notions of 'inferior races' on the other. Thus, before 1900, the Hereros were often portrayed in a positive light, as a noble warrior race, whose bodily stature and pride in their cattle and cattle-breeding knowledge distinguished them from the 'lower'

23 Otto Ammon, *Die natürliche Auslese beim Menschen. Auf Grund der anthropologischen Untersuchungen der Wehrpflichtigen in Baden und anderer Materialien* (Jena: Verlag von Gustav Fischer 1893), 1, 6, 315.
24 Otto Ammon, *Die Gesellschaftsordnung und ihre natürliche Grundlagen: Entwurf einer Sozial-Anthropologie zum Gebrauch für alle Gebildeten, die sich mit sozialen Fragen befassen* [1895], 2nd edn (Jena: Verlag von Gustav Fischer 1896), iv, 1, 5, 15, 16.

bushmen or Hottentots (Nama). But thereafter, when the Germans became increasingly frustrated by the Hereros' refusal to sell their cattle, they were depicted as wild children, whose warlike propensities made them a threat to the safety of the colonists. Rather than noble and beautiful, now they were more likely to be seen as unreliable, lazy and ungrateful for the benefits that German civilization had brought. For example, in 1896 one colonial journal asserted:

> Traits that are especially prevalent in the character of this people are great meanness and a strongly developed arrogance ... good intelligence and no modest acuteness of mind ... They possess a large capacity for carrying out negotiations ... Next to intellect, however, is an aspect of feeling also well developed in this on the whole uncultivated [*rohen*] people, namely a talent for music and song.[25]

Here we see how, from being equated with nobility in the 1880s and 1890s, Herero pride was, by the turn of the century, coming to be associated with arrogance.

A similar change in attitude took place regarding the physical characteristics of the Hereros, especially their physiognomy. Particularly after the genocide, descriptions of the Hereros took on a far more critical and condescending tone. In 1913 one journal described their physiognomy thus:

> It does not take much to imagine that foreign influences, working over centuries, have given rise not only to that fair type [*jenem hellen Typus*], but also to the frequency of traits that remind one of Caucasians and especially Semites, traits that also strike us in many eastern kaffirs [*Kaffern des Ostens*].[26]

Such depictions helped to identify black Africans, of whom the Hereros represented just one example, as an entirely separate race from white Europeans:

> In South West Africa we are dealing, as far as the natives are concerned, only with Blacks who, although they certainly belong to different peoples and tribes [*Völkerschaften und Stämmen*], all belong only to one race that is so infinitely far removed from the white race that, by comparison with this distance, existing differences within the two races totally disappear.[27]

25 *Deutsche Kolonialzeitung*, vol. 13, 1896, 298, cited in Peter Scheuler, *Die 'Eingeborenen' Deutsch-Südwestafrikas: Ihr Bild in deutschen Kolonialzeitschriften von 1884 bis 1918* (Cologne: Rüdiger Köppe Verlag 1998), 77. I am indebted to Scheuler for much of the information in this section.
26 *Koloniale Zeitschrift*, vol. 14, 1913, 342, cited in Scheuler, 151.
27 *Beiträge zur Kolonialpolitik und Kolonialwirtschaft*, vol. 8, 1906, 833, cited in Scheuler, 153.

This clear division of the races made the Herero uprising of 1904 explicable in racial terms, particularly in terms of the Africans' supposed racial hatred for the Germans: 'The real cause of this open revolt should be sought in the natural race-hatred that, having been arduously repressed for some time, had to flare up, and even in the future ought not to be left unattended to.'[28]

Furthermore, the physical prowess of the Hereros was itself problematic. Talking of the increase in physical strength encountered among the natives as one travelled southwards in Africa, Theodor Seitz, governor of South West Africa from 1910 to 1915, and previously governor of Cameroon, noted that 'with strength, however, self-consciousness and the aspiration for independence also grow'.[29] As Peter Scheuler says: 'This conception, apart from the racist-biological picture of humanity, intertwined with the Darwinian understanding of colonial expansion as the struggle by the white race for the supersession [*Verdrängungskampf*] of the black race.'[30] Indeed, the frequent use of the term *Rassenkampf* (racial struggle) to describe the uprising and subsequent genocide is an important indication of a social Darwinist framework for legitimizing atrocity.

These examples, taken from Peter Scheuler's study of colonial journals, can be backed up by looking at the writings of some of the men involved in the military campaign against the Hereros. Despite being even further removed from the anthropologists than the colonial journalists, these men's representations of the Hereros are typically based on stereotypical notions of racial character couched in scientific jargon. Not that this means that the use of 'scientific' or objectifying terminology was simply a cover for hatred; it seems rather that the work of anthropologists and racial scientists expedited the internalization of belief in racial hierarchies and thus of the righteousness of the colonists' behaviour. If anthropology *per se* cannot be held responsible for the Herero genocide, the popularization of ethnological concepts in certain circles might express the relationship more accurately.

One such popularization was provided by the military. The official history by the German General Staff of the Herero uprising, a book famous for the frankness with which it celebrates 'the end of the Hereros', provides a good example. The book, like so many on the history of the Herero uprising, begins with some ethnographical reflections on the Hereros and the other inhabitants of the region.[31] The latter are described as living, until the

28 *Kolonie und Heimat*, vol. 1, no. 18, 1907–08, 4, cited in Scheuler, 156.
29 Dr [Theodor] Seitz, *Südafrika im Weltkriege* (Berlin: Dietrich Reimer (Ernst Vohsen) 1920), 21.
30 Scheuler, 156.
31 For a typical example, see Leonhard Schultze, 'Südwestafrika', in Hans Meyer (ed.), *Das deutsche Kolonialreich: Ein Länderkunde der deutschen Schutzgebiete. Zweiter Band: Togo, Südwestafrika, Schutzgebiete in der Südsee und Kiautschaugebiet* (Leipzig and Vienna: Bibliografisches Institut 1910), 131–298.

middle of the eighteenth century, a 'wretched and contentless existence'; but the Hereros are described thus:

> With his innate wildness, his considerable bodily strength, stamina and nimbleness, as well as his war experience gained in battles with the Hottentots, the Herero is, in the fight for his cattle, an opponent not to be despised. His real character is a less pleasant mixture of cruelty, avarice, cunning and an overestimation of self, the last of which is expressed in boundless contempt for all foreigners, no matter whether black or white. ... In this warlike and free-living nature the foremost cause of the general revolt of 1904 is therefore also no doubt to be sought.[32]

Many other examples can be found. Karl Dove, a prolific writer on colonial affairs, described the positive physical characteristics of the Hereros in a book published before the uprising. But he introduced a note of caution into the description when he noted

> that the facial features, and especially the nose, very often strongly resemble south European, and even Semitic features, a peculiarity that from time to time is so marked that one could be tempted, even though any thought of a blood-mixture of recent date must be excluded, to take such a person for a mulatto.

Irrespective of these speculations, which seem to imply that theories of racial purity did not match experienced reality, Dove leaves the reader in no doubt that the uncivilized Hereros are of a very different racial make-up than Whites:

> For one should not forget that an inextinguishable hatred for the white man lives in the hearts of the Kaffirs, and that only the latter's reluctant recognition of the former's power prevents the worst. ... In war the Herero, when he gains the upper hand, becomes a wild animal.[33]

Dove's claims were repeated time and again. A major in the South West African Schutztruppe told his audience at the Berlin-Charlottenburg section of the German Colonial Society on 21 November 1907 that the Hereros

> prove to us how difficult it is to penetrate the emotional life of the Negro and to win his full trust. And the dreadful, cunning cruelty with which the Hereros

32 Große Generalstabe Kriegsgeschichtliche Abteilung I (ed.), *Die Kämpfe der deutschen Truppen in Südwestafrika. Band I: Der Feldzug gegen die Hereros* (Berlin: Ernst Siegfried Mittler & Sohn 1906), 1, 4. The section 'The barricading of the Omaheke and the end of the Hereros' begins on p. 208.
33 Karl Dove, 'Deutsch-Südwestafrika', in *Das Überseeische Deutschland: Die deutschen Kolonien in Wort und Bild* (Stuttgart, Berlin and Leipzig: Union Deutsche Verlagsgesellschaft [1903?]), 303, 306.

murdered the Germans at the start of the revolt is a vivid warning that the widely
held view that the Negro is a child needs to be fundamentally revised.[34]

And even Paul Rohrbach, one of the critics of the *Vernichtungsprogramm*,
who saw the revolt of the Hereros in social Darwinist terms as a perfectly
understandable 'national liberation struggle against German domination',
objected to the killings not on moral or even military grounds, but only
on political and economic ones: the Hereros were necessary for the
economic life of the colony 'as workers, since their old tribal independence [*Stammesselbständigkeit*] and their old property rights [*Besitzrechte*]
were here'.[35]

Perhaps the most boldly explicit racist statements are those made by
General von Trotha, the head of the expeditionary force sent to quell the
uprising. In his diary he not only justified the remorseless course of action
he had chosen, but did so with a possibly unconscious reference to the
'polluting' aspects of the foreign race, a fear familiar to students of racial
hygiene:

> I find it most appropriate that the nation perishes instead of infecting our soldiers
> and diminishing their supplies of water and food. Apart from that, mildness on
> my side would only be interpreted as weakness by the other side. They have to
> perish in the Sandveld or try to cross the Bechuanaland border.[36]

Anthropology and genocide

It is, of course, notoriously difficult to trace the influence of ideas. But even
if very few anthropologists would have happily written what von Trotha
wrote in his diary, there is no mistaking the attempt to lend respectability
to outrageous actions by the adoption of a scientific (that is, disinterested)
tone, and the employment of scientific (that is, reifying) terminology not
only by von Trotha, but by the other writers I have cited. If it is correct,
then, to say that the stated views of anthropologists were liberal, in relation
to German actions they seem decidedly resigned to, if not approving of,
the state of affairs. This does not necessarily describe an ambiguity. After
all, 'liberal' in this context means only that the anthropologists did not
hate and condemn other groups in the way that outright racists did;

34 G. Maercker, *Unsere Kriegsführung in Deutsch-Südwestafrika* (Berlin: Hermann Paetel 1908), 45.
35 Paul Rohrbach, *Deutsche Kolonialwirtschaft. Band I: Südwest-Afrika* (Berlin: Buchverlag der 'Hilfe' 1907), 352, 353, 361. See also L. Sander, *Geschichte der deutschen Kolonial-Gesellschaft für Südwest-Afrika von ihrer Gründung bis zum Jahr 1910. Band I: Geschichtliche Darstellung* (Berlin: Dietrich Reimer (Ernst Vohsen) 1912), 164-70.
36 See Gerhard Pool, *Samuel Maharero* (Windhoek, Namibia: Gamsberg Macmillan 1991), 273-4, cited in Gewald, 208.

nevertheless they firmly believed in the objective reality of race, and in the value of conducting research into it.

Besides, not all anthropologists were as ambivalent as von Luschan. Quite early on, and certainly as early as the Herero genocide, anthropologists such as Ammon were starting to throw their lot in with the racists. The founding of the journals *Politisch-Anthropologische Revue* (1902) and the *Archiv für Rassen- und Gesellschaftsbiologie* (1904) under Ludwig Woltmann and Alfred Ploetz respectively is well known, as is the enthusiasm in Germany for Francis Galton's eugenics. Eugen Fischer, perhaps the most virulently pro-Nazi of the race scientists, who became head of the Kaiser-Wilhelm Institute for Anthropology, Human Heredity and Eugenics in Berlin in 1927, learned his trade in South West Africa. His Mendelian explanation of the miscegenated characteristics of the so-called Rehoboth Bastards—the progeny of white settlers and Africans—launched his career, and on his return from South West Africa in 1909 he became president of the Freiburg Race Hygiene Society, where he was a colleague of Ammon.[37] In Fischer's case, the tension between admiration and distaste felt by the early anthropologists is entirely absent. Here we see the effects of changes in scientific emphasis from Lamarckism to Darwinism, and the consequent shift in the politics of anthropology—from liberal, philosemitic and anti-colonial to reactionary, antisemitic and racist—on the second generation of German anthropologists.

But can we be sure that anthropology actually had any relevance for events in German politics, especially German colonial politics? Is there necessarily a link between statements made by von Luschan, Ammon or even Fischer, and the attitudes of colonial administrators towards 'their' natives? On the one hand, one can argue that such men would have held a racist world-view anyway, and did not need scientific backing for it. On the other hand, one cannot dismiss anthropology as irrelevant, since the racist world-view did not come from nowhere, and German anthropologists were—once the liberal wing had been overtaken—part of a broad cultural process in which western societies legitimized atrocity in the colonies in the name of 'natural selection'. Anthropology would have been markedly less influential without the opportunities offered by the colonial enterprise. Furthermore, the specificities of German anthropology, its combination of evolutionary biology—whether based on Darwin or August Weismann, whose theory of the continuity of the germ-plasm, with its implications of an unchanging racial essence and the pointlessness of environmental reform, enjoyed a vogue in the years before 1914—and cultural evocations of racial difference, made it a potent

---

37 Eugen Fischer, *Die Rehobother Bastards und das Bastardierungsproblem beim Menschen: Anthropologische und ethnographische Studien an Rehobother Bastardvolk in Deutsch-Südwest-Afrika* (Jena: Verlag von Gustav Fischer 1913). See Weindling, *Health, Race and German Politics*, 237, and Massin, 136.

component of German thought, which was becoming increasingly resistant to notions of the equality of humanity, and more susceptible to notions of racial struggle and selection. In this sense, anthropology was one of the contributors to a broader defence of the superiority of the 'white race'.[38] The language of the colonial journals and of the military men involved in the murder of the Hereros shows them to have been influenced by such defences, and to have considered them as apodictic, requiring no special justification. The objective stance that typifies these studies, casting a dispassionate, all-embracing glance over the physical, mental and cultural characteristics of the Hereros, is one that is borrowed from the scientific approach of anthropologists, racial hygienists, eugenicists and evolutionary biologists.

Talal Asad has written:

> The role of anthropologists in maintaining structures of imperial domination has, despite slogans to the contrary, usually been trivial; the knowledge they produced was often too esoteric for government use, and even where it was usable it was marginal in comparison to the body of information routinely accumulated by merchants, missionaries, and administrators.[39]

Similarly, Woodruff Smith notes:

> It is difficult to avoid the conclusion that although German anthropology and the official apparatus of Germany's colonial empire affected one another, they did not affect one another very much. ... The theoretical patterns of cultural science were intimately connected to the political and ideological currents that shaped imperialism *within Germany*, but only tangentially to the actual administration of Germany's real colonies.[40]

---

38 German anthropology was therefore rather different in this regard to British anthropology, which developed a critique of imperialism much earlier. On Britain, see Wendy James, 'The anthropologist as reluctant imperialist', in Talal Asad (ed.), *Anthropology and the Colonial Encounter* (London: Ithaca Press 1973), 41–69; Adam Kuper, *The Invention of Primitive Society: Transformations of an Illusion* (London: Routledge 1988); Henrika Kuklick, *The Savage Within: The Social History of British Anthropology, 1885–1945* (Cambridge: Cambridge University Press 1991); George W. Stocking Jr., *After Tylor: British Social Anthropology 1888–1951* (London: The Athlone Press 1996). See also, on Germany, Paul Weindling, 'The "Sonderweg" of German eugenics: nationalism and scientific internationalism', *British Journal of the History of Science*, vol. 22, no. 3, 1989, 321–33.

39 Talal Asad, 'From the history of colonial anthropology to the anthropology of western hegemony', in George W. Stocking Jr. (ed.), *History of Anthropology. Vol. 7: Colonial Situations: Essays on the Contextualization of Ethnographic Knowledge* (Madison: University of Wisconsin Press 1991), 315.

40 Woodruff D. Smith, *Politics and the Sciences of Culture in Germany, 1840–1920* (New York: Oxford University Press 1991), 171.

Without wishing to exaggerate the role of anthropologists, I have tried to show that anthropological concepts and assumptions were indeed of some importance in legitimizing, if not driving, the work of more influential colonial actors. It is certainly hard to resist the notion of an influence in the opposite direction: that colonial practice affected the attitudes of anthropologists, which hardened at the same time as German colonial atrocities occurred. Even when anthropologists such as Virchow or von Luschan claimed that races could not be hierarchically ordered, the ease with which German colonists could contemplate the murder of a 'savage' people was one consequence of an anthropological construction of racial differences and of commensurate cultural worth.

Dan Stone is Professor of Modern History at Royal Holloway, University of London.

Index

abject Other: British view 19
abjection: physical 7–9
Aboriginal women: ill treatment 86–7
Aborigines 5, 6, 168; Australia 26–7; code 91; execution 91; extermination 173; legal status 90–1; occupants of land 13
Adorno, T. 134
Agamben, G. 7
age of enlightenment 2
Ages of Extremes (Hobsbawn) 125–6
American Holocaust: victims 159
Amherst, General J. 70
Ammon, O. 186
anamnestic solidarity 149
anthropology: German 181–94; race 183–7; switch in 187
antisemitism 156
apathy: disease 83
Arendt, H. 47, 50, 60, 132, 176, 177
arguments: legal 13
Armenians 1
Arthur, Governor 79
Asad, T. 193
attitudes: colonial administrators 192
Auschwitz 41, 115
Autobahn: network 108

Bagehot, W. 21
banishment: Flinders Island 98
barbarians: sacrifice 25
Barta, T. 168, 169
battle: Crête à Pierrot 52
Bauer, Y. 154, 155
bayonet: value 131
beauty: as virtue 9
Belorussia 102, 108; German occupation 102
Benjamin, W. 149
Berry, W. 130
bestselling author: Frenssen, G. 121
bin Laden, O. 128, 146
binary encoding: world 107
bio-power 8
biological science 36
birth rate: decline 87–8
black Africans: depiction of 188
Black Line 98; establishment 98

Black War: Extermination of the Tasmanian Aborigines (1948) (Turnbull) 71
Bolshevik power: Russia 125
bombing: high level 135; Iraq 128; Serbia 128
Bonaparte, N. 49, 56–7
Bonwick, J. 74, 95
British India Office 110
Bruni Island 80; settlement 93
Bush, President G. W. 146
bushrangers 83–4

Cambodia: genocide 55
camps: extermination 145; refugee 132
Cangé, Brigadier General 49
cannibals 12
Cap Francais 43–4
captivity: natives 93
capture: reward 78
Carr, Mr 90
Chalk, F. 163–4
channels: transmissions 115–22
child mortality 87–8
children: development 143; half-caste 87–8; killing of 88; proclamation against 88; stealing of 88–9
China: economic development 144
Chinese Communist Party 141
Christianity: doctrines 99; introduction 28
Christians: pagans 9
Churchill, Sir W. 131, 132, 159, 166–7, 172–3
civil war: European 178
civilization 32, 149; ranking 140
civilizing process 174; Flinders Island 99
cleansing: programmes 150
climate: native race 32
coffee: plantations 49
Cold War: end of 128
collateral damage 135
Collins, Captain 74, 75
Collins, D. 15
colonial administrators: attitudes 192
colonial experts: extreme claims 183
colonial gaze 9–12
colonial genocide: liberal theory 162–3; post liberal theories 165; rival theories 162–71

195

Made in the USA
Lexington, KY
01 July 2011